Hitched!

Wedding Stories from San Francisco City Hall

Edited by
CHERYL DUMESNIL

Introduction by
Rosie O'Donnell

Foreword by
California State Senator
Carole Migden

THUNDER'S MOUTH PRESS
NEW YORK

HITCHED! *Wedding Stories from San Francisco City Hall*

Thunder's Mouth Press
An Imprint of Avalon Publishing Group Inc.
245 West 17th Street • 11th Floor
New York, NY 10011

AVALON
publishing group incorporated

Library of Congress Cataloging-in-Publication Data is available.

ISBN: 1-56025-764-4
ISBN-13: 978-1-56025-764-6

9 8 7 6 5 4 3 2 1

Book design by Pauline Neuwirth, Neuwirth & Associates, Inc.

Printed in the United States of America
Distributed by Publishers Group West

For Tracie, who married me and for Brennan,
who inspires me

▼

Contents

▼

Acknowledgments

▼

My deepest gratitude to Gavin Newsom for his vision, to Mabel Teng for implementing the plan, and to the people who worked at San Francisco City Hall between February 12 and March 11, 2004, for making so many wedding day dreams come true. Much respect to the authors featured in this book for their bravery, commitment, and willingness to share their stories; to the 4,037 couples who said "I do" in voices that echoed around the globe; and to organizations like National Center for Lesbian Rights, Human Rights Campaign, Equality California, Lambda Legal Defense Fund, and Marriage Equality who have contributed so much to this movement. Thank you to Holly Near, Ann Reed, retired Episcopal Bishop John Shelby Spong, and Maura Volante for lending their words to this project. Thanks to Joann Mignano and Bobby Pearce for coordinating Rosie O'Donnell's participation, and to Rosie for her bold advocacy for equal rights. Thank you Lisa Dazols, Becky Mengarelli, and LaDonna Silva for helping me find several of my authors. Thanks to Laura Headley for her comments on early drafts of my essays, and to Judy French for feedback on the manuscript. Thanks to Catheline Jean-François for her assistance and encouragement. Thank you to my wife, Tracie Vickers, for supporting this project in so many ways—handing out an endless stack of fliers at parades, benefit dinners, and rallies; encouraging me through my pregnancy-induced energy lapses; looking the other way as the dust, dishes, and laundry piled up; and entertaining Brennan so I could get my work done.

Mahatma Gandhi's quotation first appeared in the December 23, 1939, issue of *Harijan,* an English-language weekly journal.

An excerpt from John Lewis and Stuart Gaffney's essay appeared in the June 2004 issue of *San Francisco Spectrum,* under the title "Just Married—John and Stuart, Newlyweds After 17 Years Together."

The quotations from Harvey Milk's 1978 Gay Freedom Day speech and San Francisco Mayor George Moscone's election night speech appear in *The Mayor of Castro Street: The Life and Times of Harvey Milk,* by Randy Shilts (St. Martin's Press, 1983).

The song "At Last" was written by Mack Gordon and Harry Warren (© EMI Feist Catalog, Inc.).

Dr. Martin Luther King Jr.'s quotation comes from "Letter from Birmingham Jail" (© 1963 The Estate of Martin Luther King Jr.)

The song "Chapel of Love" was written by Jeff Barry.

Lyrics from Holly Near's song "Singing for Our Lives" (© 1979, Hereford Music/ASCAP), and Holly Near and Meg Christian's song "The Rock Will Wear Away" (© 1977 Hereford Music/ASCAP, Thumbelina Music/BMI) appear courtesy of Holly Near.

Lyrics from the song "Every Long Journey," words and music by Ann Reed (© 1986, Turtlecub Publishing, appear courtesy of Ann Reed, www.annreed.com.

When the dust settles and the pages of history are written, it will not be the angry defenders of intolerance who have made the difference. That reward will go to those who dared to step outside the safety of their privacy in order to expose and rout the prevailing prejudices.

—JOHN SHELBY SPONG, Retired Bishop,
Episcopal Diocese of Newark, NJ

Introduction

ROSIE O'DONNELL

▼

A couple years ago if you'd said to me, "You're going to become an advocate for gay marriage," I'd have said, "You're crazy." Never in my wildest dreams would I have imagined this. But two events changed my mind. First, I learned that if you are a heterosexual talk show host and you're sued by a major corporation, anything you have said to your husband is privileged information—it can't be entered into the court's records and used against you. But if you are a homosexual talk show host and you're sued by a corporation, anything you have ever said or written to your partner is allowed to be entered into the record. During my court battle, we applied for spousal privilege and were denied it by the State. As a result, everything I had said to my wife Kelli, every letter that I had written to her, every email, every correspondence and conversation was entered into the record. Legally married couples don't have to testify against each other, but gay couples do. This is only one of over a thousand privileges and protections denied to gay couples. After the trial, I became and will forever be a total proponent of gay marriage.

Then, President George W. Bush proposed to write bigotry into the United States Constitution. I was stunned and horrified, hearing him say, in my opinion, the most vile and hateful words ever spoken by a sitting president. His comments inspired Kelli and me to drop everything and make arrangements to fly from New York to San Francisco to get married. On the plane, one thought ran through my mind over and over: liberty and justice for all. That's what this movement is about: equal protection for thousands and thousands of loving, law-abiding couples—like those who have shared their stories in this book—who deserve the rights and responsibilities of legal marriage. I want to thank Mayor Gavin Newsom and the City of San Francisco for taking an amazing stance, insisting that our country live up to its greatest promise: liberty and justice for all.

June 2005

Foreword

CALIFORNIA STATE SENATOR CAROLE MIGDEN

▼

San Francisco in February can be a beautiful place—cool, clear air combines with bright California sunshine to create a crisp view of a city usually shrouded in fog. Standing at the base of the steps under the rotunda of our City Hall, waiting to perform an official act, I reflected for a moment on something else that had become clear—society was changing before my eyes. I was about to perform a—for the moment legal—marriage ceremony for two women. Dressed in pink silk and champagne satin, Cheryl and Tracie were about to commit to one another "till death do [they] part."

Over the millennium, marriage has changed as dramatically as society has changed. Marriage equality opponents, fearful that extending the right to marry to same-sex couples will somehow alter the institution of marriage, seem to forget the fact that marriage has already changed, drastically. For centuries, marriage was looked upon as a business transaction that occurred between families. Depending on economic status, some families had their daughter marry the son (or vice versa) of another family to expand an ongoing concern—a farm, a fiefdom, a country. Marriages were often arranged and sometimes from a very early age. An agreement to couple could occur when two people were children, having never even met each other.

Over time, marriage evolved. Love and choice slowly worked their charms on the "institution" of marriage. In the twentieth century, the evolution of this institution followed the pace of the rest of society—a rapid series of changes, spurred on by technology, travel, and enhanced communication. And it continues to change.

California has always been at the forefront of the steady progress of American society. Around the globe, we are known as a haven for diversity, especially here in San Francisco. That is why it was of little surprise to many when, in early 2004, the city began issuing marriage licenses to lesbian and gay couples, taking the next step in the evolution of the institution of marriage. San Francisco's action sparked a wildfire that spread across the nation and around the world.

This is not the first time California has taken center stage in a civil rights movement. Long before San Francisco began granting lesbian and gay marriage licenses, California was at the center of a similar civil rights movement—the battle over interracial, heterosexual marriage. It was the California Supreme Court that, in 1948, struck down a law prohibiting persons of different races from marrying. This pioneering case ultimately led to the United States Supreme Court striking down anti-interracial marriage laws in Virginia and eighteen other states in 1967. I predict that, within a single generation, lesbian and gay couples will similarly prevail in our movement for marriage equality.

We must remember, however, that the struggle we are in today is but another step forward in the movement to seek full protections and rights for lesbian and gay persons. And civil rights movements always face setbacks. San Francisco has not always been as progressive and accepting as it is today. As recently as the late 1980s, pockets of resistance and homophobia remained in our city. In 1989, San Francisco voters rejected a domestic partnership measure on the citywide ballot—a difficult setback, but more of a political failure resulting from voters who were not educated on the subject of domestic partnerships. Just a year later, in November 1990, voters passed the domestic partnership measure. At the state level, it took three attempts before I was successful in getting California's first domestic partners law enacted. We will no doubt face similar setbacks as we progress toward marriage equality. And despite these setbacks, we will continue to progress.

Granting same-sex marriage licenses is a grassroots movement in the most noble of senses. In all, 4,037 lesbian and gay couples from forty-six states braved the February weather and lined up for days on end to get married at San Francisco City Hall. This was not a political event organized by MoveOn.org. What we saw was an organic, spontaneous act by family units of love seeking validation. It was a phenomenon sparked by couples who love one another and want the recognition and affirmation that marriage confers.

And these couples are finding tremendous support for the marriage equality movement. Public officials from both sides of the political aisle, such as New York Attorney General Eliot Spitzer and Mayor Michael Bloomberg, have expressed support for marriage equality. Our governor, Arnold Schwarzenegger, has said he would not mind if same-sex marriages were legal. Celebrities including Howard Stern and Ben Affleck have voiced their support, and Rosie O'Donnell flew out to be married in San Francisco. Indeed a groundswell of support has also risen across the country—from Seattle, Washington to Portland, Oregon to Sandoval County, New Mexico to New Paltz, New York. Not to mention the leaders across the globe who have embraced gay marriage, including the king of Cambodia and the recently elected prime minister of Spain.

Here at home, we see American attitudes changing—seven out of ten people under age thirty support gay marriage. They see marriage as a right to which all Americans should have access, and from which no American should be barred. This generation has grown up during a more open and accepting time in our nation's history, where it is more common to have a lesbian or gay person among their circle of friends and family. Children have friends whose parents are in committed same-sex relationships or relatives who are out of the closet. Popular culture has embraced the complexity of modern life, portraying same-sex relationships as the societal norm, not an aberration.

Meanwhile, American families have been redefined, and gay families are part of the new definition. In fact, nontraditional families comprise the majority of American households. These households include single-parent families, families with adopted children, multigenerational families, and lesbian and gay couples who are heads of households, parents, adoptive parents, foster parents, and stepparents. As these types of families become more common and more open, they become part of our shared, blended American experience.

In present day America, marriage is no longer a privilege reserved solely for traditional families. The true function of marriage and family must be dictated by the norm of today, not the dogma of the past. Contrary to the fears of marriage equality opponents, same-sex marriages can only strengthen the institution of marriage, for these marriages, like others, are about love, commitment, and stability—qualities that build the foundation for vibrant, healthy communities.

The stories in this book speak to the American experience. They introduce us to families and couples who found each other, fell in love, and chose to live their lives together. For these and many other lesbian and gay couples, marriage means more than gaining new rights. It means freedom from discrimination, confirmation that their love equals any other love in the eyes of the law. For gay couples with children, marriage is about providing legal rights and benefits so their children can grow up safely and securely in their homes, schools, and communities. For our nation and the world, lesbian and gay marriage is a civil rights movement that will provide equal rights to a segment of the population who has long been denied these rights, thereby strengthening us all.

Mazel tov!

Preface

CHERYL DUMESNIL

▼

I was pregnant when my wife Tracie and I got married, March 11, 2004. First trimester pregnant, which means tired, nauseous, and cautiously hopeful. Because I'd had three miscarriages prior to this pregnancy, we were not yet counting on the little one to grow. In fact, no one but Tracie and our doctor knew about the question mark floating in my uterus. On our wedding day trip to San Francisco, I nibbled on a whole wheat scone and sipped water in an attempt to steady the ground beneath my queasy belly.

Not yet believing in this pregnancy's viability, when I stood at the base of the marble staircase in City Hall that day, watching with Tracie and our friend Becky as a couple were married on the landing above us, I did not think of this moment in history relative to our unborn child's life. I absorbed the moment for myself, knowing we were witnessing a profound event, wondering how long the weddings would last, wondering how soon the opposition would try to invalidate our marriage contracts and derail our charge toward equal rights.

Months later, on June 27, no longer nauseous and now five months round with pregnancy, I hurried up Market Street with Tracie to join the newlywed contingent of the San Francisco Pride Parade. The festive atmosphere at the rendezvous point, Market and Beale Streets, felt like a replay of the wedding days at City Hall. Couples stood in the blocked off street, laughing and swapping wedding stories. Dressed in everything from shorts and T-shirts to tuxedos with rainbow cummerbunds and formal wedding gowns, newlyweds held an array of creative signs that alternately made us smile and tear up: "After fifteen years she finally made an honest woman out of me," "Justly married," and "What if they stopped *your* wedding?"

When Mayor Gavin Newsom threaded his way through the crowd toward his parade car, flanked by bodyguards, we cheered as crowds do for rock stars and heroes. Standing across from us, an elderly man held up a sign as the mayor walked by: "Together 28 years; Married February 15; Thank you Gavin Newsom." The man holding the sign must have been twice Mayor Newsom's age. Soon Assessor-Recorder Mabel Teng and California State Assembly-member Mark Leno made their way through the throngs of newly-weds, receiving the same expressions of gratitude as they walked to their parade floats. As we waited for the parade to begin, Tracie and I struck up conversations with strangers and saw again some couples we had met at City Hall. For the first time, people noticed I was pregnant without us announcing it. People I have never met offered their congratulations. And this time, as he announced his presence by turning flips and half gainers in my belly, I thought about this historical moment relative to our unborn child's life.

We conceived this baby on February 12, the day the first same-sex couple, Phyllis Lyon and Del Martin, were married at City Hall. On February 20, not knowing if I was pregnant or not, I took BART into the city to volunteer at the Clerk's Office. Those were the days when City Hall was ringed by one thousand-person-long lines and fleets of media satellite vans, when bride and groom hopefuls waited upwards of eleven hours for a chance at a wedding license, when City Hall employees scrambled to marry as many couples as they could, multiple hundreds a day. From the time I left the train that morning until I returned to the station late that afternoon, I had not sat down for more than five minutes. Swept up in the excitement, I worked nonstop, shuttling couples from the Clerk's Office where they got their marriage licenses, through the crowded hallways, out to the rotunda where they would be married. My job included not only guiding the newlyweds, but also carrying their belongings so they could have their hands free to wave to the cheering crowd as they walked down the hallway, flashing their marriage licenses. Many of these people had been camped out since the wee hours of the morning. They had a lot of stuff—duffle bags, coolers, cameras, folding chairs. Had I known I was pregnant, I might have been more cautious about the weight load I carried. Occasionally remembering that possibility, I did pause for bites of a fruit salad, an energy bar, or a muffin. And I made sure I drank my water.

Four months later, preparing for the Pride Parade, I looked through our wedding day photos where my pregnancy was invisible under my size two pink silk dress—the dress that no longer fit over my belly by Pride weekend. Looking at the photos, I remembered leafing through family albums with my mom when I was a kid, how she would point to some snapshots and say, "You were in my tummy then." I marveled at that thought—how I was both present and not present with my mother when she posed beside a canyon, sat on a couch in my grandmother's living room, stood on the sidewalk next to a café. If my older sister pulled age rank and argued, "You weren't there," I'd fight back, insisting, "Yes I was, in Mom's belly."

So in that way, yes, our son was there, sitting on the couch, watching the news with us when we first heard that San Francisco was issuing marriage licenses. He was at City Hall as his mom volunteered to guide newlyweds through the wedding process. He was on the rotunda steps when his moms were married on the morning of March 11, and he was in the Castro later that evening, after the courts ended the weddings, when we returned to the city to protest their decision. Our son has heard it all.

Within a year surrounding my own birth, John F. Kennedy was killed, Dr. Martin Luther King Jr. was killed, the Stonewall Riots energized the gay and lesbian community to fight for their rights, and our government landed a man on the moon. I was born during the Viet Nam War and at the height of the civil rights movement. Because of my birth's proximity to these events, even in childhood I felt connected to them. Maybe the timing of my birth is a source of my drive for social justice: this is what was happening in this country when I was born; this is what I was born out of, born into.

And so I was thinking about our son as I sat on the hardwood floor in our living room, making our sign for the Pride Parade, gluing a Kelly Moore Paints stir stick to the back of a piece of poster board, affixing a copy of our Marriage Certificate to the front, lettering Married March 11th in permanent ink. I was thinking about our son at the Pride celebration as the music started on Beale Street, cuing the newlywed contingent to march up Market.

Parade watchers filled the sidewalks five rows deep. They raised their hands high in the air, applauding. They leaned over the police barricades, waving flags and blowing whistles as we walked by. Some wiped tears from under their sunglasses; others pointed at my belly and yelled, "Congratulations!" And I thought, *This is what my son will be born out of, born into—this love, this encouragement, this celebration and struggle to create positive social change.*

I remember childhood family dinners, sitting at the table with my folks, listening to them tell stories about what the world used to be like. As a young girl, my mom was warned not to drink out of public fountains "because you don't know who has been drinking out of there." When he attended a small college in Texas, my dad, a San Francisco Bay Area native, learned about segregation when the buddies he had played basketball with couldn't come get a beer after the game because "their kind" were not allowed at the bar. When Dad told them, "Then I'll go with you wherever you're going," he learned that "his kind" was not allowed where his buddies were headed. I always had the same response to my mom's and dad's stories—an incredulous *"Really?!"* As a kid I could not believe the injustices of the world they had lived in. Looking ahead, I hope my son, his generation, and those who follow will have the luxury of that reaction: *"Really?! Gay people couldn't get married back then? Why?"* And I hope people of our generation will look back and come up with the same response my parents did: "I cannot think of a single good reason why."

That hope inspired me to compile this book, to record the truth of our history, and to help push us toward that future. These stories offer detailed, personal accounts of our experiences at San Francisco City Hall, as newlyweds, volunteers, and witnesses of the historic weddings. This book introduces the newlyweds to the world, reminding readers that our commitments to each other differ very little from the commitments of legally married couples—if anything, our commitments are stronger, tested as they are by bigotry rooted in ignorance and fear. Finally, this book celebrates the strength and courage of the 4,037 couples who were married and the city and county officials and volunteers who helped those weddings happen, continuing the outpouring of love that began in San Francisco on February 12, 2004.

The Marrying Machine

FROM AN INTERVIEW WITH CALIFORNIA STATE
ASSEMBLYMEMBER MARK LENO

▼

For months I had been planning to introduce my Marriage License Non-Discrimination Act to the California State Assembly on February 12, 2004, National Freedom to Marry Day. I was working toward that goal when, on Monday, February 9, I heard from San Francisco Mayor Gavin Newsom about the plan to issue marriage licenses to same-sex couples. His news took me a bit by surprise, and I was excited that we were going to do this very dramatic thing, making marriage equality a reality in San Francisco. On Monday, Mayor Newsom was still looking into whether we really could move forward with this plan. He had to talk to the City Attorney further and see what changes needed to be made to the marriage license forms at the County Clerk's Office. He learned that, because the city charter states that the Recorder directs the County Clerk, not the mayor, his power was limited. So all the mayor could do was urge the County Clerk to make preparations. Then things moved pretty quickly.

On Wednesday, February 11, I heard that Del Martin and Phyllis Lyon, together fifty-one years, would be married the next day. I had a floor session in Sacramento on Thursday morning, so I couldn't be in San Francisco for their wedding. That morning, I put my bill across the desk of the Assembly Clerk and received a number for it: AB1967. These numbers are handed out in chronological order. Coincidentally, 1967 was the year that the United States Supreme Court ended the ban on interracial marriage.

Having filed the bill, I jumped in my car and raced back to San Francisco as quickly as possible. Outside City Hall, hundreds of couples were gathered. A podium was set up at the top of the staircase where Supervisors Tom Ammiano and Bevan Dufty were speaking. I stepped up to welcome everybody and share the good news about the Marriage License Non-Discrimination Act. Then I proceeded inside City Hall and met with Mabel Teng who had a press conference assembled in her office. When we finished with the press, we began performing weddings. I spent the next five hours marrying couples throughout that afternoon. It was thrilling. It's hard to describe how thrilling it was.

Seen with hindsight now, clearly our actions on Thursday, February 12 were the beginning of something big. We didn't yet know how big. With Mabel, I married the second and then the third couple. The second couple were two women, one of whom is the offspring of one of the very first interracial couples to be married legally, so there was that wonderful connection. In those early hours, the wedding activities were makeshift. We moved out of Mabel's office into the rotunda, and this line began to form. To give you a sense of how free form and spontaneous it all was, I stood in pretty much the same spot in City Hall for about five hours. My staff brought me a sandwich on a plate, and between couples I would take a bite, then take a sip of my drink, and then I would keep on marrying people. I was a marrying machine.

We were moving awfully quickly, so there wasn't a lot of time to learn many details about the couples I was marrying, but I tried to add a little something personal to the ceremonies. I asked each couple how long they had been together. One of the last lines of the service that the clerk provides for the Deputy Marriage Commissioners is, "Now that you have joined yourselves in matrimony, may you strive your entire lives to meet the commitments you have made today with the same love and devotion that you are possessing at this time." Since all of the couples I married had been together a minimum of five to ten years, in some cases twenty or thirty, I would change the words to, "with the same love and devotion that you possess at this time and have possessed for the past eighteen years."

Many of the couples I knew. And many of the couples I was meeting for the first time. I married two men from Sacramento who had been together for fifty years. One of the most memorable experiences for me was standing before those two seventy-eight-year-old gentlemen who had been together for fifty years, looking them in the eye and saying, "Now do you promise to love and comfort, honor and keep, in sickness and in health, for better or for worse, for richer or for poorer, to be faithful as long as you both shall live?" And they'd been doing it for fifty years. It gets a little silly.

Also memorable were the people who said, "Excuse my appearance, but I didn't know I was getting married today. We came to City Hall to protest the fact that we weren't getting a marriage license." They had just come to protest and then were issued their marriage certificates. They had no idea that would happen. They proceeded to the "altar," embarrassed by their very casual clothing. And then of course there were people who were arriving breathlessly, saying, "We heard it on the radio," or "We saw it on the Internet." They had picked up their phones, called their partners, and said, "Meet me at City Hall." People were jumping on buses, rushing over to City Hall to get there before five o'clock. Their urgency about it called to mind the image of what Ellis Island must have looked like in times of intense waves of immigration—people longing and yearning and rushing to get this taste of freedom that they had been denied for eternity. So the floodgates were being opened.

On that first day, we had no idea that the weddings would continue for a month. A couple hours into it, we learned that our adversaries were stymied. Marriage equality opponents were looking for an immediate injunction to stop the weddings, but they couldn't file their papers because it was Abraham Lincoln's birthday. The courts were closed. Also, the courts require a twenty-four-hour notice period. So our opponents couldn't take any legal action until Monday. But Monday was a legal holiday, President's Day, so the opposition were stalled until Tuesday. We learned all of this information between wedding ceremonies, as the afternoon unfolded. By the end of Thursday, Mabel Teng, a Deputy Marriage Commissioner, and I had performed weddings for the ninety-five couples who got married that first day. And that was just the beginning.

By Friday, couples were not just jumping on buses, but jumping on planes and flying across the country to get to City Hall before the curtain came down. On Friday the mayor announced

that the doors of City Hall would remain open all holiday weekend long, with the weekend services operated by volunteer assistance. We deputized many, many more people to perform
weddings. On Monday of that holiday weekend—on that one
day—eight hundred and fifty marriage licenses were issued. So
you can imagine the mania that was going on.

I HAVE TO tell you, politics aside, I'm very drawn to all of this. I'm
a single guy, but I had a partner for ten years, from 1980–1990.
So I feel very blessed—I know what that thing is. And I am fascinated by that thing—what is it that two people are able to see in
each other's eyes that draws them together and makes them
decide they want to commit their lives to each other? It's a fasci-
nating thing. Clearly, more books have been written about it
than anything else. It is one of the least understood human experiences. It has produced incredible works of art—musical, visual,
dance, literary—through the ages. Since my partner's death, having been single all this time, there've been some flirtations and
there've been some crushes, but I realize that whatever that thing
was that happened with my partner has not happened for me with
anyone else since. So I'm continually fascinated by it. I think it's
magic that falls from the sky. I just don't think there's anything
else you can say about it. And isn't it an amazing and wonderful
thing? And so I'm very drawn to the fact of these commitments
of love. I feel enormously privileged to have been present and not
only witnessed but officiated for more than one hundred couples.
It's really been exciting and thrilling in a personal way, inde-
pendent of the political thrill of it all.

Soon after the weddings ended, I had a packed schedule. I
hadn't had a day off for a long time. One Sunday I had finally
cleared some time for myself. But then I got an invitation to be
at the Unitarian Church at 9:00 that morning. A reverend friend
of mine was consecrating twelve recently married couples. He
asked if I would come say a few words. So, that was going to be
my morning to sleep in, but I wanted to be there. I didn't want
to miss it. I felt that drawn to it.

OF COURSE, AT the other end of these wedding stories, we see the
heartbreak of the 2,700 couples who had made reservations to be

married in San Francisco, and of the untold thousands who won't have that opportunity.

I was in Sacramento on Thursday, March 11, when I heard about the court decision to end the weddings. I was disappointed when I heard the news, but it got more disappointing when I arrived in San Francisco and actually met some of the couples who had been turned away from the County Clerk's Office. Two fellas had driven across the state in their tuxedos and wanted to know if the city would pick up the cost of the rented tuxes. Then they realized that they were not the only ones turned away, but that thousands of couples were in the same position. I believe that the images of the couples who walked up to the counter at the Clerk's Office and were told they could not get a marriage license will help move us further politically. It's one thing to deny rights, it's another thing to take something away. There is a mean spirit-edness about it, a cruelty.

In the political realm, when the weddings ended we saw an interesting shift. Whereas on February 12 the shocking story was "Oh my god, look what's happening, they're issuing marriage licenses to same-sex couples," by March 12 it was, "Oh my god, look what's happening, they've stopped the weddings." Many people, not just those who were closely involved, felt disappointed that the weddings ended. We moved public opinion in those thirty days, in unknown ways, in unfathomed ways, and com-pletely without design. Mayor Newsom did what he did because he knew in his heart it was the right thing to do. And he knew he was going to have hundreds of same-sex couples descending on City Hall on February 12. He as mayor was in a position of turn-ing them away as always, or issuing licenses. He decided to issue licenses. What he couldn't have known at the time was the power of the images that were flashed around the world endlessly for week after week after week.

The fact of those photographs and videos changed people's minds and hearts rather quickly. Dazzlingly so. A field poll con-ducted here in California soon after the weddings ended showed 52 percent of Californian Republicans in support of civil unions. In the history of California there's never been a Republican in the state legislature who has ever supported any GLBT right. The polling results teach Republican legislators that they're not representing their constituents, a majority of whom now support civil unions. We didn't have one Republican in the state legislature this past year supporting our AB205, the comprehensive domestic partnership bill. The Republican constituents probably didn't know a year ago that they supported civil unions, but as a result of the actions in San Francisco, they support it. Because San Francisco moved all the way to demanding full marriage equality on February 12, the middle ground got dragged all the way to supporting civil unions, almost overnight. Public opinion is a dicey thing. It's hard to understand how you move it. But we moved mountains in those few weeks in San Francisco. Quite unexpectedly.

PUBLIC OPINION SHIFTS in response to national news like the San Francisco weddings, but it also shifts one person at a time, in response to individual experiences. When marriage equality became a front page item about four or five years ago, and I was already involved with the issue as a legislator, I asked my parents to tell me their feelings about the subject so I could benefit from their views. We'd never really talked about the marriage issue, though I'd been out to them as a gay man for thirty-five years and I have a lesbian sister as well. Though they're very familiar with my being out, my parents expressed discomfort about same-sex marriage, and again, even though I'd been out all these decades, shame still came to the surface. So we flushed all that out and I thanked them for their honesty. It was a tough conversation, but it was important. And then I said, "But listen, if Doug were alive"—and they loved him like a son—"and we decided we wanted to get married, are you telling me you wouldn't be the first ones to uncork the champagne and throw the biggest party anyone ever imagined and join in the celebration?" They were silent for about five seconds, then they were in tears, saying, "Of course we would!" They were there, like that. Two days later, I overheard my father on the phone with a friend of his, arguing, asking, "And who is my son not to have the same rights as your son?" So he had become an activist. My parents are eighty-three years old.

In recent months, some of my own thoughts about marriage have changed as well. As an advocate for marriage equality for the past six or seven years, I had reached a point where I wanted the bottom line, the benefits, the privileges, the rights, and I wasn't interested in fighting a war over a word. I was not that attached to the word "marriage." But my mind changed completely after the Massachusetts State Supreme Judicial Court ruling, which had poetic wording in it. They said first and foremost there is no constitutional basis for this discrimination, and that our history teaches us that separate is seldom if ever equal. But they went on to say that only marriage and marriage alone would remedy the situation. A parallel track would not do. And that's where they differed with the Vermont State Court which said civil unions will work if that's what you choose to do. But the Massachusetts State Court told their legislature that *only* marriage will do, because they said—and this is what impressed me so incredibly— these four heterosexual justices said that anything short of marriage "perpetuates a destructive stereotype that communicates that there is something inherently inferior and unstable" in the way I love, as a gay man, compared to how a heterosexual person loves. They said that the destructive stereotype must end. The ramifications of their statement are huge.

If I settle for civil union, I am accepting a premise that there's something inherently inferior and unstable in the way I love. If I settle for that premise, then why should I be afforded any equality? Lawmakers could use that inferiority to deny all of us any rights that are afforded any other American. So no, civil unions will not do. They imply an inherent inferiority. The Massachusetts justices made me realize that, and that realization gave me impetus to introduce my bill when I did. A lot of folks are saying, "No, not now, it's not a good time, what about the backlash? Wait until after the election." No. We have got to do it now. There's no perfect time to further the cause of civil rights. Neither is there a wrong time.

While we see that opinions about marriage equality are shifting, I would rather not wait for the shift of public opinion. History shows us that, in this country, civil rights are not granted through shifts in public opinion. We didn't abolish slavery by taking a vote of the people. We didn't give women or people of color or people who are eighteen years old the right to vote by a vote of the people. These changes occurred either through the courts or through constitutional amendments, which happen through a legislative process. When the U.S. Supreme Court ended the ban on interracial marriage in 1967, a Gallup Poll that showed 74 percent of Americans opposed that decision. It has taken decades for the populous to catch up with that strict reading of the constitution, which states that there are no grounds for this discrimination and lack of equal protection.

To THE COUPLES who are still waiting and fighting for the right to marry, I want to say be patient. Count your blessings. The biggest blessing you have is each other, and no one can take that away from you. Sustain each other in your disappointment. This is part of an ongoing battle and we won't rest until it's won. And we will win. There's no doubt in my mind that we'll prevail. I can't tell you the date. I know from looking at the polls that gay marriage is the future of the United States, not just California. People who are over sixty-five oppose marriage equality more than the general population, and those under thirty-five support it more than those over sixty-five oppose it. So it's only a matter of time before the demographic shift occurs. One generation passes, another comes into its majority. One day the legitimacy of marriage equality will not be debated anymore. Of course, we want to speed up that process because there's no reason on earth that loving couples should be denied a marriage license.

On March 12, the day after the weddings ended in San Francisco, I read a quotation in the newspaper: "I'm a law-abiding, tax-paying adult citizen in this country. Explain to me why I am denied this marriage license." I've said it all along—try and name one other license that the County Clerk issues that is denied to an entire group of people. There isn't one. Licenses are not denied to entire groups of people. And that's what we're talking about: a marriage license. That's why the title of my bill is the Marriage License Non-Discrimination Act. We're talking about a legal document being denied to a group of people.

Adversaries want to talk about the sanctity of marriage, the sacredness of marriage. No. A marriage license is a legal document not a sacred document. What makes a marriage sacred is that which the couple invests into the marriage. Our government can't issue sacred documents. We are a democracy, not a theocracy. We go to war to fight theocracies. So if you want to quote scripture, I recommend that you don't use the Bible or the Torah or the Qur'an. Use the holy books of our democracy, which are the Bill of Rights, the Constitution, and the Declaration of Independence. And when you come at it from that direction, there are just no grounds for denying same-sex couples the right to marry. I'm an ardent supporter of separation of church and state. I would never begin to tell a church what they should or should not do. But we're talking about marriage licenses—legal documents. I'm saying that it's my job as a legislator to make sure that all Californians are treated equally under the law.

Spouses for Life

PHYLLIS LYON AND DEL MARTIN

▼

When we became the first couple to be legally married in San Francisco, on February 12, 2004, we had no idea of the consequences it would have—the worldwide publicity and the tremendous responses congratulating us for once again paving the way for equal rights and justice for Lesbian, Gay, Bisexual, and Transgender people.

Early in February, we had heard that our mayor, Gavin Newsom, had attended the State of the Union address in Washington, D.C., and been distressed by President George W. Bush's call for an amendment to the U.S. Constitution to ban same-sex marriages. Bush's announcement inspired Mayor Newsom to reflect on his recent swearing in as mayor in January 2004, when he took an oath to defend the California and U.S. constitutions. In those documents he found language prohibiting discrimination against any citizen or group of citizens. It was obvious to him that same-sex couples who wanted to get married were being discriminated against, that separate but equal is not equal.

When Kate Kendell, Executive Director of the National Center for Lesbian Rights, phoned us on February 11, she asked us if we would agree to be the first couple to get married in San Francisco. Without hesitation, we said, "Yes." Kate explained that she didn't know exactly when the ceremony would take place—it might be the same day. But it wasn't. She made a date to pick us up at 9:00 the next morning.

So on February 12, we got up early and started getting dressed, when the phone rang. It was Kate—the pick-up time had been changed to 10:30. "Okay," we said, and began to have coffee and read the paper.

Then the phone rang again. "How soon can you be dressed?" Kate asked us.

We said, "In half an hour."

"Okay," she said, "I'll pick you up at 9:30."

So it was going to happen.

We arrived at City Hall and made the long trek through the halls to the office of our assessor-recorder, Mabel Teng. There was an aura of secrecy in that morning's adventure. Our marriage was to be secret because City Hall officials didn't want the "anti" people to rush into court and file a lawsuit. (Later we all found out that the courts were closed because it was President Lincoln's birthday.) So we sat around and chatted with some friends, and finally filled out an application form for a marriage license. The form had been changed to drop the terms "bride" and "groom" and replace them with "Applicant No. 1" and "Applicant No. 2."

It turned out that Mabel was going to perform the marriage. A little after 11:00, we all got up and formed a small group, and heard Mabel announce that we were "spouses for life." During the ceremony there were camera flashes going off and a video-tape was being made. But we were really only aware of the words of the wedding ceremony and each other. One of the photographs of us, taken by a *San Francisco Chronicle* photographer, made the front page of the *Chronicle*, and it seems to have been reproduced on the front pages of most large papers in the U.S., plus many foreign papers.

After the brief ceremony, we thanked everyone for being present and went upstairs to see the mayor who gave us congratulations and a paperback book containing the text of the constitutions of the U.S. and the State of California. Then Kate swept us away, down the front stairs, past numerous members of the press—newspaper, radio, and television—to whom we could say only a few words. Then Kate drove us home.

We assume this abrupt ending was meant to protect us from

encountering any negative reactions from a gathering crowd. This precaution seemed rather strange, since the whole event had supposedly been kept secret. But once the word was out—as it would be soon, considering the media presence—it was evident that a crowd would gather, whether they were for or against same-sex marriages. Still, we were used to being called names, being told that marriage between one man and one woman was sacred, and hearing that we were doomed to hell. Perhaps it was due to our ages—Phyllis, seventy-nine and Del, eighty-three—that people felt a need to protect us.

Kate drove us home and there we were, safe and sound—and hungry. It was past our lunchtime and we didn't have anything to eat in the house, so we headed to Delancey Street and celebrated our new status at our favorite table by the window overlooking the San Francisco Bay. While we were well known as patrons of Delancey Street, at that time no one there knew anything about the wedding.

On Saturday, February 14, Valentine's Day, we celebrated our regular anniversary at home, alone, over champagne. Phyllis asked, "Which of our anniversaries are we going to claim as the one?"

Del responded, "This one, of course."

We first moved in together into an apartment in the Castro (way before it went gay) on Valentine's Day in 1953. So we have been together fifty-one years as of this marriage year. We were also "Domestic Partnered" by then-mayor, Willie Brown, on March 26, 1999, on the stairs under the City Hall dome, along with hundreds of other couples. A few years later, on March 2, 2002, we became California State Domestic Partners. But we intend to keep February 14 as our official anniversary, since that's the date we first committed ourselves to each other.

We have many fond memories of our lives together, including the house we bought in June 1955, which we dubbed Habromania Haven, named after a type of insanity or madness of a pleasing nature. It is also the home where many events of the Daughters of Bilitis were held in its formative years. D.O.B. started as a secret social club for lesbians but soon blossomed out into the first national Lesbian organization. D.O.B. was also the beginning of our activism in the Lesbian-Gay movement, which led us into involvement in many civil rights movements, especially the women's movement. We might add that Habromania Haven is still our home.

But getting back to the same-sex marriage issue. We took our vows seriously. We are committed to follow through on the case against the state and to promote the cause of marriage for everyone, even if that means being available to the media, attending fundraisers, appearing and testifying in court if necessary, and whatever else will enable us to explain and educate people about equal rights. Our children need to be accepted for who they are and who their parents are. They should have the same opportunities as other children. Too many have been ridiculed, taunted, and physically harmed because they have two moms or two dads.

At the beginning, we figured our current crusade for equal rights would be confined to California. We had never dreamed that we would marry, so we were overwhelmed when the concept swept across the country—and out of the country—like wildfire. We were not prepared for the positive reaction to the photo of our marriage, nor for it to be published in newspapers around the world. We were deluged by congratulatory phone calls, letters, and cards from friends and from strangers. Our house filled with bouquets of flowers, mostly roses, and we almost ran out of spaces on which to display them. We received communiqués and handmade valentines from youngsters, and buttons that had "the photo" on them, or slogans such as, "So you finally made an honest woman out of her." Then we began to get requests from organizations in other states to attend their events.

On Sunday, February 22, the Bay Area Community of Women, along with many other friends and organizations, hosted a wedding reception at the Hyatt Regency for us and all the other couples who had been married. It was fantastic. Two thousand people showed up. We were escorted to a stage from which various friends spoke about us and about the necessity for marriage equality. More photos were taken, and Olivia Cruises and Resorts offered us a free cruise. After the events on the stage, we were again escorted to another room where we could talk with people. And talk we did, with people we had never met, and with friends we hadn't seen for ages. In the days after the event, we found out many of our friends had attended, but the crowd was so large that we hadn't seen them.

Our Olivia cruise starts in Boston, in the state that is continuing to conduct same-sex marriages. We are hoping to meet those who are making this happen and find ways in which we can combine our efforts to keep the momentum going. The cruise will also take us to Provincetown where we will no doubt meet others who are also legally married.

All of our traveling requires more energy from aged bodies that require more rest, as well as more time to adjust to time differences. This is not to say that we are complaining. We know that we will be well taken care of and will enjoy the experience and the fun. It is just that our calendar is getting pretty full, and the thought of what it entails is exhausting.

Since we married, the California Supreme Court has already ruled on one legal issue, whether Mayor Newsom had the power to ignore a state law he found to be discriminatory. On August 11, 2004, they ruled that Mayor Newsom did not have legal authority to issue marriage licenses to same-sex couples, and they invalidated the marriage licenses issued between February 12 and March 11 in San Francisco. Soon after we were married, a different lawsuit was filed on behalf of several same-sex couples, including us. This lawsuit questions the constitutionality of the California law that offers marriage rights only to heterosexual couples. Our lawsuit will continue at the California Superior Court level, and it will be some time before our case is heard. However, the reality is that the ultimate decision on the constitutionality of our marriages will be made by United States Supreme Court. The lawsuits brought in other states and in other areas of California will give us more chances to challenge existing laws prohibiting same-sex marriage. We are hopeful that the ultimate decision will be in our favor.

"Joy Lies in the Fight"

JULIE HENDERSON

▼

On the evening of Tuesday, February 10, I received an e-mail
from Marriage Equality California, an organization that I
signed up with two years ago during Pride Weekend in San Francisco. Although I'm a youngin' at eighteen years of age, I have
been very active in the gay community and I fully support those
couples who are serious about making a lifetime commitment to
each other. The e-mail announced a rally celebrating National
Freedom to Marry Day, scheduled for noon, on Thursday, February 12, on the steps of San Francisco City Hall. I was eager to
participate in what was dubbed "lunch hour activism" and to
extend my support to couples like Phyllis Lyon and Del Martin,
and Molly McKay and Davina Kotulski, who have led the efforts
both locally and nationally to acquire the right to marry. I quickly
forwarded the e-mail to my partner at the time, Ariel, who lives
in San Francisco. We both wanted to participate, and even though
doing so meant cutting classes, we planned to take off Thursday
morning to join in the festivities.

Mahatma Gandhi once said, "Joy lies in the fight, in the
attempt, in the suffering involved, not in the victory itself." My fight
began at school that Thursday morning. It was easy for Ariel to get
out of her morning Music History class at the San Francisco Conservatory of Music, but my ditching required a little more effort.

I had two big tests in my first two periods, not to mention I was walking on thin ice with my Catholic high school's administration for having ditched classes previously to travel to the city on a school day. If I were caught leaving school grounds this time, expulsion would surely follow.

After a morning of chaos, stress, test-taking, and examination of my priorities, I notified the teachers of my remaining classes about the event and got their permission to go to City Hall. Before I knew it, I was in the front seat of my girlfriend's car, on our way to help make history.

We parked near Ariel's place in San Francisco's Sunset District, collected our camera, keys, money, and Muni change, checked to make sure we had our "Freedom to Marry" game faces on, then hopped on a streetcar, headed for downtown. While walking down Market Street toward Civic Center we were scoffed at by a few passersby, but were quickly reinforced by the show of love and support from many others. When we finally arrived at the steps of City Hall, we were disappointed by what was, compared to the antiwar rallies we'd participated in and witnessed in San Francisco, a small crowd. We made our way up to the steps where we saw same-sex couples holding signs reading Justly Married and We Are All Human. With them stood Mark Leno, the California State Assemblymember who is trying to write justice and equality into our state constitution, and San Francisco Supervisor Tom Ammiano. Guards secured the front entrance to the building until the rally subsided.

Close to 250 people attended the rally, each one willing to take a stand for the right to marry legally in our state. The message was simple, as it always has been and always will be in the fight for gay rights. What lies at the core of any struggle connected to the greater gay rights movement is the desire to be recognized as human. That is, we wish to be treated with the respect that we, as human beings, all deserve.

Our efforts met the dissent of only one protester, a middle-aged man who called out that the reason why Molly had been denied a marriage license to her partner of eight years, Davina, was because she was not "a husband." He argued that his nine-year-old son is what kept him from being confused about his sexuality, and while he squealed ignorance, the rest of us drowned him out with cheers, laughter, and roaring applause for the couples and community leaders who spoke about love, hope, and courage on the steps of City Hall.

Initially the rally had been organized simply to protest the inequity of California State marriage laws. What many of the protesters did not know was that Mayor Gavin Newsom and Assessor-Recorder Mabel Teng had their own plans for February 12. Earlier that day, thanks to Mayor Newsom's commitment to justice, Phyllis Lyon and Del Martin had gotten married. Now, much to their surprise, protesters who had come to City Hall expecting to have their requests for marriage licenses turned down were welcomed into the building to get married.

Ariel and I clung to each other as we entered City Hall with everyone else, eagerly awaiting the moment when the City Clerk would unveil the new and improved marriage licenses that would permit same-sex couples to get married. We waited with nearly forty couples in a line that extended beyond the corridor leading up to the office where each couple received their marriage license. Reporters hovered above and below, asking us all questions, digging into couples' personal stories, and documenting this exciting, monumental moment in history with their cameras. As each new couple walked out with their marriage licenses, none having imagined that they would truly make such a bold move on that day, we cheered and extended our good wishes. Nothing could have made the smiles on our faces fade now that *finally* someone was willing to stand up against the barrier of hatred, ignorance, and fear that engulfs so many political institutions in this country.

While waiting in line we spoke with many couples who had traveled near and far to participate in the rally. The couple to our left had been together eight years, the couple in front of us for fourteen, and the couple directly behind us had been together four years. It was encouraging to know that in a society where marriage is regularly demoralized by heterosexual couples, namely Britney Spears and her husband of roughly fifty-eight hours, there still exists so much love and compassion between partners who have truly committed themselves to one another.

We were at City Hall that day to support the marriage equality cause, to show the world that love is love. I look forward to making this lifetime commitment to my own partner someday, when the state finally recognizes that the sanctity of marriage lies in its availability to all human beings, not in its limited access to men and women who hardly honor it as a "special" or "solid" commitment.

After witnessing a wedding ceremony officiated by Mabel Teng near the entrance of City Hall, Ariel and I made our way toward Mark Leno to thank him for the courage and effort that he has contributed to our community's movement. We congratulated Molly and Davina and the other couples who were married that day and then left the building in a state of euphoria. We felt empowered knowing that we had stood up not only as representatives of the GLBTQ community, but as representatives of all human beings who are denied their rights. As more people try to strip us of our natural human rights, it is even more crucial that the community stands together on the issue of gay marriage. I extend my full support and gratitude to anyone who is willing to sacrifice so much in order to work for the freedom and liberty of so many people.

Newlyweds After Seventeen Years

JOHN LEWIS AND STUART GAFFNEY

▼

MARCH 17, 1987

For nearly as long as we can remember, we each wanted to meet someone to fall in love with and start building a life together. It happened March 17, 1987.

It was a Tuesday evening, and an exciting time in San Francisco politics. The politically powerful Philip Burton, and then his wife Sala, had held San Francisco's seat in Congress for years. But now the seat was open due to Sala Burton's untimely death. Harry Britt, the openly gay president of the San Francisco Board of Supervisors, was running to become the first openly gay member of Congress. His primary opponent in a crowded race was a new face in electoral politics, Nancy Pelosi.

John, who was twenty-eight, had just moved to San Francisco after graduating from law school the year before. He was clerking for a federal judge, and some coworkers had invited him to go to a small fundraising party for Britt at a mutual friend's house. John decided to join them. He was interested in getting involved in local politics—more importantly, he wanted to make new friends or even meet someone to date.

The party turned out to be more a social event than a political fundraiser. However, John remembers that Carole Migden, then chair of the San Francisco Democratic Party and now a California State senator, told those gathered that we had a rare opportunity to elect a truly progressive, openly gay man to Congress. On election day, Nancy Pelosi won narrowly. Little did we know that Pelosi would become the highest ranking woman in the history of the House of Representatives and a champion of lesbian, gay, bisexual, and transgender (LGBT) rights.

As the party went on, John's friends decided to go home, and at first John gave in to shyness and told his friends that he'd go home with them. He knew no one except the busy host at the party. But then John said to himself: "No. I'm new to the city. I'd really like to meet someone. I've got to take a risk and stay."

John saw the host, a casual friend, talking to a young man, and went up to them. The host, clearly wanting to talk *neither* to John *nor* to the young man, exclaimed upon John's approach: "Why don't I introduce the only two people I *don't* know at this party to each other?" Before John could say, "Wait! You're the only person I *do* know at this party," John saw the young man offer his hand—right over the fruit bowl—and say, "Hello, my name is Stuart."

We talked for hours that evening. Stuart, who was twenty-four, was also a relatively recent arrival to San Francisco. He had graduated with a degree in English literature from a college back East a few years before. Now he was working in San Francisco while pursuing his passion—film and video making. We ended up being the last guests to leave the party.

We continued our conversation at the Elephant Walk bar at the corner of 18th Street and Castro. Although neither of us was much of a drinker, it *was* St. Patrick's Day. Finally, before hopping on different buses to go home, we memorized each other's phone numbers—and when we got home called each other to make sure we had them right.

On Thursday night, John called Stuart, and we talked again—for hours. John asked Stuart if he would like to do something that weekend—perhaps go to the congressional candidates' debate. Stuart replied that he'd "*really* like to get together over the weekend," but that his best friend from college and his family were all in town for the weekend. Giving in to insecurity, John feared Stuart was actually rebuffing him, despite all the wonderful hours of conversation. "Just friends?" John thought.

But on Sunday night, Stuart called John, announcing "they're finally all gone." We each jumped on Muni to rendezvous for our first official date: the candidates' debate.

After the debate, Stuart showed John a photograph of his family that he had taken earlier in the day with his brand new Polaroid camera he'd bought for a dollar at a garage sale. The photograph was of the Chinese side of Stuart's family, and we talked about Stuart's experience of being mixed race, Chinese and white. John, himself white, had recently returned from working at a refugee camp in Asia and traveling in China, which at the time had just opened its doors to the West. We talked and walked, and found ourselves an hour later happily enjoying a meal of bean curd, black mushrooms, and bok choy at a nearby Chinese restaurant.

Afterward, we walked back down 18th Street near the intersection of Castro, and we kissed simply and sweetly for the first time. You know it's true love when you *both* want to go to the candidate's debate.

For our second date, we both thought it would be fun to try the brand new Chinese herbalist restaurant in North Beach. An acupuncture convention was in town, and the restaurant was filled with doctors of traditional chinese medicine. We tried our best at dishes made from ingredients such as swallow's nest tree bark and deer antlers, but we must confess we left the restaurant a bit hungry. We then took a long stroll up Telegraph Hill, past Coit Tower, and down the picturesque Filbert Steps overlooking San Francisco Bay. On the way back, we passed a hole-in-the-wall pizzeria, and when Stuart eyed some bacon pizza in the window, we did not hesitate.

John felt as if he had already known Stuart forever. To this day, when we visit old places from Stuart's childhood, John feels like he was there with Stuart. And even before our second date, Stuart had already told his best friend from college, "I've met my future husband."

FEBRUARY 12, 2004

On Thursday, February 12, 2004, the unimaginable became reality. We married each other at San Francisco City Hall in the first hours that San Francisco performed same-sex weddings.

A lot had happened for us in the intervening seventeen years. New friends and family members were born or adopted. Others died. We worked jobs, backpacked around the world together, cared for family, hiked in national parks, enjoyed friends, shopped for food, cooked dinner, and did the laundry. We started living together in our apartment at the beginning of 1988 and started sharing finances in 1989.

The legal and social status of LGBT people also changed dramatically over those years. John remembers attending a protest in the Castro the day the United States Supreme Court decided the notorious *Bowers v. Hardwick* case in the summer of 1986, just months before he met Stuart. In that case, the Supreme Court held that the United States Constitution permitted states to imprison lesbian and gay people merely for physically intimate expression of their love for each other. Warren Burger, then chief justice of the United States, seemed to forget the separation between religion and state, when he justified the decision by stating that "condemnation" of "homosexual conduct" is "firmly rooted in Judeo-Christian moral and ethical standards."

Emotions ran particularly high at the time because HIV/AIDS was ravaging our community and President Reagan could not even say the word *AIDS*. The late lesbian and gay rights attorney Mary Dunlap, who had argued the unsuccessful "Gay Olympics" case before the high court the year before, stood up and addressed the rally. She shouted to Justice Sandra Day O'Connor, over 3,000 miles away in Washington, D.C.: "Have you ever had oral sex? If you have . . . you're a hypocrite! If you haven't . . . you're ignorant!" Dunlap then ripped a copy of the opinion into pieces and threw it to the crowd.

It took seventeen years—our entire relationship—for the United States Supreme Court to rip the *Bowers* opinion into pieces itself. In summer 2003, the Supreme Court overruled *Bowers* in *Lawrence v. Texas*. In a stunning reversal, the court, recognized same-sex couples' love for one another, noting that the sexual expression was "one element in a personal bond that is more enduring." The Constitution protects "personal decisions relating to marriage . . . [and] family relationships," which are "matters, involving the most intimate and personal choices a person may make in a lifetime, choices central to personal dignity and autonomy. . . ." The court stated that people in same-sex relationships should have the same right to autonomy in those decisions as people in different-sex relationships.

As the years passed by, we became increasingly conscious of the disparity between our legal rights and those of married different-sex couples. We were angered when we arose from the kitchen table after figuring our taxes due in 2003: We were paying almost 40 percent more in taxes than if we had been able to file jointly. Over the years, that added up to thousands of dollars of hard-earned money that we could have used for retirement or a down payment for a house. We also found it humiliating to be forced to check the "Single" box on separate income tax returns when we knew it did not reflect the true nature of our relationship. We asked why any newly married different-sex couple—who may have known each other for just a matter of months—could receive the over one thousand benefits of marriage while we, who had been together for seventeen years, could not. We had already registered as California Domestic Partners, but we wanted full equal rights and full legal recognition of our relationship.

In November 2003, we were elated by the news that the Massachusetts Supreme Court had ruled in *Goodridge v. Department of Public Health,* that the Massachusetts Constitution required the state to permit same-sex couples to marry on an equal basis to different-sex couples. Same-sex weddings would begin in Massachusetts in May 2004.

Then in January 2004, President Bush in his State of the Union address proposed amending the United States Constitution to ban same-sex marriage and enshrine discrimination against LGBT people in the Constitution itself. Bush's words were like a dagger through our hearts. We felt as if the President of the United States had attacked us personally. The idea that the Constitution of the United States would forever declare our relationship inferior and treat us as subhuman was anathema to us.

The *Bowers* decision and the federal government's inaction on HIV/AIDS had led us to activism in the late 1980s. It was time to act again. We made a simple New Year's resolution: Get involved with the growing movement for marriage equality—now.

We learned from a local gay newspaper that February 12 was the annual National Right to Marry Day and that the groups

Marriage Equality and Equality California would be holding a noon rally on the steps of San Francisco City Hall. We decided that John would attend, because Stuart would be tied up with work all day. We had heard rumors that the newly elected mayor of San Francisco, Gavin Newsom, might soon direct the City to issue licenses on an equal basis to lesbian and gay couples. Indeed, Bush's attack on lesbian and gay San Franciscans in the State of the Union address so disturbed Newsom himself that he was motivated to act. But the night before, we checked the Internet and read that the City would not be performing marriages that day. We made no plans for contacting each other. Stuart had a 1:00 p.m. meeting at work, and John would report back to him that evening.

When John arrived at the rally just before noon, he approached Molly McKay, Executive Director of Marriage Equality, to ask her the latest news. She exclaimed: "They're issuing licenses!"

"What?"

"They are issuing licenses!"

Disbelief, joy, and then adreneline shot through John. Thank goodness we had had no idea the night before—we never would have been able to sleep. Not knowing that February 12, Lincoln's Birthday, was a state court holiday, John thought that anti-gay groups could be in court at that very moment, trying to halt the marriages. There was no time to waste. But could John catch Stuart before his 1:00 p.m. meeting?

A sympathetic newspaper reporter lent John his cell phone, and he was able to find Stuart, who dropped his work and ran to the subway. As John stood waiting on the City Hall steps, he could sense that something truly historic was taking place. The local, national, and even international press were starting to descend.

When Stuart arrived, we dashed into City Hall, but—perhaps, not surprisingly—we had no idea which office to go to. We had never dreamed that *we* would be able to get married. We eventually made it to the Clerk's Office and found other couples already in the process of getting licenses, and we saw a crowd of reporters and TV camera operators starting to assemble.

The initial application we filled out specified "Bride" and "Groom," but we didn't care. We were getting married. But seconds later, after we had paid our fee and received the license, the deputy clerk asked for it back. We thought, "No, you can't take this away from us. You don't know how long we've waited for this opportunity." But the deputy clerk told us her boss had just informed her that the form needed to say "Applicant No. 1," and "Applicant No. 2," not "Bride" and "Groom." The Clerk's Office had given us pregnancy and family planning information, too—just part of the standard packet. We returned the form and, after a nerve-wracking half-hour or so, we received the new gender-neutral one.

Then, it was off to the Assessor-Recorder's Office where the first ceremonies were being held. As we entered, CNN was televising live the wedding of the couple that got married right before us. A family member soon thereafter called them from New Jersey, and told them: "I just saw you getting married on TV!" The atmosphere was electric and surreal. What had seemed impossible just hours before was actually happening.

We married a few moments later in what we can describe only as a sacred experience—even with a *San Francisco Chronicle* reporter scribbling notes and an *Examiner* reporter snapping photos. Not a single friend or family member was in attendance, and we didn't know if a court injunction would interrupt us in the middle of saying "I do." But there we were—the two of us, holding hands and getting married. During the ceremony, we reexchanged the rings we had originally purchased outside a crowded temple in India in 1998 and then exchanged on an Indian bus. In a sense, the experience at City Hall was no less impromptu and chaotic than the one in India, but this time the City would issue us a certificate showing we were legally married. We were no longer outside the temple—we were inside City Hall.

When we heard the city's tax counsel, who presided over our wedding, announce "by virtue of the authority vested in me by the State of California, I now pronounce you spouses for life," we felt something transform within us. We experienced for the first time our government treating us as fully equal human beings and recognizing us as a loving couple worthy of the full respect of the law. And then we kissed—and held each other—for a long time. "Never, *ever* let you go."

The *San Francisco Chronicle* reported our kiss and the rest of our wedding story as front page news the next morning. Thanks to the

Internet, friends and family across the country learned the news quickly and began sending us congratulatory e-mail messages and gifts. One gay male friend, not prone to sentimentality, wrote that reading the *Chronicle* article is "actually . . . making me cry—with happiness for the two of you and for what it means for all of us." A straight friend wrote that she, her husband, and their kids "are jumping over furniture because we're so happy for you two!!!" Stuart's best friend from second grade, from whom he hadn't heard in over thirty years, sent a bouquet of flowers. A straight male friend reported: "I cried with bittersweet happiness for you two and for the countless years of hiding and suffering that same-sex couples have had to endure."

This outpouring of joy and support from friends and family made us realize how much we had missed by not being able to marry. Friends, family, and coworkers all seemingly knew how to respond to the news of our wedding. One of our most politically active friends asked, "Are you registered?" We first thought she meant "registered to vote," but soon realized she meant "registered at Macy's." Our seven-year-old niece, who knows us only as "Uncles John and Stuart" and knows nothing about marriage discrimination against same-sex couples, revealed the simplicity of the instinct to celebrate love. When we told her about our wedding, she asked simply, "Why were we not invited?"

Shortly after we married, we walked past the Botanical Gardens in San Francisco's Golden Gate Park, where we noticed a young, straight newlywed couple taking pictures on their wedding day. We had witnessed this scene in the park hundreds of times before. But this time it was different. We looked them straight in the eyes and gave them broad, knowing grins. Even though the circumstances of our wedding differed greatly from theirs, our minds immediately flashed to *our* wedding day, and all we could do was smile. Only then did we realize that for years we had ever so slightly averted our eyes when we passed newlyweds in the park. They were doing something that we thought that we would *never* be able to do. Although we had not realized it before, we had felt a tinge of inferiority, jealousy, and resentment. Those painful feelings had now lifted.

We believe strongly that marriage equality for same-sex couples is one element of a broader effort to attain full equality for all

LGBT people, coupled or not. Breaking down the barriers to marriage is a very powerful act, because marriage discrimination against same-sex couples is such a powerful expression of the view that LGBT people are "less than equal." Indeed, the straight, sixteen-year-old son of some dear friends wrote in a traditional pink newlywed card, "Congratulations on your marriage in defiance of an unjust law."

It did not take us long to realize that we were able to marry not only because of Mayor Newsom's incredible leadership, but because of many people's hard work and activism. We recognized that it was time to give back. Instead of an out-of-town honeymoon over the Valentine's Day weekend, we stayed home and wrote a legal declaration for the ACLU, National Center for Lesbian Rights, and Lambda Legal Defense to use in court to defend our marriage. Getting out of town was the last thing we wanted to do anyway; San Francisco was alive with love, jubilation, and freedom, and we did not want to miss it. Over that weekend, seemingly every nook and cranny of San Francisco City Hall was filled with couples professing love and commitment to one another. Such an unending spontaneous expression of love and joy was unprecedented.

Together with all the San Francisco newlyweds, we were venturing into uncharted legal, personal, and political territory. We truly had no idea what lay ahead. We did not even know that thousands of same-sex couples would stream into City Hall in the coming days and weeks to get married. Ironically, Republican Senate Majority Leader Bill Frist put it best when he said that same-sex marriage was primed to spread "like wildfire" across the country.

FEBRUARY 2005

A year has now passed since those joyous days at San Francisco City Hall. Sadly, the California Supreme Court ruled that Mayor Newsom could not independently enforce the California Constitution to stop marriage discrimination. The Court declared our marriage "void from [its] inception and a legal nullity." As far as the government of the State of California is concerned, our marriage never happened.

But when the Court declared our marriage void, we took refuge in the sacred vows we made to each other on February 12 in San Francisco City Hall: "to love and comfort" and "honor and keep" each other "for better or worse." When we married each other, we committed to stand by each other and support each other no matter what comes—even a court's declaring our marriage a legal nullity against our will.

And we have taken action. After the court invalidated our marriage, we became plaintiffs in the lawsuit that challenges the constitutionality of California's denial of access to marriage for same-sex couples. We have lobbied the California legislature to amend the state statute that prohibits same-sex couples from marrying. We have participated in grassroots activism to educate people about the harm that marriage discrimination causes real people. In October 2004, we joined over forty other married couples and supporters on the National Marriage Equality Caravan from San Francisco to Washington, D.C. In towns like Laramie and Akron, we shared stories of our wedding day and spoke out against amending the constitution to deny lesbian and gay couples access to marriage.

Our being denied the right to marry carries particular sting for our family because Stuart's parents were an interracial couple who married here in California fifty-three years ago, in 1952. At the time Stuart's parents married, the California statute books said that interracial couples could not marry, just as today's California statute books say that same-sex couples cannot marry. But in 1948, the California Supreme Court had become the first appellate court in United States history to rule that the laws banning interracial marriage are unconstitutional. Without that ruling, Stuart's parents would have been prohibited from marrying, and we would not be here today.

As we witnessed so much lesbian and gay dignity and love fill San Francisco City Hall during those amazing days in February and March, we could not help but be reminded that Harvey Milk, the first openly gay member of the Board of Supervisors, and Mayor George Moscone were assassinated twenty-five years ago in that very building, largely because of their commitment to lesbian and gay freedom.

We realized that Harvey Milk's 1978 Gay Freedom Day speech opposing the Briggs Initiative, a proposed amendment to the California Constitution that would have banned lesbian and gay teachers from public schools, had striking relevance today. On that day, Milk urged lesbian and gay people to "fight to preserve your democracy from [those] who are trying to constitutionalize bigotry." He vowed, "We are not going to sit back in silence as 300,000 of our gay brothers and sisters did in Nazi Germany. We are not going to allow our rights to be taken away and then march with bowed heads into the gas chambers. On this anniversary of Stonewall, I ask my gay sisters and brothers to make the commitment to fight."

In November 1978, California voters defeated the anti-gay Briggs Initiative by a 2-1 margin. On election night, Mayor Moscone proclaimed in the Castro that from then on "emblazoned upon the principles of San Francisco" will be "liberty and freedom for all, forever. . . ."

We hope that all people who are San Franciscans in spirit and purpose will join us in working for equal access to marriage. Our extraordinary experiences at San Francisco City Hall in February 2004 sustain us. We've tasted the freedom to marry, and there's no going back.

Someone You Should Know

J. E. FRANET

▼

*W*hen *I met* Jenna in the winter of 2000, love no longer interested me. My marriage had ended in August of 1999, and I was enjoying that valuable solitude that Virginia Woolf describes in *A Room of One's Own*. I was still married at the time I read it, living under my husband's oppressive micromanagement. Now I had what I'd yearned for: the freedom to think, to daydream, and to write, while spending time with my two young children and finishing up my bachelor's degree at UC Berkeley.

Suddenly, I had so much more than a room of my own. I had a vast castle spanning 655 square feet: two small bedrooms, a kitchen counter expansive enough to squeeze two baking pans side by side, a battered white desk and a secondhand loveseat, and a dining room table with mismatched chairs.

The living room window of my family housing apartment looked out onto the courtyard, where all the children played. My little white desk faced this window, and when I was tired of transmogrification, or triangulation, or reification, I could turn away from my computer screen and fill my sight instead with sparrows hopping up and down in trees, forbidden cats skulking through the courtyard, and children digging in the lawn with spoons, then filling the cavities with water to turn them into gaping pits of mud.

I was not at all lonely, but I was solitary in a way that I had never before been. My relationship choices had left me with serious doubts about my own judgment, and I vowed not to be wooed by another pauper with an infectious smile and pockets full of lint. Next time I would snag a rich old man, make a fiscally sound decision that would hold up in a capitalist society. That way, when the inevitable occurred and the whole thing plummeted to the ground like a fighter plane shot from the sky, I would be able to tally up the smoking pieces and say it had been worth it.

But then I agreed to cat-sit for my neighbors.

It was Thanksgiving. My family had invited me to dinner, but I chose to be alone, pretending it was just another day that my children were with their father. I decided to drown my holiday sorrows in the speedy euphoria of my neighbor's DSL connection. Perhaps I could expand my circle of women friends to include some other writers.

In my optimistic past I'd browsed Planetout.com looking for romance, never coming across Jenna's profile. Now, looking only for friends, her prescient title appeared to me: "Someone You Should Know." I read on. Among a dozen other things, she liked "kids, poetry, thunderstorms, books, running, animals, the smell of my nana's house . . . what I love most is spending time with the people I care about." In the rest of her profile, the woman I should know sounded intelligent, witty, and honest. There was a hint of sexiness about her—"the small of a woman's back" made it onto her favorite things list—but above all, she sounded *nice*.

By this time, it was past midnight. I kept my introduction brief:

> There is something nice and gentle about your interests . . . friends, conversation, reading. . . .
>
> Wish I had the energy to write more, but it's late and I'm tired, must get some sleep so I can return to Zora Neale Hurston's *Dust Tracks on a Road* and Maxine Hong Kingston's *Woman Warrior.*
>
> I write short stories and read all sorts of books, spend time with friends and my two young children, like animals and sunsets, eating good food and drinking hot apple cider in the wintertime. Please stop by my profile, write back if you like what you see.
>
> Take care,
> Basil Blue

As we became acquainted through a series of e-mails, it seemed that God had cultivated my Caucasian twin in the Midwest and transported her here to California. There were superficial coincidences: we were both named Jennifer, we came from Catholic families, we had brunette hair and brown eyes, we were five foot three. Then there were coincidences of personality and choice: we loved rats, had worked with developmentally disabled children and adults, majored in English, enjoyed foreign films and international literature, valued honesty and humor. . . .

I literally felt my heartbeat quicken every time I saw an e-mail from Jenna, but I struggled to hold onto a healthy disbelief. She was poor, she worked in social services, she was a woman—which meant my children would be ostracized simply for my dating her: she was not my rich old man. Plus, just because she seemed interesting and kind by e-mail didn't mean that she wouldn't turn out to be some New Age freak, or, even worse, that by phone there would be awkward silences, uneven speech patterns, that our symphonious online duet would deteriorate into chaotic dissonance.

Then we talked, and she was wonderful, hysterically funny. She spoke to me in accents—German, Indian, Irish—and I felt as if I were in junior high, being flirted with by the funniest boy in class. We spent hours on the phone, stayed up nights and felt bleary-eyed but happy in the mornings. She'd never even seen my picture, but when she discovered that we both took most of our phone calls in the bathtub, she said we should take a bubble bath together someday—with swimsuits on, just like you do when you're a kid in the tub with a friend.

I reminded myself that sure, she was great on the phone, but what about the time I tried to date that guy I'd been friends with? He was compelling from a distance, but in person I didn't even want to hold his hand.

While talking with Jenna, I did make a friend, a poet with whom I'd been corresponding. Robyn and I met the day before Jenna and I did. Afterward, I felt a little defensive. "I want you to know that I hung out with a woman I met through Planetout," I told Jenna. "And she's just a friend . . . not that it matters . . . because *we're* just friends. . . ." The call was short, awkward. I'd just called up a friend to tell her not to worry because I'd spent time with another friend.

The next night I met Jenna: December 17, 2000. Clearly following the admonitions of online safety, we met at my house. She knocked at the door, and when I opened it, there stood not the sweet disembodied voice that I knew, but a stranger, with a *body*. Jenna wasn't plump at all, as she told me she'd recently become, but thin and wiry in her overalls, biceps and triceps moving visibly beneath freckled skin. No plush nymph. *Who is this?* I thought. We hugged hello, and then she walked in, talking nervously. She'd brought a bottle of Petite Syrah.

"I'll get a corkscrew," I told her.

"No, that's okay," she said, walking past me and into the kitchen, where she began opening my drawers, "I need to learn my way around."

I WAS SIXTEEN when I first kissed a girl. Her name was Maggie. She was one of my boyfriend's friends, and we would hold hands in back of our high school, near auto shop, and sneak little kisses. My boyfriend thought it was cute.

Kissing girls did not present me with any moral qualms. I had grown up in the San Francisco Bay Area with two parents who were young hippies, and my mother took us to church only twice a year, on Christmas and Easter. I was five when my sister Julia was born, and my parents prepared me by giving me a book on where babies come from. It talked about love—not marriage—as the necessary precursor to sex, and showed a drawing of a naked man and a naked woman lying modestly side by side in a garden.

By the time my second sister, Rachael, was born, Julia and I had discovered our father's old *Playboy* and *Penthouse* and *Hustler* magazines in cardboard boxes in the garage. Nearly twenty years later, I carry with me the vision of dairy maids tipping their steel milking pails over each other, creamy white milk flowing over the swell of their monumental bosoms. Cornucopia.

My wife's childhood was different. Jenna was born in the Midwest, into an actively Catholic family. She spent a happy boyhood swimming shirtless on the lake where she grew up, until puberty hit her with certain unfortunate news. Around the same time, her eldest sister began teasing her about being a lesbian. Jenna spent the next decade praying to God and the Virgin Mary and practicing the delicate art of always having a boyfriend while trying never to have sex.

After graduating from Drake University and returning home from Iowa, Jenna finally came out at age twenty-three, having never held hands with a woman despite her attractions from elementary school onward. Incognito in her parents' minivan, she would drive an hour to a lesbian bar called Paris Dance. There she hid behind her Fileofax, pretending to get work done while trying to breathe. At age twenty-four she fell in love for the first time—with a politically active ice bitch—and quickly discovered why her friends would cry when their boyfriends dumped them.

Comparing our coming out experiences, we were two travelers from different lands:

> JENNA: Straight girls would come onto you and actually do stuff?!
>
> ME: You lived in a sorority—and you didn't make out with any of the girls?!

Despite our differences, we merged more than we diverged, and even our divergences were complementary: I was messy whereas she was neat, she was a fool soon parted from money whereas I was Ben Franklinesque in holding onto mine. Each of us was truly the better half to the other.

It was not, however, a fairytale melding of lives. The first year, and certainly the first six months, challenged us. Before settling into a stable relationship, I first had to a) realize that despite societal prejudice, my children gained more by us being together than they lost, b) figure out that using certain props in the bedroom did not mean I was actually attracted to men, and c) finally trust that Jenna was as wonderful as she appeared. Additionally, we had to work out issues that can come up for any couple: d) she wanted a baby and I was all done with them, e) she hated paper clutter and I fancied myself the curator of North America's largest private library, and f) despite having loved cats all my life, I hated hers. Perhaps because I was engaged on a level much deeper than necking, moral issues finally popped up for me as well. But though I contemplated and prayed about them, they were never quite as urgent as the other issues, certainly not the cats.

The problems we did anticipate, however, never came. We were sure my children would have trouble adjusting, not only because Jenna was a woman, but also because general stepparenting issues were so commonplace they seemed compulsory. Instead, our love and the happiness it brought into the house seemed to wrap itself around all of us. Unprompted, my daughter Sage began proclaiming to neighbors, friends, and school staff that we were her parents, that she had two moms, and that her mommy had a wife. This five-year-old cut through any possible confusion or hesitation, explaining our relationship to people, even us. My son Zachary, being older, was a little concerned about what some of his friends might think; aside from that, both children slipped into our new family roles with ease.

One afternoon I received some random insight on our children's stepparenting views. By then Jenna and I had been living together for about a year, and I was driving the kids home from school. Somehow the conversation turned to their dad.

"I hope Daddy falls in love and gets married again someday," I said to them.

"Daddy won't do that," Zachary told me.

"Oh no? Why not?"

"Because he's not rude."

I sucked in my breath. "Do you think I'm rude because I'm with Jenna?"

"No, because Jenna's not a man."

No, because Jenna's not a man. Jenna, as a woman, couldn't take their father's place. She had slipped under the radar. Later I relayed this to Jenna, and we laughed at the thought of my straight ex-husband not being able to date anyone but men. While it would be rude for Dad to bring in a woman to replace me, mom herself could bring in another mom and there were no torn loyalties. Jenna wasn't replacing Daddy, and she wasn't replacing Mama either. She was just another mom that their mom loved, and they loved, too.

My family and friends were also welcoming. "You and Jenna better never break up," my friend Lia joked with me one day, "Because I sure would miss you."

My mother, though she liked Jenna, needed time to adjust. This surprised me, because Mom had married outside of the social norms—a white Catholic girl from the suburbs marrying a mostly African-American Protestant boy. Gradually Mom acclimated to the sight of her daughter with a woman, and a year later she told me that she had never seen me so happy. Jenna was wonderful with the kids, Mom said, and our family loved her. I shared that we'd been thinking about getting married. That, for my mother, was different. Marriage was for people who could create children together. And why would we want to have a wedding when it wasn't legally binding?

It was my mother's parents that I planned never to tell. They knew Jenna from our family gatherings, but only as my friend. "My grandparents will go to their grave without knowing!" The cliché flew from my mouth. But I have never been good at keeping my own secrets.

My grandfather was a little confused at first. "Which one's the boy?" he wanted to know. "Neither of them are, Fran," my Grammy chided him, "They're both women. That's the point." As for Grammy, she delighted in her new granddaughter.

When they found out about our wedding, Grandpa went out and got his hair cut. Grammy brought out something she had been saving for fifty years, from her own wedding: two small pearl hearts on pearl stickpins, framed with tufts of tulle. They had been in her bouquet, and before our wedding ceremony began, she tucked them into ours.

Hallelujah. Rather than waiting until my children were grown up and moved out of harm's way, here I was—now!—sharing my life with a woman. And we were not miserable, mucking about in some well of loneliness, but happy, loved by family and friends, active members of the PTA, with children who adored and depended upon us. When we went to church, two moms and their two kids, no one cast stones at our heads. God was good; our lives were blessed.

EVENTUALLY JENNA FOUND my corkscrew, and we enjoyed our first evening together. It turned out she was just nervous, and when she's nervous, she talks a lot. While she talked I noticed the thin pale scar that cut across her upper lip. I caught myself watching it move, watching the corners of her mouth as she smiled. But what I noticed most about her were her eyes. It was not their color or their shape, but somehow their intensity. They were bright, sparkling, *alive.* To look directly into them was almost startling.

We talked candidly about our lives: my children, my divorce, the recent loss of her grandmother. Jenna touched my leg while we sat together on my loveseat, and I gave no indication that I was aware of her touch. *If I ignore it,* I thought, *it'll go away.*

When she left, I turned on some music and danced alone in my tiny living room, pretending that she was holding me, looking at me with her bright eyes. I tilted my lips up to her phantom mouth and kissed the sweet scar in the corner.

I was filled with a sensation I hadn't felt in five years. Not since I last prayed deeply, not since I last let God reach in and rustle my spirit did my breath feel effervescent and solid at the same time, did my forehead fill with lightness. How can one explain what God's Spirit feels like? And yet I felt its promise, there again after I had been gone from it so long.

The next time we met, it was at Jenna's house. She had cooked dinner for the two of us. We sat across from each other at the simple oak table in her kitchen, and I was too flustered to meet her gaze the entire meal. In fact, I was unable to meet her gaze at that table for the next couple of weeks; she finally resorted to sitting beside me so I would not feel so shy.

We were, at that second meeting, still struggling to be just friends. Jenna carefully proclaimed her joy at having made a new friend in me, and I seconded the sentiment. After dinner she put on Van Morrison's "Into the Mystic" and asked me to dance. Our bare feet whispered together over the Oriental rug, and she moved her cheek closer and closer to mine, finally caressing my face with the velvety warmth of hers. Through the entire song, I thought, *Oh shit, oh shit, oh shit.* . . . I was so afraid she would try to kiss me. And she did. And I spent the night.

I awoke in the darkness, and while it could have been because I was sleeping in a foreign place, I know what powers summoned me: the spectre of the lesbian U-Haul, its black wheels creaking outside in the street. Six months later, my children and I moved in.

I tell people that when I met Jenna I was just looking for friends, and that's true. But something in me must have yearned for more, because I found it. I also tell people that Jenna and I met online. But just as true is this answer: we met in that mythical place, where the childhood friend is reborn in the soft curves of a woman's body; in that space where hands touch breasts touch lips touch dreams touch laughter.

Twenty-five years had steadily sloughed away my naivete, until I knew that lesbian relationships were just as flawed as heterosexual relationships, that soul mates did not exist, that the concept of marriage was optimistic but flawed. And then I met Jenna, and I learned that I had not learned anything at all.

We were married July 19, 2003. The night before, Zachary and Jenna stayed nearby, and my two sisters came over to spend the night with Sage and me. When we arrived the next day at Fuchsia Dell, I was greeted not by my boyish sweetheart in her baseball cap, but by the most elegant bride I have ever seen. Jenna wore a simple, strapless white gown that graced her figure. A silver crystal choker skimmed her collarbone. And of course, those brilliant eyes, smiling just for me.

Despite minor mishaps, such as momentarily misplacing our wedding bands in a San Francisco gutter, our wedding day was pure bliss. Our friend Lori sang Etta James's "At Last" as Jenna, on Zachary's arm, and then Sage and I, holding hands, walked down an aisle of meadow grass and miniature daisies.

Robyn began the wedding ceremony with an excerpt from Plato's *Symposium.* "Do you desire to be wholly one, always day and night in one another's company?" she asked us, and finished it by reminding that "human nature was originally one and we were whole; and the desire and the pursuit of the whole is called Love." When Robyn asked who blessed our marriage, Zachary and Sage leapt from their chairs to chorus, "We do!" Turning to each other, Jenna and I exchanged vows and rings. Then the four of us jumped the broom within a circle of family and friends, sweeping away the past to make room for our lives together as a new family. And then we kissed.

By then, Jenna's surprise for me had arrived: a horse-drawn carriage. We rode through Golden Gate Park, waving at passersby who turned to greet two brides and their children on their wedding day. A champagne and strawberry toast awaited our return to the dell, where we floated around for photos and then headed to a little French restaurant nearby. After the brunch reception, Lori whisked away our kids, and Jenna and I checked into The Inn on Castro.

The white gowns came off; the kisses began . . . and when the sky outside began to darken we put on our black evening attire: a svelte strapless dress sprinkled with starlight for me, a handsome suit for her. We dined at Ma Tante Sumi, and sitting across the table from Jenna, I met her eyes every time.

We walked back to our suite, made love, and fell asleep holding hands.

I have always been a restless sleeper, full of dreams so vivid they sometimes compel me to answer them aloud. But the night of our wedding brought me the sweetest sleep; and in the morning I awoke gradually, married and filled with the deepest peace, as if lavender dreamers had painted with ostrich feathers inside my skin: softest purples and blues, oceans and skies and beds of crushed lilac.

Soon after our July wedding—eight days later, to be precise—Jenna and I began trying to get her pregnant. Up until April, two years of painful and earnest conversations had gotten us nowhere. All her life Jenna had wanted to have a baby, but I found the baby years long, and was terrified that having one would jeopardize our happy status quo. The change came when, out of financial necessity, we took separate spring breaks. Jenna and Zachary flew off to visit her family while Sage and I drove up the redwood coast to see Julia. Returning home to each other, Jenna and I discovered that we'd both been envisioning a new baby the whole time we'd been gone.

We tried getting pregnant at home for four months. Bisecting her cycles into two-week intervals was draining: the rush of insemination followed by the crash of her periods left us in a state of near-constant anxiety. We'd begun sweetly, with massage lotion and candles and baby movies for her to watch with her bottom propped up on pillows; but by the fourth month we were sick of movies about talking babies and pregnant men. It was time for a sabbatical from sperm.

Married life rolled along. In the winter, for the first time we went all together to see Jenna's family. We stayed first in Illinois, with Jenna's mom and stepdad—"Kiki and Papi" to their grandkids. Zach and Sage were delighted by their first snowfall, ephemeral flakes so tiny the locals called it "spit." Papi hitched up the wooden sleigh to their little tractor, and onto the rickety flatbed we piled with Aunt Meghan and Kiki. Zachary and Sage took turns in the seat with Papi, and we all sang Christmas carols.

When we stayed with Grandpa and Grandma Smith in Wisconsin, our kids' first snowfall was followed by their first snowball fight. Grandma took photos from the balcony as Jenna, Zach, Sage, Jenna's niece Alexis, and I all pelted each other. Then we crunched down the hill and slipped around on the lake until I heard the ice crack and shooed everyone off.

That Christmas my daughter disproved the theory that being raised by gay parents disrupts the natural order of things: Sage had resolved to get her ears pierced with ocean blue studs, but buckled instantly at the sight of pale pink rhinestones.

At the end of our ten-day vacation, Zachary and Sage didn't want to say good-bye to their newly discovered family. They wanted to live in the Midwest. Despite their protests, Jenna and I hustled the kids into the car and off to the airport, where we flew back home to our San Francisco lives.

When the City Hall news came, it came fast and without warning. It was Wednesday, February 10, 2004. Jenna heard on the radio that Mayor Gavin Newsom planned to perform marriage ceremonies for some gay couples. Thursday he did. We called City Hall, but no one could tell us if more marriages would be granted the next day. We decided to go anyway.

Arriving at City Hall, we were absolutely ecstatic. With more than a thousand rights and responsibilities, legally recognized civil marriage would allow us to protect our children and ourselves. Jenna had suddenly become our family's sole provider in 2003 when the budget cuts hit and I lost my teaching job. Without civil marriage, she couldn't properly provide for us: She had to mark "single" rather than "head of household" on her taxes. Employers did not have to extend family health benefits to us. Social Security would not recognize me or Zachary and Sage as her beneficiaries, nor could Jenna contribute to an IRA for me as many spouses do when the other is home taking care of the kids. What Newsom was doing at City Hall held incredible ethical, civil, and financial importance for us.

Jenna and I arrived at City Hall just before it opened, taking our place in what seemed at the time a sizeable line. Forty minutes later we had our marriage license, and after waiting five minutes in a second line we were married by a city official. Then we spotted Mabel Teng, the county assessor-recorder, and ran over to thank her.

While we were still waiting in the first line, we made several brief, happy phone calls, telling family and friends. Then I called my mom, whom we had not invited to our wedding because she never could understand our decision to have a ceremony. Standing in the court hallway, I told her our news. I didn't know what she would say.

"When I heard about the marriages," Mom told me, "I almost cried." Before we hung up, she said, "Jenny, I love you both."

That evening Jenna and I took our children to the City Hall reception. Zachary pushed his way through the crowd to shake Mayor Newsom's hand. Then Sage reached Newsom. "Thank you for letting my parents get married," she told him. "We were already married in God's eyes, but when we heard you were doing this thing here, we thought we would come get married here too."

I wish I could say that February 13, 2004, did not change our lives. In many ways it didn't. We got married, Jenna went off to teach school, I went home. We still had dishes to wash and cats to feed and bedtime stories to read. But it did change things. I suddenly loved my city with fierce pride. My wedding ring carried new dignity. My fellow Americans had finally deemed my humanity important enough to defend.

For our children, the legal process has been riveting, but the outcome is not very important. When a reporter asked Zachary how he would feel if President Bush wrote us out of the Constitution, Zach replied, "It wouldn't matter. They're still married."

He has a point.

Better Than Winning the Lottery

DIEGO FRANCISCO SANS

▼

The first time I laid eyes on Jon-Ivan at the Rich's downtown store in Atlanta, a building that has since gone with the wind, it was 1975 and I thought he was the most beautiful creature that I had ever seen. I fell into his aquamarine eyes and I've been drowning ever since. Because he kept staring back at me, I thought the feeling was mutual. But sometime later, when a mutual friend finally introduced us at Backstreet and we overcame our timidity, we reflected back on that near encounter. Jon simply told me, "I thought you were security."

But he must have decided that there was something about me worth a trial date. And then another. By the first weekend of March 1976, after a few of those trial dates and a trip to Panama City, Florida, in an Orkin pest control truck with a friend named Lamar, we figured our relationship could go nowhere but up from there. The rest is history.

Could it have been mere chance that brought a Cuban refugee from the small town of Manzanillo, who had lived in Miami, New York (I was there in 1969, the year of the Stonewall riots), Boston, Los Angeles, and San Francisco, together with a young man from Powell, Tennessee, who had never lived outside of the southeastern United States?

Many years later, after living together in glorious San Francisco for five years, with the date of our twenty-eighth anniversary approaching, we heard the unexpected but wonderful news that we could actually get legally married at City Hall. We felt so lucky.

Early in the morning on Friday, February 13, though in a rush to get to City Hall, we debated about our clothing. Jon had changed his mind about what he was going to wear: a blue turtleneck. I had also picked a blue turtleneck the night before, and after some discussion, I wound up pressing a green shirt in a hurry.

By the time we arrived at City Hall, our friend Kevin, who had gone to the University of Tennessee with Jon many, many years before, and who now works with me at the San Francisco AIDS Foundation, was already there, waiting. He seemed even more excited than we were.

By 9:30 a.m. we were married!

A little over a week later, I got up one morning and realized that I couldn't see at all out of my right eye. It was a temporary condition, but my doctor was understandably concerned and asked me to come in and see him right away. He did some preliminary checking in his office and referred me immediately for an eye exam, a head MRI, blood tests, ultrasound tests, and I forget what else. I spent the entire day waiting to be squeezed in between appointments and then being poked, tweaked, bumped, battered, kneaded, and rolled by different specialists all over town.

All the test results came out negative, so maybe I'll never know what caused that weird episode. But I do know that through all this, Jon refused to leave my side. He drove me around, sat with me for long hours in waiting rooms, then waited patiently still some more while the examinations where being carried out. He helped me fill out forms after my eyes had been dilated and called my boss two or three times to update him on what was going on, never showing the slightest impatience and never losing his sense of humor. In short, he turned what could have been an unbearable ordeal into a reaffirmation of our love and support for one another.

How lucky is it to fall for a man because he's beautiful, and then find out that he's even more beautiful inside? After twenty-eight years living together through discrimination; after losing uncountable friends, my brother, and one cousin to AIDS; after political activism that made Jon a favorite target of local, national, and international reporters for many months in the mid-nineties; through difficult relationships with both our families and finally relocating to San Francisco, ending more than twenty-five years in the South—after all this I regard our union as stronger than the Rockies and more beautiful than the California coastline on a clear, sunny day. Marrying Jon-Ivan is better than winning any lottery, it is far above the tired rhetoric of those who attempt to render our marriage invalid.

Two Umbrellas and
a Couple of Plastic Laundry Bags

KATHLEEN DONNELLY

▼

*K*aren and I eloped—we got legally married in San Francisco on Valentine's weekend. After twenty years as best friends, eighteen years as lovers, and nine years as domestic partners we really rushed this momentous event. The week before we had been traveling separately—I was in Southern California taking care of my sister's kids, and Karen was in Atlanta on business. While I was babysitting, I stayed at my parents' posh, high-tech mansion down there. Maybe it's an L.A. thing, but my folks have televisions in every room, so I couldn't help but catch a lot of news shows. I eagerly watched the possibility of same-sex weddings in San Francisco swiftly develop from Gavin Newsom asking Assessor-Recorder Mabel Teng to look into what needed to be changed on their license form, to actually marrying our super-dyke activist heroines, Phyllis Lyon and Del Martin (fifty-one years together).

By the time Karen arrived at my sister's home on Friday night, I was raring to get to San Francisco ASAP. I was on my knee proposing the moment she walked in the door. There were three eager children under six hanging onto Karen, trying to get her to play trains and read stories, but she managed a casual, "Yes, of course, dear," before going to build a fort with the kids. I was feeling pooped after the week of babysitting, so I was glad for the reinforcements, but I was concerned by Karen's relaxed response. She obviously wasn't aware of the radical political love fest going on in San Francisco, despite the fact that she had been at CNN headquarters all week.

After putting the kids to bed we went out to dinner with my parents, and I announced that I had proposed to Karen. We revealed our plans to get married in San Francisco as soon as possible. When my mother asked about the date for our wedding, Karen continued to be laidback about the timing. After watching the news for days, I was crazed about getting to San Francisco immediately, but I seemed alone in that burning desire.

When we got back to my parents' home that night, Karen watched the news coverage with me and she finally understood the gravity of what was going on. We sat clicking through the news stations, bawling over the stories unfolding in front of us. It turns out Karen thought the news coverage she had clicked past that week was only about Valentine's domestic partner ceremonies, so she didn't understand my urgency—we've done those ceremonies before. For me, it was amazing to watch the festivities on television, but unnerving to be so far away.

That evening, the county clerk was announcing that they would keep City Hall open all weekend, including the President's Day holiday, to accommodate the weddings before the opposition would start battling it out in court that Tuesday. I absolutely could not sleep that night, fretting that we would be too late or the courts would stop the weddings early. I woke up Karen with CNN coverage at 5:30 the next morning, and she got right to calling the airline to change our flight back to the Bay Area. We had some family obligations we wanted to follow through with for Saturday, and some to get out of for Sunday, so we managed to book a flight early in the day on Sunday.

On Sunday morning, I woke up with a 102° fever, laryngitis with a super sore throat, and the beginnings of bacterial pneumonia. I felt miserable, but I knew this opportunity was a fluke and it was very likely that the court case on Tuesday would end this possibility for a legal wedding, so we just had to get hitched now. From the morning newscast, we learned that ceremonies were being performed from 10:00 a.m. to 4:00 p.m. on Sunday, and that hundreds of queue numbers had been passed out at the end of the day before so people didn't have to wait all day. We were feeling gleeful when we landed in San Jose at 2:30 p.m. and sped off to City Hall.

Unfortunately, in San Francisco we were met with torrential rain and a crowd of frustrated/angry/sad people, most of whom had been turned away that morning and were anxiously waiting in the storm all day just in case. Quite a few people were going to ignore the "no camping" warnings and stay overnight to insure their place in line, but that just wasn't a possibility for my ill self. Instead, Karen booked us into the W Hotel and called into work voice mail as "getting married" for the next day.

At the hotel we ordered chicken soup from room service and neurotically watched all the local news. At 6:00 p.m., one hundred couples were waiting in line in the pouring rain, most with minimal coverage, like trash bags covering their shoes and umbrellas for shelter. By the ten o'clock news, two hundred couples were lined up in the nasty storm. Some were more organized by then with tents and tarps, but most were just braving it. It struck us both how many of the campers had children with them, desperately wanting to legally protect their families with a marriage.

Rumor claimed that City Hall computers could only handle four hundred licenses a day, so we were stressing as we slept until 4:30 a.m. We got back to City Hall by 5:30 a.m., only to find a line wrapped around the building in the downpour. We uneasily took our place and chatted up the couples around us, determining that we were around couple 350 in line. (Well, Karen chatted, I could only squeak at that point with my raging fever and chills.) Karen and I didn't have much time to plan anything so we felt lucky to have two umbrellas and a couple of plastic laundry bags from our hotel for weatherproofing. We put our chic W laundry bags down near the cold, wet marble wall and sat under our umbrellas. The people around us started wishing aloud that City Hall would open early for us. I'm sure all of us drowning bride and groom wannabes were praying for the same thing, but we were all ready to wait in line right where we were for the four and a half hours before the County Clerk's Office began to start processing the first wedding licenses of the day.

Karen went in search of Starbucks and came back an hour later, soaking wet, with not only some piping hot coffee but also a rumor that City Hall was going to open early. After we spent another hour sitting in the deluge speculating, a Deputy Marriage Commissioner came by to tell us that hundreds of volunteers were coming in two hours early on their President's Day holiday to start marrying us so we wouldn't have to stand in the rain much longer. Such an unbelievably kind gesture touched us all.

I felt a roller coaster of feelings during those first few hours, from the bliss of bride-to-be excitement, to the fury at having to wait in this inhumane line, to the anxiety of maybe not making it, to humility in the face of all the random acts of kindness, to the joy of seeing enormous love and commitment everywhere I looked. All morning, drivers were honking and cheering us on as they passed by, and by commute time we watched a constant parade of well-wishers roll by. It was uplifting to have the support of our community in San Francisco, and it certainly helped pass the time.

By 8:00 a.m., the first one hundred couples who had spent the night were officially welcomed into the building, so our line moved for the first time. Unfortunately we moved to an unprotected corner of the building, which provided a new level of discomfort after two and a half hours of cold water and wind pounding down on us. Since City Hall decided to open early, lots of the overnighters left their camps for breakfast and lost their places in line, and, conveniently for us, they left behind a gold mine of tarps, tents, and other gear. Karen scored a roll of black trash bags during our move, which caused a joyful celebration. She made everyone around us ponchos, skirts, and various waterproof fashion statements.

Then the strangers started showing up offering kindness. People who were watching the morning news felt moved to support our motley images of love, and gay couples who had married in the previous days wanted to support our experience. It was awesome. It started with a couple of people carrying soggy cardboard Peet's Coffee to go trays, and it progressed to people pushing a wire cart carrying all the coffee, juice, sweets, and breads we could eat. Then the businesses showed up—Noah's Bagels employees driving up in a pickup full of bagels and schmears, then the Krispy Kreme folks throwing open a truck full of hot donuts. The circus of kindness was just jaw dropping.

Meanwhile, we started slowly moving a few inches up the line at a time. None of the couples around us were sure how close we were to the four hundred couple cutoff, but we knew that one thousand people were lined up behind us, so we tried to stay optimistic. The stories around us were tear-jerking—ten, twenty, thirty, forty years of love in every tale, and people from everywhere: Mexico, Germany, Holland, and all over the United States. All of us were soaking wet and feeling more anxious and joyful as the time ticked.

Around 9:00 a.m. we noticed another line up against the building. Folks around me began speculating: "Who are they?" "A special group?" "Insider weddings, maybe?" Some of the coffee delivery newlyweds went over to check it out and came back, announcing that it was the volunteers also waiting in the rain for orientation. It was yet another touching moment of unreal kindness—these ordinary people taking this time from their families to come down to City Hall on a holiday early morning and stand out in the rain so we could have the chance to get married. Wow.

By 10:00 a.m. we'd all had enough coffee, and the last of the free "honeymoon biscotti" was a hard sell, but we could see the front door, and the rain had eased up a bit—not that it stopped or warmed up at all, but it was a little less torrential. At 11:30 a.m., Karen and I walked into City Hall and started the four-hour, indoor, warm, and dry wait. Inside, we got our paperwork and waited in line as hundreds of volunteers checked and rechecked all our applications, where they had made the change from "Bride" and "Groom" to "Applicant No. 1" and "Applicant No. 2." We were ecstatic by then, since we knew it really was going to happen.

Karen and I were officially couple No. 310 for that day when we picked up our license at the County Clerk's Office around 12:30 p.m. All through the process, City Hall staff and volunteers were celebrating our relationships with lots of "congratulations" all around. When we left the clerk's office with the first of our official papers, we walked the gauntlet of well-wishers cheering us on as we wiped away still more joyful tears.

By 1:00 p.m. we were deliriously waiting in yet another line that yet another volunteer had sent us to, when we were asked if we had a witness with us. We'd been standing for nine hours by then and were barely keeping it together (me with my cough-sniffle-hot-cold-achoo, and Karen's sopping-wet exhaustion), so the kind volunteer usher introduced us to our volunteer witness who walked us up the grand marble staircase to our official Deputy Marriage Commissioner.

This was it—our big moment. Karen managed to pat down our hair and rearrange our soggy outfits. We were getting ready to do our bit to make history when our officiator asked for our rings. "Rings?" Karen wasn't wearing hers. (Again, what's up with that?) So, he adjusted our ring exchange to a kiss ceremony. I wasn't so sure kissing me was a great idea considering the hot-cold-cough-sniffle-achoo, but history was calling. I made it through my part okay, without too much crying, but Karen sobbed. It was so sweet sad beautiful touching glorious ridiculous: "With this kiss I thee wed," and "By the virtue of the authority vested in me by the constitution of the State of California, I now pronounce you spouses for life." Far freaking out.

On our way back down the staircase to the rotunda, we passed dozens of other couples who were simultaneously having ceremonies all over the beautiful hall. Finally, we moved onto our last line to have our officiated, witnessed, and signed license recorded. This line was full of glowing, mostly coiffed, dry, and coutured couples. How was that possible? Two beautiful women in full-on Mexican mariachi wedding dresses waited in front of us in line. Karen later told me she'd run into them in bathroom, where they had a whole makeover setup with blow dryers, curling irons, a bag of makeup, and those gorgeous formal dresses.

When we finally walked out of the courthouse with our honest-to-god legal marriage license, we stumbled past the rice-throwing drag queens and through the tunnel of drama queers in silver sequined tap shoes and top hats, and we walked into those smashing looking cholo chicks who were met by a full mariachi band playing the Mexican wedding song. The girls were dancing and singing. Spectacular.

Karen and I walked on air to our car, snatched the parking ticket off the windshield, and drove back to lovely Watsonville, grinning ear to ear to ear to ear. Back home, some friends had let themselves in to our place to put (nonalcoholic) champagne on ice and lay out chocolate-covered strawberries, which we devoured with the last bits of joy we could muster. I was so sick by then that I stayed in bed for two weeks before jetting off to

Hawaii where Karen's mom and stepdad surprised us with another wedding ceremony full of white linen Hawaiian marriage shirts, many meaningful leis, significant candles, various shell bracelets, and countless kind words.

We were surprised that our marriage was not annulled the day after our wedding, and as time passed, it was harder to deal with the prospect of having it taken away. When Karen and I were waiting in line to get married, it was mostly a political act—we wanted to put faces on the issue of gay marriage for all of America to see. But as we celebrated our weekly and monthly anniversaries, it became more about having a relationship completely equal to our heterosexual friends' and family members' relationships. Although I logically knew that the California Supreme Court would rule against Gavin Newsom's actions, it still broke my heart to hear their decision to void our marriages almost six months after our wedding. We look forward to our opportunity to legally marry again. I hope next time we will have some time to plan out our big event.

One Day at a Time

MOONYEAN

▼

FALL 1989

The leather jacket and motorcycle boots, the pressed jeans and sparkling white T-shirt, the man's haircut—I was intensely attracted to Lakke's appearance. I was proud to be in the company of this clearly butch lesbian, and it didn't bother me at all that she said she never dressed up for Halloween. I hoped she didn't think my witch's costume was too ordinary.

We were in Lakke's tiny Volkswagen Bug. It was dark outside, and pouring rain. I had no idea where we were, just that we were going to a Halloween dance in Healdsburg. This was our second date; the first, a week before, had been to see a mediocre movie. We talked for hours afterward.

"So, tell me about this dance," I said.

"Well, it's an NA dance. I go to meetings every day. There'll be a speaker meeting first, then the dance. It's not a gay dance or anything—"

"What?" I was startled. In all my adult years, I had never been to a "mixed" dance. "What do you mean, it's not a gay dance?"

"All kinds of people go. All ages. It's fun, you'll see."

I was not convinced. If I'd known it wasn't a gay dance, I probably would have declined the invitation. I tried not to show my annoyance.

"So, what exactly is NA?" I asked.

"Narcotics Anonymous. It's like Alcoholics Anonymous, but for drug addicts. I'm a recovering addict."

I digested this information. "How did you become an addict, if you don't mind my asking?"

I listened attentively to her story of childhood abuse, times in jail, mental institutions, and drug use. I was fascinated by the story of her first long-term relationship with Laura, whom she had met while she was living at a halfway house in Denver. Laura encouraged her to get her GED and attend college, where she majored in mathematics. But then I began to get more and more uncomfortable as Lakke described how she dropped out one semester short of graduation. It reminded me of a former relationship.

Two years earlier, I had left someone I loved dearly who was an alcoholic. I'd been with her for eight years and I had supported her financially while she returned to school for a master's degree in engineering. She dropped out just one paper short of graduation.

I started to panic. I did not want to be anywhere near someone whose recent history so closely mirrored my experience with my ex-lover. The emotional agony I had already experienced living with an active alcoholic was enough for one lifetime. I stared out the window. I wanted to run away, but I didn't like the idea of being lost in the pouring rain, more than forty-five minutes from home. We appeared to be in a rural area, with no lit public places or phones nearby. I resisted the urge to demand that Lakke stop the car and let me out.

It'll be fine, I told myself. *It doesn't really matter how attracted you are to her. You'll just go to this dance and you'll never see her again. It's only one evening. Just relax, and try to have a good time.*

The dance was held in a Veteran's Hall auditorium. Big and drafty, it was filled to capacity. On the stage, the DJ played a mix of modern and oldies music. Several people dressed in costume, and some were very inventive. One person was dressed half as a woman, in a short skirt, frilly blouse, and one high heel, and the other half as a man, in dress pants, shirt, and formal jacket. I marveled at the time spent sewing the outfit together, and the makeup was superb. It was hard to tell if the person wearing it was male or female. Most of the women's costumes tended to be skimpy, and most of the men seemed to share Lakke's aversion to costumes.

There were old people, middle-aged people, teenagers, and

youngsters. The kids ran around like crazed Energizer bunnies, darting between dancers, racing along the edges of the room, hopping up and down on the dance floor. The teenagers tried to appear cool, but seemed very caught up in dancing to the latest hip-hop. The oldest crowd flooded the dance floor for the swing numbers. Everybody crowded in for the Motown songs. I was impressed with Lakke's smooth and coordinated dancing. She made me feel as if I knew what I was doing.

The DJ announced a "mixer" dance. The women formed a circle, facing outward. Then the men formed a circle around them, facing inward. Lakke was in the men's circle. Music started and everybody danced—until suddenly it was quiet. The DJ told the women to stay put and the men to move three people to the right. He started the music again. On and on it went, with everyone changing partners about every ninety seconds. I was astonished to see gray long-haired fifty-year-old men with potbellies, tattoos, and motorcycle boots taking part in a corny ritual that forced them momentarily into a social situation with a teenager or a middle-aged housewife. Although everyone appeared to be slightly self-conscious, we were all laughing.

When a slow song came on, the Temptation's "My Girl," Lakke took me in her arms. I was conscious of her freshly showered smell, and the scent of hair mousse. I felt her jaw muscles move as she chewed gum. I felt the tiny hairs on the back of her shaved neck. I was aroused, yet completely comfortable in the circle of her arms. She guided me confidently, never stepping on my toes. I felt myself melting. Something special was going on here.

When Lakke took me home, I was surprised she didn't kiss me goodnight. But she did invite me to another dance the following Saturday night. I said "Yes!" before I remembered my earlier panic and my decision that this would be our last date.

FOUR DAYS BEFORE Halloween, this dance was held in San Rafael. I felt more daring than the week before, and wore a "working girl" outfit—a very short red skirt and a slinky black blouse, too much makeup, fishnet stockings, and heels. Lakke wore a sports coat, dress shirt, and tie, and her slacks fit like they were made for her. I thought the Stetson she wore was her concession to costume, but I later discovered she wore it a lot.

The crowd was so boisterous and rowdy that I had to remind myself that these people were not using drugs or alcohol. I saw a few people I recognized from the week before, and more people were wearing costumes. I was very taken with the Robert Palmer look-alike, complete with a bevy of scantily clad, coordinated backup singers. But I stopped noticing the other costumes after we started dancing.

We danced every song as if it were a slow song and we were in a room by ourselves. We were feverish with sexual heat, twisting and sliding and rubbing against each other. Later, Lakke said it felt like making love standing up and with clothes on. I was dimly aware of other dancers, but felt no hostility or disapproval from them. Rather, I felt glances of acceptance, perhaps even encouragement. No one rushed their kids away, made comments that we should leave, or whispered about perverts. That rather surprised me, when I thought about it later. Of course, I was so enveloped in a world of sensual desire, I might not have noticed.

The DJ took a break, and so did we. We went outside for some fresh air, standing in companionable silence, leaning against a rail. I heard a fountain splashing nearby. Lakke took me in her arms and whispered, "I want to take you home and fuck you."

I looked at her, surprised by her direct approach. "Mmmmmmm," I answered, nuzzling her neck. "But I will only do safe sex." After all, she was a former IV drug user and I wasn't about to risk the rest of my life for a night of passion.

"Okay, that's fine," she replied.

As we drove to my apartment—a 25-mile drive that seemed to take six hours—she asked me, "What's safe sex?"

I chuckled, touched that she had agreed to it without even knowing what it was. I explained about not exchanging bodily fluids. She didn't seem at all upset by it.

OUR PASSIONATE LOVEMAKING lasted most of the night, and after only a couple of hours sleep, I had to get up to get ready for work. When I came out of the shower, I was astonished to see that Lakke had made breakfast for us.

"I didn't think I had anything in the fridge!" I said.

"You had eggs, cream cheese, and leftover moo shu. So now

you're out of everything, because I used it all in this scrambled egg creation."

Sex all night and she makes breakfast in the morning, too! I thought. *Maybe I should keep her around.*

And that's what did it. We settled into a routine of spending as much time as possible together, considering our work schedules and various other commitments. Lakke worked split shifts, weekends, and evenings as a bus driver for the county transit system. I was a bookstore manager and often worked evening shifts and usually at least one weekend day.

One of Lakke's commitments was her daily attendance at NA meetings. "It seems like you've just switched your addiction from drugs to meetings," I said. Once again, she was leaving bed to attend a meeting.

"Look at it this way: the meeting is only an hour long. I have twenty-three other hours in the day to drive myself crazy," she replied.

That certainly gave me something to consider. I started attending meetings with Lakke, just to be with her and to see for myself what it was about. I was impressed with the level of honesty I heard at the meetings. I heard men say things I would not have thought them capable of saying, and it humbled me to realize my own prejudices. I learned a lot about addiction. Gradually I became aware that I looked forward to particular meetings, because I was getting something out of it for myself. I was slowly developing a spiritual base, something I'd never had in my life before. I was learning an attitude of gratefulness that nourished me.

Lakke and I continued to date, and many of our dates consisted of group activities with other NA members. We often went to speaker meetings, followed by a dance. Sometimes we went out for coffee with a group of NA friends after a meeting, or for a meal before. I met people who were accepting and encouraging of our relationship and of us as individuals.

Just after Christmas, we met eight other women at a popular Chinese restaurant near the bookstore I managed. I joined them directly after work. As I slid into the chair next to Lakke, I said, "I've got unbelievable news to tell you."

"I ordered for you already," she said, taking the menu I was just opening. "So what's up?"

"Emily was sporting a big ring today," I said. "Flashing it all around, pointing it out to everyone who came into the store. She said Cheryl asked her to *marry* her!" Emily was my ex-best friend; Cheryl was my ex-lover. It was an exercise of self-control to work with Emily. My emotions veered from anguish to hatred, and often changed from moment to moment. It would have been a lot easier to accept the change if I didn't have to see Emily every day. The store atmosphere often crackled with hostility, and I knew the customers noticed. Of course, I felt better now that I was seeing someone, but it didn't lessen the pain of betrayal.

"Don't worry," Lakke said solemnly. "Whatever happens, I'll never ask you to marry me."

Why not? What's wrong with me? I thought. But I smiled, and said, "Good. I never wanted to get married, anyway."

As the months passed, it became apparent that Lakke and I had a lot in common. When we weren't in bed, we talked a lot—about our dreams for the future, our past relationships, our families, and our work. We shared a love of reading and liked the same books. We had similar values and opinions, so much so, that at times it felt eerie. We felt an extraordinary and unexplainable kinship, as if we had known each other before we met. We were surprised by our level of honesty. I felt I had little to lose by telling the truth and it became apparent that was another thing we shared.

ONE DAY I asked Lakke why she had not asked me for a date first.

"The femme always makes the first move," Lakke said.

"What's that mean?" I asked.

"The femme lets the butch know she's available. Like you did, calling and asking me to a movie."

"Wait a minute," I said. "Let's be clear about this: I wasn't calling for a *date*! I was just calling a friend to go to a movie. Besides," I added, "if I'd thought for one minute that it might develop into something, I would never have had the courage to call. Really. I was just tired of going to the movies by myself."

Lakke smiled. "Sure," she said. "Whatever you say."

"I DECIDED IN third grade that I was never going to get married," I told Lakke. "I watched my mother start arguing with my father midweek to get him to part with enough money for groceries by

Saturday, and I knew then I never wanted to share my checkbook with anyone."

"Me neither," Lakke agreed. "I like being a bus driver, having my own money, paying my bills, being responsible for myself. It's new for me. As an addict, I always seemed to have someone around who would take care of all that for me. And after a while, I felt powerless around the issue of money."

"My parent's divorce had a huge impact on me," I said. "They say the kids always know, but I sure didn't. I was thirteen, my brother was seven, and three days before I was to start high school, my mom ordered us into the car and we left. We moved to Fresno and lived with relatives. There was no discussion, no explanation, no time for good-bye—it was horrible. Somehow I figured we were just visiting relatives, not moving there. I didn't realize what was happening until my mother took me to register for high school. I knew then that I never wanted to be divorced, and the only way to make sure of that was to never get married."

"I don't believe in divorce either," Lakke said, " but it's because of my parent's marriage. They did not have a traditional marriage, and they were not the most functional people, but I always knew they loved each other, and they loved me. My dad stayed with Mom through her asthma and diabetes, even when they didn't sleep together any more. He was devastated when she died."

"My mom told me I was a butch," Lakke said. "I was about twelve or thirteen, and she sat me down and said this is what you are, and this is what it means. She said I needed to find some rich woman who wanted a butch, and I would be taken care of. She and my dad were both totally accepting of me."

"Really? How did you feel about that?"

"I already knew I was attracted to women. I thought she was probably right."

"That's amazing," I said. "I can't fathom that level of acceptance. It sure is different in my family. I told my parents, but they never talk about it, they never ask anything about my life. It's just not an acceptable topic of conversation."

In the fall of 1990 we decided to look for a place to live together. We were tired of dragging our clothes—and our pets—

to each other's apartment for the night. It seemed Katie, Lakke's shepherd dog and Marbles, my Goffin cockatoo were tired of the constant change, too. I circled classified ads for possible places, and Lakke agreed to make the phone calls.

She called me at the bookstore the next day, excited. "I think I've found it! It's in Sebastopol and it has everything we want and then some."

"Not possible," I said flatly. "It just doesn't work that way. You have to look and look, sometimes for weeks."

"I've already seen it. It has a backyard space for Katie, with a bunch of apple trees, a garage we can use for the TV room. It's on a little rise; there's a wonderful view from the sliding glass door in the dining nook." She paused for a moment, knowing the next feature would interest me. "It's even got a built-in bookcase in the living room. You need to come see it. Can you leave the bookstore early?"

And it really was perfect, and that easy. The rent was affordable. We moved in together the following month.

SUMMER 1991

I was sitting on a loveseat in a bookstore with a book of Pablo Neruda's poetry. Lakke was standing behind me, listening as I read aloud a gem I'd found. She leaned over and kissed the top of my head. "Will you marry me?" she asked. Time slowed, and my surroundings receded into the background. My heart pounded, and I was flooded with a sense of certainty. I knew this was absolutely right. I looked up at her, brushed her cheek with my hand, and without hesitation said, "Yes."

We held our first marriage ceremony at our home a year later. We hired Gwen Avery, a popular lesbian singer/songwriter, best known for her song "Sugar Mama," to play the music. Our invitations were a half sheet of stationary with femme and butch cows on a motorcycle in the lower corner. In lieu of gifts we requested people make a contribution to the local food bank. Two dear friends, ministers who had been together for more than fifteen years, officiated and helped us write the ceremony.

I wore a sleeveless red dress with a deep v-neck cut and lots of fringe from the waist down, and my only pair of black heels. Lakke wore a black tux with a red bow tie and cummerbund and I thought she was the handsomest butch I'd ever seen.

People crowded into our living room emptied of furniture and stuffed with folding chairs. We were thrilled that about fifty people, some of them relatives, came to see us formalize our commitment to each other. Neither of my parents came, and although I was disappointed, I wasn't surprised. Lakke's parents had already passed away, and she placed pictures of them on the altar table; our ministers spoke movingly about their spirit presence. Several people commented later on how much the ceremony moved them, and many were surprised to learn that it was not a legally recognized marriage.

It was a participant-catered affair, otherwise known as potluck. Our wedding cake was a chocolate sheet cake with white cream frosting, and a motorcycle on it. We ate and danced and celebrated for hours.

EIGHT MONTHS LATER, Lakke was injured at work. She slipped and fell. She came down hard, twisting her foot badly. This inauspicious beginning changed both our lives, dramatically and irrevocably.

The initial injury was diagnosed as a sprained ankle. "It would have been better if you had broken it," the doctor said. It soon became apparent something more was going on as the swelling and extreme pain continued. We rented a wheelchair, and Lakke used it whenever we left our place. At home, she used crutches.

After ninety days, a case manager was assigned. She made an appointment with Dr. Richards, a specialist at Stanford. He diagnosed it as Reflex Sympathetic Dystrophy, a chronic neurological syndrome characterized by severe burning pain, pathological changes to bone and skin, excessive sweating, tissue swelling, and extreme sensitivity to touch.

Lakke was determined to return to work, and she was discouraged that her efforts in physical therapy and sheer will did not make the pain lessen. A year or more later, she finally reached the conclusion that she could not return to bus driving. She threw herself into vocational rehabilitation training, electing a six-week crash course in computer tech training. When she completed it, she was hired at the first job she applied for, as a phone tech support person for a local software company. Lakke pushed herself to work, but after two months, she reluctantly resigned because she was in too much physical pain to continue.

Lakke's and my belief in "one day at a time" allowed us to maintain a breezy and nonchalant attitude for quite some time. Friends were sympathetic at first, but as the months wore on, they experienced compassion burnout. Some seemed to think she was malingering, but I saw how much she pushed herself every day, willing herself to accomplish things despite the pain.

One friend left a message on our phone answering machine: "I can't see you any more, Lakke. You're just too wrapped up in your disability. I volunteer with men who are dying from AIDS, and they are more involved with life than you are."

Another friend, a nurse, asked how long I was going to stay with Lakke. "I didn't marry her because she was healthy," I said. "I'm not going to leave her just because she can't walk now."

Weeks turned into months, and then years. Our circle of friends changed. The condition spread and Lakke was eventually pronounced 100 percent disabled. We learned more about disability, workers' compensation insurance, and medical stuff than we ever wanted to know.

We each experienced periods of depression, and somewhere along the line, we quit being quite so truthful with each other. I became afraid that Lakke would die, and that fear filled me, suffocating my joy in our relationship and in my life. My world narrowed as I spent all my time obsessing about and trying to be prepared for the unbearable. I was scared to tell Lakke about my fears, and she didn't want to tell me how much pain she was in.

This dynamic did not change until Lakke and I quit being so protective of each other and started taking risks to talk honestly with each other again. It was more difficult than it had been a decade earlier. The disability is a third presence in our relationship, and we spent far too long denying its impact while still trying to cope with its effects. We began to see a therapist who specializes in helping people who live with chronic pain.

Lakke now uses a motorized wheelchair. She has a van with a wheelchair lift that she drives using hand controls. She has an aide who takes her to physical therapy twice a week and helps her with shopping, cooking, and laundry. Our home was renovated to be accessible with ramps, widened doorways, a roll-in shower, and a lowered kitchen countertop and cabinets. All of this is thanks to workers' compensation insurance, but it was not given without a fight.

It has taken us a while to come back to ourselves, to grieve the losses that the disability has caused, and more importantly, to learn what new things are possible, and to find joy in our lives again.

FEBRUARY 2004

Although Lakke and I arrived early in the morning, two hundred people were already waiting in line at San Francisco's City Hall. The crowd's mood was jubilant, and not in the least affected by the rain or the long wait. Some were dressed in wedding finery, some were dressed in work clothes, and some looked like they had just rolled out of bed and thrown on the closest sweat clothes. Some came prepared with raincoats, umbrellas, and collapsible canvas chairs. It was the second week marriage licenses were issued to gay couples by order of Gavin Newsom, San Francisco's mayor.

Lakke looked handsome in her black tux with a white shirt and a cream colored scarf, and her wheelchair shone. Shadow, her black Lab service dog, was her "best man," with a red bow tie that made his working demeanor look formal. Lakke had worn that same bow tie at our first commitment ceremony, some twelve years earlier. I wore a full-skirted sea blue dress with a bright pink flower print, and a fuchsia silk flower in my hair that matched my lipstick.

As we waited to enter City Hall, an elderly black man with a huge Afro skipped down the line offering plastic garbage bags for people to sit on. A bicycle courier passed out steaming Starbucks coffee from a huge tray balanced on his bike's handlebars. A woman came by holding a white wedding dress on a hanger, announcing it hadn't been worn in ten years and she'd give it to the first person who wanted it. A florist delivered bouquets to some surprised couples, from kindhearted midwesterners who wanted a part in the celebration.

Conversing with the couple in front of us, we learned they had driven in from Sacramento early that morning. The young Latino couple behind us could have passed for brothers, and were accompanied by a family of parents, younger siblings, and a grandparent.

When the doors opened at 8:00 a.m., we all inched forward. Mayor Newsom's spokesperson strolled by and told us that the first fifty couples would get a marriage license that day, and after that people would be taken in groups of ten. I sighed. At number 204, we would be waiting awhile.

Lakke took Shadow for a walk, while I held our place. She called me on the cell phone from the other side of the building. "Come on up here! We get to cut in line, because of the wheelchair!"

The security guards waved a wand over us, and we were directed to the room for marriage license applications. Someone handed out application forms and we barely had time to complete it before we were whisked to the front of the line again. We paid the fee and the clerk entered our information in the computer. Lakke's eyes danced with excitement. I squeezed her hand, and realized my heart was racing.

Our wedding ceremony was in the beautiful City Hall rotunda. It was performed and witnessed by strangers to us, but that made it no less moving. "Do you, Moonyean, take Lakke to be your wedded spouse, to love and to cherish, to honor and to comfort, in sickness and health, until death do you part?"

"Yes, I do." I nearly choked with emotion. Looking at Lakke, I saw tears in her eyes. It seemed unbelievable that this could really, finally, be happening. We exchanged the same rings we had given each other more than a decade earlier.

Then we were off to the Assessor-Recorder's Office to get an official copy of our marriage license. Last week, I framed it.

When we left, people still waiting clapped, cheered, and whistled for us. Some snapped pictures. No one seemed the least upset that we had been allowed to cut in front of them.

We are thrilled to be part of this historic and political event, but that's not why we did it. We are still very much in love and committed to each other. Our fifteen-year relationship has survived some dramatic life-changing events. We are married, and want to enjoy the same legal rights and responsibilities other married couples have. For us, this is a dream come true, and something we had not thought possible in our lifetime.

Refusing to Sit in the Back of the Bus

ADRIENNE L. BLUM

▼

Brenda Hatten and I have paths that have crossed for years. When I was about twelve years old and Brenda was eighteen, my mother dated the minister of Brenda's church back in New Jersey. One Christmas Eve, my mother took us kids to her boyfriend's church, and Brenda remembers seeing us sitting in a pew. On April 3, 1991, Brenda came out to San Francisco, and coincidently, I arrived in San Francisco one month and one day later. We met one night, two years later, in The Café, a bar in the Castro. She asked me to dance and I turned her down; I hated the song. When she asked me a second time, that was it—we were inseparable.

Our wedding story began on Thursday, February 12, 2004, when Mayor Gavin Newsom announced that the City of San Francisco had begun marrying same-sex couples. Almost everyone I know was in shock. People in my office couldn't believe it was happening. It was all over the news that night and we were riveted by each story, especially the tale of Del Martin and Phyllis Lyon who have been together for fifty-one years.

The next day, February 13, Brenda and I celebrated eleven years together. We had decided that we would go to our favorite restaurant, Catch, for dinner. Everyone there congratulated us on our anniversary. During dinner we started discussing the marriages. A judge had refused to hear the anti-same-sex-marriage case until Tuesday, so we had four days to decide if we wanted to participate. Should we? Shouldn't we? On the opposing side, we wondered why do we need to get married? Would we want to get married this way? Brenda had never been married before, so did she want the fanfare, or was rushing to City Hall the way she wanted to wed? I had been married before, and had sworn I'd never get married again, so did I want to do this? Since my first marriage ended badly, I've been soured on the practicality of marriage. I always felt that couples stay happier when they live together and don't wed. On the other hand, we thought about how great it would be to be a part of history, how we could make a statement. We already love each other, and we have already been a couple for eleven years. Maybe we should try it? By the end of our conversation, we decided that I should check out what we needed to get married.

When we got home that night, the news was full of reports that the City of San Francisco would be going to court twice on Tuesday to defend the same-sex marriages and that the marriages could be stopped. The City announced that it would be marrying people all weekend with a volunteer staff. Brenda and I went to sleep tossing and turning, not sure what to do.

On Saturday, February 14, 2004, Brenda and I went to the bank to get my divorce papers. To get married a second time, I had to know the date of my divorce. Since I don't keep that date in the frontal lobe of my brain, we had to get the papers from my safe deposit box. That made it impossible to get married on Valentine's Day. We also assumed (correctly) that Valentine's Day at City Hall would be madness. At home, the discussion continued: Should we? Shouldn't we? We went to sleep having decided that we would wake up and check out the line in the morning.

Sunday morning, February 15, 2004, we woke to the sound of rain. Not just drizzling, but downpouring, so we rolled over and went back to sleep. All day we discussed what to do. Then, around 3:30 p.m., we drove down to City Hall to check things out. In the rain, some people were gathered on the steps and others were sitting in line. We walked over to ask about the process of getting married and found out that starting Monday marriage licenses would be issued on a first-come, first-served basis. The people in line were planning to camp out until Monday morning to get married, staying out overnight in the rain and cold. Brenda and

I looked at each other and said, "Love you but not that much." We were not ready to sleep outside. We went home and started to get a little depressed. We thought we were going to miss this amazing opportunity.

On Monday, February 16, I went to work. At about 3:30 p.m., I heard a report that City Hall was going to marry couples until 8:00 p.m. That was it—I picked up Brenda and we rushed down to City Hall. Unfortunately, we were given misinformation. The only people there were those planning on staying outside overnight. You've heard that story about the woman who never wanted to have kids, who suspected she was pregnant, then found out she wasn't and felt sad? That was how we felt—depressed that we didn't get to participate in something that we didn't know we even wanted.

By Tuesday, February 17, weddings continued despite the court hearings at 11:00 a.m. and 2:00 p.m. that day. To our surprise, both judges refused to stop the marriages. At home, Brenda went to get something from her wallet and couldn't find her ID, ATM card, or library card. She tore the house apart looking for them. I came home and looked also. She realized they had not been in her wallet since Friday night. We knew we couldn't get married without her ID. For the tenth time in the last five days, we listed off the names of couples who have stayed together for years without getting married: Oprah and Stedman, Susan Sarandon and Tim Robbins, Goldie Hawn and Kurt Russell. See, we didn't need to get married! Look at Helen Hunt and Hank Azaria—they got married after about ten years of living together and they lasted about six months before they got divorced. We didn't need to get married!

On Wednesday, February 18 I went to work and called our friend, Eddie Phillips, who works at City Hall. The night before, I had seen him on TV marrying people. I just wanted to know if he could marry us. He said he couldn't help us get in, but once we got in, he could marry us. He also said that if Brenda could find her expired ID she could use that to get married. About two hours later, Brenda came home and found a piece of mail with no return address. She opened the envelope and out fell her ID, ATM card, and library card. Somebody found them and mailed them back to her! Now we could get married! That person will never know that they were part of a special moment for us.

After getting the ID back, karma told us we had to get hitched now. At work I told three people that if I didn't show up the next day, I was probably getting married. After work, I picked up Brenda and we went to the Serramonte Mall. Why? I did some research and found it had the largest concentration of jewelry stores of all the local malls. At the first jewelry store, Samuels Jewelers, the saleswoman was very nice but laughed when we told her we wanted two matching rings, not too expensive, in white gold, in our sizes, oh, and tonight. When she stopped laughing, she explained that it had been only five days since Valentine's Day, and all jewelry stores were sold out of everything. She helped us find two rings, but they cost more than we wanted to spend, so we said we would come back after dinner. At four more jewelry stores, salespeople laughed when we told them what we needed. We ended up back at Samuels, in time to watch some customer pitch a fit because they didn't have a hinged box to give her. The salespeople patiently explained that it was right after Valentine's Day and they were out of boxes, but they would call her when they got them in. The customer was not happy and would not leave.

While that drama played out, our saleswoman begged us with her eyes not to leave. Finally, she helped us. Before we plunked down our money, I looked in the display case and found a ring that matched one we had tried on earlier. This made us happy. At the cash register, she noticed that one ring was more expensive. It turns out that one was a little bit "better," but the manager told her to charge us the same price for both rings. Then we insisted on a box. Just joking!

After our shopping trip, we came home and set out the clothes we were going to wear for our wedding. Dressing for warmth and comfort were foremost in our minds. Looking nice was secondary, since we might be standing for many hours in line in the cold. We both had a sleepless night.

At 5:15 a.m. on Thursday, February 19, we woke up. Brenda went straight out to the living room to turn on the news and saw that the line of people waiting to get married was already very long. We got dressed quickly. By 6:15, we were in a taxi on our way to City Hall. Our driver told us he had been married but wouldn't do it again. He was excited that we were getting married, though. He dropped us off at City Hall after wishing us luck.

At that point, the line started at City Hall, continued down Polk Street, and turned onto Grove. We joined the line about halfway down Grove Street. By the time we went in to get married, the line had wrapped around another corner, onto Van Ness Avenue.

While we passed time in line, a video documentarian began talking to Brenda. Later, she called her mom, who quoted Martin Luther King Jr to us over the phone: "A just law is a man-made code that squares with the moral law or the law of God. An unjust law is a code that is out of harmony with the moral law. To put it in the terms of Saint Thomas Aquinas, an unjust law is a human law that is not rooted in eternal and natural law." And we struck up a conversation with the guys in front of us, Matt and Chuck, who had flown all the way from Cleveland, Ohio, the night before. Their witness, Shawna, was expected to join them later that morning. We became fast friends since we stood next to each other for hours.

At 7:00 a.m. we called our friend Eddie in City Hall to let him know where we were in line. After a while, we heard some commotion on Polk Street—a Bible-thumper spewing religious rhetoric. Shockingly, he looked a bit like San Francisco's previous mayor, Willie Brown. We joked that he had come back to haunt Gavin Newsom. Brenda decided to walk over and check him out. After a few minutes, she started following him up and down Polk Street. Later I found out she was singing, "Jesus loves the little children, *all* the little children of the world" to him. He began to avoid Brenda and stopped pacing. He made a turn onto Grove Street, and Brenda was right behind him. He called Brenda over to talk one-on-one, and the next thing we all knew, he got in his car and left. Brenda successfully chased off the Bible-thumper! The crowd applauded and cheered! In fact, days later a guy who had been in line with us saw Brenda in the Castro and thanked her for chasing the Bible-thumper away.

At 8:00 a.m. we heard that Mabel Teng was outside addressing the crowd. The line contracted and we moved forward. When we arrived in the application office, we called Eddie while we filled out our application and paid $144 for the license and ceremony. We received our souvenir marriage certificate, our marriage license, a booklet on family planning called, "Your Future Together—Health Information You Need To Know (previously titled: If There Are Children In Your Future)," and a list of providers for family planning and pregnancy testing in San Francisco. Funny, huh? After the clerk took a picture of us posing with our souvenir wedding certificate, Eddie told us to follow him down a hall. As we passed the people on line they all cheered for us!

Since we had no witness, Eddie asked Daniel Homsey from the Mayor's Office of Neighborhood Services to assist us. It turns out he was also a photographer and took many fantastic pictures of our wedding ceremony. Together we walked up to the fourth floor of City Hall, where we found a beautiful hallway with big windows and these magnificent sculptures. From there we looked down on the rotunda where all the other couples were getting married. Eddie told us to put our stuff down, reminding me to get the rings out of my bag.

Then, next thing we knew, Eddie was reading off the vows and we were repeating after him, saying, "I do." It all happened so quickly—we exchanged the rings, kissed, and it was over. After, we took pictures with Eddie and Daniel, signed the papers, kissed and thanked them both, then headed downstairs to the Assessor-Recorder's Office to file our license.

When we got to the office, we stood in line behind a female couple who had just gotten married. One of the women was the rabbi from the Temple Emmanuel in San Francisco. They had an entourage with at least four photographers. We followed them to another window to pay $13 for a copy of our marriage certificate. We saw piles of papers in that office—licenses waiting to be sent to the State of California, that now can't be sent because the lovely State of California refuses to process them. While we were waiting for our copy, we met Wendy, one of the photographers with the rabbi's entourage, and she asked if we wanted our picture taken. After receiving our copy of our license, we walked out into the rotunda with Wendy, excited to stand on those steps and get our picture taken.

When we finally gathered our stuff together and exited the front door of City Hall, the line of people waiting to get in cheered and clapped for us. It was such a rush! We found Matt and Chuck from Cleveland, and we all hugged. Brenda and I wanted to go somewhere and warm up, so we got on MUNI and rode the train to the Castro. We went to Café Flore to eat and make some calls. We called Brenda's mom, and our friends Natalie, Katherine, and Paula. After breakfast, we went home to call more friends and print out wedding pictures. There we found a note and present our next-door neighbor, Mike, had thrown on our balcony—a wedding Beanie Baby.

At 5:30 p.m., we went to our favorite restaurant, Catch, to celebrate. Everyone was so fabulous when we arrived, wishing us well. There were other couples celebrating their marriages also. It was quite festive. We sat down and all of a sudden in walked Matt and Chuck from Cleveland, with their witness Shawna. We all moved to a larger table so we could sit together. We had quite a celebration with other diners sending us glasses of wine and roses. We have never had such a good time. After two and a half hours we called it a night. Matt and Chuck had only had about four hours of sleep in two days and they were exhausted.

The next day, Friday, February 20, we wrote Just Married on my car. In the drizzle, the writing dripped as I went to work for half a day and Brenda went to her class. After work, I drove Brenda over to our friend Mickey's house. Outside of his house we rewrote Just Married on the car window and took pictures. We left that message on our car for five days, just for fun. People beeped at us everywhere we went.

Our wedding experience didn't stop there. We were involved in a photo shoot at the Conservatory of Flowers with some women from the Art Institute. We have participated in demonstrations to protest the end of the marriages and to counter the hate. We were interviewed for a documentary on same-sex marriage, *I Will, I Do, We Did.* Glide Memorial Church included us in their same-sex marriage blessing ceremony. Having all those people cheer and sing for us got me teary-eyed. We have received wedding gifts and cards from friends and family all over the world. We have been very lucky.

We had decided before we got married that our wedding was not going to change our relationship. What we didn't realize was that our marriage would take on a greater resonance, becoming meaningful even for absolute strangers. We are becoming a face, a recognizable symbol, for those who couldn't or didn't get married. This unplanned decision to get married has not only made us individually stronger but has made us realize that we are at the forefront of the new civil rights fight. We are refusing to sit in the back of the bus.

Couple #A169

REESE JOHNSON

▼

I met Tolver in late October 1985. He called himself Matthew then, and had long, dark brown hair and the muscular upper body of youth. It was usually hot in the fall in Austin, Texas, and Tolver was wearing a pair of very revealing, cutoff denim shorts. I was dressed, I'm sure, in some high '80s, Flock of Seagulls, fashionable getup, probably a bit of eyeliner, and definitely a lot of hair spray. It was at *The Rocky Horror Picture Show,* the midnight movie, at the Northcross Cinema 8. The theater was at the end of one of those long, multiplex hallways. I had been attending (and performing in) showings of *Rocky Horror* there for almost three years at that point. I had played many roles in the cast, and had graduated to the level of "god" among my Transylvanian peers ("god" defined as one who has been around long enough to know everyone and everything about the clique). Tolver was a newbie—obviously not quite old enough to be there, but definitely not the youngest there, at seventeen. I had started at fifteen.

We first laid eyes on each other at the entrance to that theater, at the end of that long hallway, where it was customary to step out of the movie and smoke cigarettes during the lame scenes. I was talking to someone; he was leaning up against the opposite wall. I was obviously checking out his quite obvious basket. When I looked up at his face, he smiled at me and said, "I think I'm in love."

I smirked back, "You don't want to fall in love with me," very coy, but superior and snide.

Tolver didn't miss a beat. I felt the tremendous power of his animal magnetism engulf me as he replied, "Oh, I've already fallen, and I'm in no hurry to get up."

I HAD NEVER considered myself attractive. I'm not sure why, exactly. I was always skinny and scrawny, and saw no chance of growing into one of those big, masculine guys whom I found so attractive. I had been in a few relationships by that time, with girls and boys, even a couple of older men, but I had never been given the sense it had been because I was cute. (I know I was really naive.) Tolver was the first person to tell me that I was beautiful. He was attracted to the fact that I was skinny and scrawny. In those first few minutes he gave me more confidence about myself than I had ever felt in my entire life. I was eighteen, a leader among my peers, but had never realized it. I was smarter than most, but had no basis for comparison. And I was completely unaware of my potential. But here was this little guy, younger than me, yet obviously wiser, smaller than I was usually into, but still very attractive, hinting that there could be so much more to my world.

I spent the rest of the movie with Tolver, talking, and kissing, and groping, and fondling. But we parted that first night, and I went back to my life already in progress. I was in the middle of trying to figure out where I was going to live at the end of the year when the lease was up at the two-bedroom apartment I was sharing with three of messiest people on the planet. And I already had a boyfriend. Well, sort of. There was this guy, whom I had dated a year earlier, that I was sort of trying to get back together with, kind of. See, I was pretty secure and settled into my sexuality by eighteen—I had come out to my parents at sixteen, and had already spent time living on my own and dating. Still, it was the early '80s, in Austin, Texas, and the gay life was basically this: find the first person that you are even partially compatible with, have sex, and go directly to a relationship.

THE WEEKEND AFTER I met Tolver was Halloween, better known as *Rocky Horror* High Holy Day. Halloween fell on Thursday, but it wasn't until Friday night that we were back at the theater, ready to do *Rocky*. For some reason, maybe because it was Halloween, this night was extra special in our minds, so everybody was all stressed out. Most of the kids who performed *Rocky Horror* in front of the screen during the movie were a close-knit troupe, always on each other's nerves and fighting. And there in the middle of all of this stress, I saw Tolver again.

It hadn't been a good week; I had had a big fight with the guy I was seeing. I wasn't the type to let a fight stop me from trying to have a relationship with the guy, but it had gotten physical, and I was leery of entering an abusive relationship. Here in the middle of all of this peer stress, I wasn't ready to face my love issues. I was also scared to death of this little guy who had shown me more passion than I knew what to do with, so, I made a point of avoiding him. Until my friend Joseph came up and grabbed me by the shoulders and said to me, "Look, you unhappy little boy, there is someone down there who is really into you, who has got to be better than that scum you been messing with, so you have to go get him right now and have fun while you can!"

I walked down the aisle of the theater alone. Tolver was sitting down in the front row, where all of the Transylvanians hang out, watching me progress toward him. All of the shyness and inse-curity welled up in my throat as I met his eyes. Looking back, I realize that I was like a bride walking toward my waiting fiancé at the end of the aisle. I sat down in front of him in the seat, between his legs, and he started rubbing my shoulders and purring in my ear. I turned to him and asked, "Do you want to go somewhere to play?"

He replied, "Yes, but I have to tell my mom where I'm going."

"Um, okay . . . Uh, your mother?"

"Don't worry, it's cool."

In my experience, by that time in my life, moms could be "nice," but never "cool." Yet, Tolver grabbed me by the hand and quickly dragged me halfway back through the theater, where his mother sat in an aisle seat.

"Hey Mom, this is Reese, we're going out to his car to have sex," he whispered to her, loud enough to be heard by everyone in the surrounding seats.

"Sure," she said, and then returned her attention to the twenty-something stud sitting next to her.

As Tolver pulled me out of the theater and the mall to the parking lot, I was in a blur. I was trying to comprehend what had just happened. Was I going to get in trouble because he told his mother?

"How old are you?" I asked.

"Seventeen," Tolver replied.

"Whew." Okay, we're less than a year apart; they won't arrest me.

And then we were in the car, a tiny Toyota Celica with a stick shift. And then our hands were all over each other, and then our lips, and oh my God, this is what *good* sex is like!

Tolver went home with me that night, November 1, 1985, after we had said our farewells to his mother, and dropped off all of my friends who needed rides home. We ended up back in my bedroom that I shared with another gay guy, whom we let join in out of politeness. The next morning, my roommate left and I spent the next four hours trying to wake Tolver up. He had forgotten to mention that he has a sleep disorder, and without his before-bed medication, would sleep as if in a coma for twelve hours. He had mentioned that he had to go to work that afternoon, so I dutifully tried to wake him. And tried to wake him, and tried to wake him, to the point where I started getting really scared. But he was obviously still alive, just a heavy sleeper, so when the time that he was due at work came and passed, I just gave up, and went on about my day, cleaning up around him. He finally woke up and explained his condition, and then we spent the rest of the day together, until it was time to get ready to go to *Rocky* again that night.

We went to the theater together, and spent very little time participating in the movie. About halfway through, the other guy showed up looking for me. Tolver got all puffed up and gallant, and wanted to go beat the guy up, but I stopped him and sent the other guy away—he'd had his chance, bye-bye. Tolver took me to his house that night, and we slept and made love in his bed, with his family locked safely on the other side of the door.

FROM THAT POINT on, we found a way to spend every night together, switching off houses. By mid-December I had secured an apartment of my own, and without question Tolver moved in immediately. We have spent very little time apart since. Yet, we were pragmatic in the beginning. Before we had moved in together, we had had that moment when we decided it was okay to start using "I love you" with each other. I remember that first time, in bed together saying, "I don't want to say I love you, I don't want to say I love you, I love you." Still, we decided that we wouldn't "marry" until we had been together for at least a year.

During that year, Tolver learned as much about my wants and desires as he could, and did everything he could to nurture them. He bought me a synthesizer and encouraged me to make the music that was in my head. He taught me to love myself, so that I could allow him to love me. And, he taught me I could love, without pain, and without the fear that the person I loved would take me for granted.

The next Christmas, I gave Tolver an engagement ring. I hid the box among the ornaments on the tree. When he found it, and I asked him to marry me, the glee and joy on his face became the picture of him that will always be in my mind.

WE WERE MARRIED on March 22, 1987, in front of about seventy of our peers. People from our jobs, and *Rocky Horror,* and even some of Tolver's family were there. His mother gave him away, and his big sister took photos. Our best friends Patti Platt and Stephen Carver, as best men, performed the ceremony that we had written ourselves. We held the ceremony in the backyard of a condominium complex where a friend lived, while his neighbors peeked out their windows at us in our matching gray tuxedoes. We had one bottle of champagne per guest. Some called it "white trash," but we prefer "white recycling." We were definitely ahead of our time in the gay community. Even then we were out to show everyone that a gay relationship could be the same as a heterosexual relationship, while the gay community at large was still working on just getting the word "gay" uttered on TV. We had (and still have) every confidence that we have always been spouses for life.

We spent the next seven years in Austin, with a little stint in San Antonio to be near my father after my stepsister died. My father and stepmother were always accepting of my relationship to Tolver, although it wasn't ever really a topic of discussion. My father gave Tolver work at his construction company while we were in San Antonio. Tolver says that, after seeing my father with his shirt off, he knew he would find me attractive as I aged. While we were in Austin, we lived mostly in Tolver's mother's rental properties, and were very close to his family. In 1993, his mother paid for us to fly out and visit his sister in San Francisco, and thus began the next chapter in our relationship.

WE VISITED SAN FRANCISCO, but we didn't really see much. I mean, we went to the Golden Gate Bridge, and we cruised the Castro, but we didn't have a guide, so we didn't really *see* San Francisco. Yet, I felt it immediately—this was where we needed to be. Back in Texas there may be nothing but wide open spaces, but there was no place for us to grow. As we looked at the city skyline from his sister's backyard in the Berkeley Hills, I said to Tolver, "We should move here." When we got home, he made it his mission to get us here.

We moved to San Francisco at the end of October 1994, the beginning of our tenth year together, and the beginning of a new life far beyond anything we had yet imagined. It took us a couple of months to get started, but I eventually found the perfect job making lots of money, at the beginning of what became the dot-com era. In March of 1996 we were honored to take part in the first government-sanctioned Domestic Partnership ceremonies and licenses in the United States, recognized and presented by the City of San Francisco. While the transition to the city had been hard, and Tolver and I had probably gotten very close to splitting up not too long before this, when offered this first chance to have our relationship recognized by our society, we moved without hesitation to reaffirm our love. Then again, for the one year anniversary in 1997, we joined with even more new Domestic Partners to have our relationships recognized by the State of California.

WE FELT SO lucky to live in San Francisco then. I know that most people in the United States do not understand what it means to live in a community where each individual is respected for their uniqueness. In most of our country people live their lives afraid of "what the neighbors will think." In San Francisco we have been fortunate to find a place where our neighbors think we have the right to be happy being who we are. Through our domestic partnership rights we believed we had reached the pinnacle of acceptance, at least as far as we ever expected. Along with the powers of legal and medical attorney, and the wills we had drawn up, we were practically equal to legally married couples. In fact, we had been together longer than my siblings' first marriages, or either of our parents' first marriages, and we were finally afforded many of the same rights they had been granted just by following tradition.

Then the carrot of marriage was dangled in front of our heads. It came out of nowhere; we were completely taken by surprise. Sure, we jump at the chance to be recognized, but it's not like we've been super involved in the gay and lesbian movement. So, all of the sudden we hear that San Francisco's new mayor, whom we hadn't voted for because he was too "Republican," was issuing marriage licenses to same-sex couples. Well that was great, but unfortunately we were broke. My dot-com job having fizzled out, and it being a particularly bad month, we didn't even have the $95 to pay for the marriage license.

To the rescue comes our good friend Marq Coburn. I've known Marq longer than I've known Tolver (although he did have a habit of missing our weddings). I moved him out here from Austin when business was good, and he has since come into his own in San Francisco, finding a good job and a boyfriend of almost two years (the longest relationship I have ever seen him in). Well, Marq came over Friday night, after the second day of weddings at City Hall, and said we "*have* to do it!" In fact, he was going to marry his boyfriend, too. So, he loaned us the money, and after staying up half the night, we headed out for City Hall at 8:30 on Saturday morning. I'd been so busy with the rest of my life that I didn't even notice it was Valentine's Day.

WAITING IN LINE was the most unbelievably joyful five hours you can imagine. Everyone was smiling and happy—a happiness mixed with surprise and disbelief, like when you are a child and you first see the huge mound of Christmas presents under the tree. As we waited, children played around our feet, and the sun was shining brightly, and the spirit of San Francisco spoke to me again, probably for the first time since our trip here to visit Tolver's sister. "See," I said, "I told you we needed to come here."

I'll admit it—as I stood there in line to get married on February 14, 2004, to the man I had been with for eighteen and a half years, and been through three ceremonies with, I was flippant. I acted like the marriage application was just another form to fill out. Even our number was a joke: we were couple number A169. Yet, when Bill Haley, who officiated our marriage, said, "I now pronounce you spouses for life," all of time stood still and I was able to see our whole life together so far, and our whole life together yet to come, and I understood what they mean when they say "it feels like your heart will burst from the joy." I saw a tear of happiness come to Tolver's eye; I could tell that he didn't want to cry, but in that moment we became one, and it didn't matter. Nothing mattered but the love that we share.

Tolver and I know that we are lucky ones. Before we met, we had a mutual friend who had mentioned to each of us that she knew "someone perfect for you." This was before we even knew each other existed. A few years after we had gotten together, she saw us and said, "I told you so." We had found each other on our own. Since our beginnings, we made it through some pretty hard times. We have learned that, when you spend a lot of time with someone, like with your family, occasionally you have to agree to disagree. We have found a nurturing society to live in here in San Francisco, and we have good friends to share it all with. After our wedding ceremony, Tolver and I witnessed for our friends Marq and John, who had witnessed for us. To see Marq so happy—the friend I thought would always be single—to see that he has found someone also gives us joy.

However, we also are aware that, as a community, we have a long road ahead. "Gay marriage" is not the whole issue. We are fighting for the separation of our government from the tyranny and superstitions of religious zealots. We are fighting for equality for all partnerships. We truly believe that "marriage" is a religious institution and should be left to the religious to bestow as they see fit. But we also believe that religious marriage should not be connected to rights granted by the state. Instead, our government should offer civil unions to all couples who wish to participate in the legal rights and responsibilities of committed partnership.

Since getting married by the City of San Francisco just two weeks ago, we—Tolver especially—have gotten involved in the marriage equality movement. Tolver has volunteered at the mayor's office, setting marriage appointments, and handed out information and his own buttons at rallies. We have watched the news coverage constantly, and recorded all the good bits for later editing. Tolver wrote e-mails to several stars, including Rosie O'Donnell, who came to San Francisco to marry her partner, and Penn and Teller, who sent flowers to random people waiting in line. We have sat and strategized, and thought about the consequences of the changes we have helped to perpetuate in the world. We have prepared ourselves for the backlash sure to come. I am not an activist, but I am the patron who will sponsor Tolver as he works the system, and I will write my feelings down, documenting each step. Together we feel privileged to be alive during this renaissance of mankind, when information and society are evolving toward freedom for all.

The Luckiest Woman Alive

Renee Potter Olson

▼

This past weekend was the best Valentine's Day of my life. On Thursday evening my partner came home from work, and I tossed out an idea. I told her about Phyllis Lyon and Del Martin, about how the mayor of San Francisco was letting lesbian and gay couples marry.

We thought for a moment and decided we needed to hit the road. My friend Clayton Kroh accompanied us on our journey to make history. At 11:00 p.m. we told our sixteen-year-old daughter we were off, headed out on the eight hour drive from Poway, California, to San Francisco.

We arrived in the city at around 8:00 a.m., rented a hotel room, showered, and headed down to City Hall. Being unfamiliar with the city, we looked at a map and thought it was a short walk. Instead we ended up walking nearly twelve blocks to the building. Only one protestor stood on the steps, shouting, "Homosexuality is a sin." We took our place in line behind hundreds of gay and lesbian couples, all waiting for someone to burst in and slam the doors shut on us.

After two long hours we reached our destination, the Clerk's Office. A freshly volunteered clerk took our application and our IDs, beginning the wedding license process with a short smile and an, "Isn't this a great day for us?"

We took our license and were cheered on by the ever-growing number of brides and grooms as we made out way to the rotunda for our ceremony. There we were greeted by a very happy gentleman in a long black robe who introduced himself to us with a, "My partner and I have been together seventeen years, isn't this wonderful?" We nodded in agreement.

Brought to tears by the moment, we looked into each other's eyes and pledged our love to each other. We kissed and then were whisked away to the registrar where we had to file our license to make it official. There we were, Hattie and Renee Olson, signed, sealed, and delivered.

By 1:45 p.m. we were on our way back to the hotel where we collapsed in exhaustion. We slept a few hours and the headed out to a lovely seafood dinner on Fisherman's Wharf.

IT TOOK US nearly ten hours to get back home in Valentine's Day traffic. We stopped in here and there to get gas and to pick up another city's newspaper to have the clippings for our scrapbook. As we walked through the door at home, our sixteen-year-old daughter, Lacy, greeted us, excited and pointing us to the kitchen counter. She had bought us a wedding card. Also on the counter, I saw that my little girl had done one more thing that was, to me, more rewarding than everything I had experienced up to that point. She had taken an old T-shirt and some rainbow markers and created a shirt for school. The front of the shirt said, "I have two Mommies and they are getting married today in San Francisco." On the back it said, "I have two Mommies and they CAN get married today in San Francisco."

My heart and eyes filled as I realized I was truly the luckiest woman alive. My daughter had worn this shirt to school as my wife and I stood in line waiting for our chance to be just like everyone else. What courage it took for her, a straight teenager, in her junior year at a new high school, to show up with that shirt on.

I've folded up the shirt and placed it in a box with the cork from our wine bottle, our hotel bill, and the newspaper clippings that will commemorate this Valentine's Day 2004. What a great day for everyone.

My Life, My Wife, and Our Family

MARA McWILLIAMS

▼

On a warm evening in September, I was on my way home when
I decided to stop into a local nightclub for lesbians and
get a little dancing in. I don't know where the idea came from. I
wasn't dressed or made up to go dancing, but this voice whispered, "Go to The Savoy." So, I listened and pulled my car into
the parking lot. I got out, walked into the club, and wandered
around, but I wasn't feeling the groove, so I simply decided to
leave. Feeling somewhat foolish for even stopping into the club,
I let myself into my car, backed out, and just as I was about to roll
forward, this beautiful woman stepped in front of my car with her
arms outstretched in front of her yelling, *"Stop!"*

It was the funniest thing. There I was, sitting behind the steer-
ing wheel, and this gorgeous woman walks to the car door, asking me to roll my window down by rotating her wrist. I opened
my window about three inches—enough to give us space to talk,
but enough to keep me protected as well. This sexy blond woman
asked me to pull in so she could talk to me for a moment. I figured, *Why not? I have nothing to lose and she is hot!* She leaned into
my window and asked, "Can I buy you a drink?"

I looked up into her big brown eyes and said, "I don't drink."
She didn't skip a beat, sweetly offering, "Let me buy you a Coke."

I was impressed that she wasn't thrown off by my telling her I didn't drink, which was usually met with odd looks and the question, "Why?" She told me I was the most beautiful woman in the bar and she just wanted me to talk to her for a few minutes over a drink. It seemed innocent enough, and incredibly enticing.

THAT WAS OUR beginning, over four and a half years ago. The start of our journey together was overwrought with challenges. We were dating for only a little while when, on an overcast day in February, my apartment burned down. My four-year-old daughter Serena and I lost everything we owned. In shock, I called Renee from the fire scene, and time must have slowed, because the next thing I remember, she was walking up to me, trying to hide her own disbelief. Realizing that we had nowhere to go except a homeless shelter, Renee graciously moved my child and me into her home. Initially we didn't know if we were going to end up being lovers or roommates, but Renee assured me that Serena and I had a safe home and we needn't worry.

After the fire, I suffered post-traumatic stress and went spinning headfirst into a serious bipolar depression. For the first time in my life, I became agoraphobic, unable to leave our new home. This lasted for nine months. It took me six months to work up the courage to venture out of the bedroom. I was mentally and physically incapable of taking care of myself. My weight quickly plummeted and I began suffering from fainting spells due to malnutrition. Renee, bless her heart, nursed me back to health and took care of Serena as if her own. Overnight Renee transformed from a single lesbian who never wanted children to a stepmom and mental health provider.

It took five doctors and approximately two years to find the right medication regimen to balance my condition. Many of the medications they prescribed had side effects too unbearable to live with. Renee religiously researched all my medications and potential side effects. She drove me to appointments, reminded me to eat, and assisted me in applying for Social Security, as I was too ill to understand all the paperwork. When I was at my weakest, she would draw a bath for me, walk me to the bathroom, and get me into the tub where she would then wash my hair. Even in my weakest and most bipolar of moments, this woman truly loved me.

Very few people are willing to go into a relationship with someone who is either terminally ill or who is diagnosed with a mental illness. Understandably, the stress and strain is often too heavy
for the caregiver to continue to carry for a long duration. Yet my
wife has stood up to the demons of my illness, fighting beside me
for mental health, and has continued to love me through it,
even in my scariest moments. She has somehow found a way to
separate my true self from my illness, which is a gift for which I
am forever grateful.

We were together twenty months when Renee proposed to me
in the woods beside a beautifully flowing stream. Before we
arrived in that spot, her friends had set up a romantic picnic,
complete with blanket, a basket filled with gourmet delights,
candles, and a vase of white roses. When we approached the picnic spot, I was about to walk around the blanket, fearful we were
intruding upon someone else's party, when Renee took my hand,
stopping me. She looked into my eyes and told me all of the beautiful things she saw in me. Then she went down on her knee, presented me with an open blue and white ring box, and asked me
to marry her. Without hesitation, I answered, "Yes." We hugged
for an eternity and then Renee said, half-laughing, "Don't you
want to look at your ring?" Of course I did, but it didn't matter.
What mattered was her love for me; the ring was just a symbol.

Seven months later, on February 9, 2002, we eloped to Las
Vegas. Upon our arrival, Renee searched most of Vegas, looking
for Will Smith's "Potnas" and "Crash and Burn" by Savage Garden for us to walk up and back down the aisle to—not such an
easy feat in a city filled mainly with casinos, yet she succeeded in
her quest. We had our commitment ceremony at the Bally's Wedding Chapel. Our ceremony was wonderfully simple with only
the two of us, the minister, and a witness attending. We spoke the
vows we had written, committing ourselves to our love and our
family before God, the world, and, more importantly, each other.

After our ceremony, we danced and pranced through the
casino. I shouted to passersby that the beautiful woman next to
me was now my wife. We were congratulated and cheered on. The
people who saw us supported our love and decision to wed; they
didn't care that we were two women. We continued our celebration over coffee and ice cream sundaes. We enjoyed a night full

of love and romance where no one and nothing could distract us. We never dreamt that we would ever experience a wedding more real than the one we had just participated in together. To us, this *was* our wedding day, despite what the law said and recognized.

THEN CAME SAN FRANCISCO Mayor Gavin Newsom.

Thanks to Mayor Newsom, his administration, and Assessor-Recorder Mabel Teng, Renee and I were legally married on Monday, February 16, 2004, in San Francisco City Hall. The event itself was beautiful from beginning to end, despite the pouring rain and freezing cold. Hundreds of us camped out around City Hall in the lousy weather, hoping for the opportunity to be issued a marriage license and get legally married, even if the marriage might be considered legal only for a few days.

I have heard the same-sex weddings in San Francisco described as a media circus of marriages that aren't worth the paper on which they're printed. That is not what I experienced when Renee, Serena, and I stood in the pouring rain and bitter cold on that blessed Sunday night.

We showed up outside City Hall at 10:15 p.m. to stake out our spot on the cold sidewalk surrounding the building. Luckily, we were able to park directly across from our little area, which was perfect for our daughter, who was camping in the back seat with the doors locked. Not that we had anything to fear. I've never felt so safe on a big city street in the middle of the night. Within five minutes of our arrival, the rain started to trickle down and resigned moans filled the air. We thought we were prepared, bringing sleeping bags, padding, a camping chair, a propane heater, thermoses of coffee and soup, a small ice chest, and a few snacks. We didn't expect the rain, but were grateful for the single mini-umbrella that we found in the trunk.

The couple next to us, William and Eddie, were less prepared than we, as were many couples who had flown in from around the world. They huddled together under a single large umbrella with a shared sleeping bag covering their legs. Eddie had flown in from Utah to marry his love, William. We talked about the adventure we were all embarking on in the name of love, and although drenched, everyone was excited.

While we waited on the sidewalk, Serena remained snugly situated in a sleeping bag in the back seat of our car, watching a DVD, calling us on her walkie-talkie, taunting us about how dry she was. Couples around us laughed, and we bonded like family. She soon fell asleep in the back seat, and Renee and I settled in for a long, wet night.

The City of San Francisco responded to us with compassion, doing their utmost to meet the needs of those waiting to be married. Within half an hour of our arrival, supportive San Franciscans began passing out bottled water, cookies, and chips. The individuals handing out these simple luxuries believed not only in our commitment to each other, but our commitment to equality for all. By midnight the City had Porta Potties delivered to the corner, and not a moment too soon. A police van slowly circled the building all night, ensuring our safety, and the night passed in peace.

Throughout the night, people, just regular people who wanted to help, continued to come around, passing out free coffee, hot chocolate, oatmeal, umbrellas, trash bags so we could try to stay dry, hot pizza, juice, donuts, and muffins. We were so deeply moved that these individuals and couples, straight and gay alike, were willing to brave the elements with us in order to show their support. When I thanked a man for his generosity, he said, "I'm not ready to get married yet, but I wanted to thank you all for what you're doing for us."

Again, I said, "Thank you."

He replied, "No, thank *you.*"

That night, love was a living, breathing entity surrounding all of us and bonding us together for what I imagine will be a lifetime.

I HONESTLY DON'T know what time City Hall opened on Monday morning. I was exhausted and excited, hoping that we would be able to get married. We had been turned away the previous morning at 9:00 a.m. because City Hall was processing licenses as fast as possible, but could not keep up with the overwhelming demand. We were anxious and fearful that we might again be turned away.

We had gotten a mere two hours of sleep when, at 7:15 a.m. we were told that the line would start moving soon. We woke Serena up around 7:45 and initially, because the car was so crowded and wet, we could not find her pants. It was looking as if she was going to have to wear her PJ bottoms under her jacket. Luckily she was able to find them, and we were all greatly relieved.

When the line began to consolidate, we jumped up, leaving our sleeping bags and everything on the sidewalk (I didn't care if the stuff would be there when I returned, yet it was). As we moved closer to the door, my heart started pounding loudly, so loud I thought those around me could hear it. We were all focused on crossing the threshold from concrete walkway to marble floor. That in itself was a conquest. It was a glorious thing to be greeted in a dry, warm building by smiling and supportive city workers and sheriffs, all of whom had volunteered their time to help marry the gay and lesbian couples who had waited through the night.

Inside, the halls were quickly filling with anxious brides and grooms. Shouts of congratulations echoed throughout the building. Ladies rushed to the bathroom to dry off and fix their makeup; many held flowers that they had brought with them the night before. The building was alive with exhilaration and love. Again, volunteers walked the line serving orange juice and water.

City workers seemed determined to process as many marriage licenses as possible that day. The atmosphere in the Clerk's Office was downright festive. Volunteers called out "Next patient!" or "Next victim!" to keep the applicants and paperwork flowing quickly.

When we received our marriage license tears of joy filled my eyes. As we walked down the hall, license in hand, passing the line of people still waiting, people cheered and yelled their congratulations. We proudly held up our license for all to see. We were quickly escorted to the rotunda and had our ceremony with Serena as our maid of honor. Despite the scores of people in the building, it was as if the only people there were my new bride, Renee, Serena, our Deputy Marriage Commissioner, David Owen, and myself.

After taking our vows with tears streaming down our cheeks, we proceeded to the Assessor-Recorder's Office to file our license, a room overflowing with newlyweds and the media. We received our marriage certificate and proudly walked out the front doors, down the steps of City Hall. People shouted their good wishes, while passing cars honked their support. I was elated, walking down the steps of San Francisco City Hall with my new bride and our daughter, marriage certificate in hand. Had we really just been liberated?

My heart ached to personally thank Mayor Newsom, the City of San Francisco, and all of the generous volunteers who made 4,037 marriages possible in February and March. They are all my heroes. We received such support from the people and City of San Francisco. This city of dreams and miracles has again shown the world just how compassionate and accepting people are capable of being. I hope the rest of the world will follow its gallant lead.

Watching the hundreds of volunteers process licenses and hand out simple comforts restored my faith in humanity. I was taught that God is love. Witnessing humans committing truly selfless acts was watching God in motion.

We drove home from San Francisco in the rain-drenched interior of my car, but our exhilaration kept us warm. Leaning forward, I turned on the CD player and put on "Crash and Burn" by Savage Garden, our Las Vegas wedding song. Renee and I both teared up and held hands. We were *really* married, just like other married couples. No different. Nothing more, nothing less. Simply equal.

The remainder of our wedding day, night, and "honeymoon" we spent in our wonderfully comfortable king-size bed covered with soft, patterned quilts. Together we cuddled, following the news, overjoyed that San Francisco was still marrying same-sex couples, but fearful that the courts would shortly invalidate our licenses and marriage certificates. We somehow transformed from a loving couple to same-sex marriage activists overnight. We felt there wasn't any time to relax, and I know many other San Francisco newlyweds felt the same. We joined newlywed e-mail lists. We began organizing and attending peaceful protests and rallies. When President Bush came to Santa Clara, California, for a fund-raising event, I spoke on behalf of Marriage Equality California at a protest against his proposal for a constitutional amendment that would ban same-sex marriage. Our president completely sidestepped his constituents at that rally. Going in a back entrance, President Bush did not face the peaceful protesters who stood outside with signs and banners, signing songs, asking our president for the right for same-sex couples to marry, for funding for educational programs for our children, and for a stop to bloodshed overseas.

But why had Renee and I become activists overnight? We did so because we were graced with the ability to marry, and we believe it is our responsibility to stand up, to make our voices heard, and to represent the countless other GLBT couples who want to wed now and in the future. Legally wedding the woman I love in the center of the rotunda at City Hall gave me a feeling of liberation and equality which I believe all people, regardless of sexual orientation, are entitled to as United States citizens.

A FEW DAYS after our wedding, we heard through the Internet grapevine that the Bay Area Community of Women (B.A.C.W.), presided over by Mindy Bokser, was hosting a reception for not only Del Martin and Phyllis Lyon, longtime lesbian activists and the first couple to be married, but for all the S.F. newlyweds, on Sunday, February 22. I RSVP'd immediately, securing our two spots for the party at the San Francisco Hyatt Regency. B.A.C.W. went above and beyond the call of duty when they organized this event. Just as City Hall opened its heart to us, San Francisco invited us to attend the biggest reception I have ever seen. I was honored to donate a couple of my original paintings to the silent auction. So much work went into organizing this event, it seemed the least I could do to contribute.

While Renee was parking the car and I was setting up my artwork for the silent auction, I had the most horrifying moment. I looked into my bag and realized that our marriage certificate, which I had brought with us, was gone. I cannot describe the overwhelming anxiety I felt at that moment. Here, everything we wanted and stood in line for in the pouring rain for thirteen hours, was *gone*. Before I knew it, the room was swimming and I started to sway, the woman next to me saw something was wrong and grabbed my arm, steadying me. She asked me what was wrong and, panting, I explained to her that I had lost our marriage certificate. She did her best to calm me down until Renee came into the room. As she walked over to me, I told her, "I lost it. I lost our marriage certificate." She hugged me and told me it was okay, we could get another from City Hall. But in my heart,

I knew it wouldn't be the same. As it turned out, the paper slipped into the back of the frame of a painting. "Phew!" I was relieved.

After that, the reception continued without a hitch. Volunteers from several GLBT organizations staffed the check-in tables while the line outside grew longer. I was grateful we had showed up early and didn't have to wait in another line. At one point rather early in the reception they had to stop allowing people in because we were about to exceed capacity.

The Grand Ballroom was beautifully decorated. White and purple balloons and gorgeous floral bouquets of all colors and designs were thoughtfully placed in the centers of all the round tables. The dance floor was crammed with loving newlyweds holding each other or cheering on the speaker. The room was filled with joyful and grateful couples, some of whom brought their children. Most were dressed in formal attire. At one point, I took a deep breath and looked up, noticing all the balloons surrounding the exquisite chandelier that hung proudly in the center of the ballroom. Empowerment filled the air.

As we walked about the softly lit ballroom I was taken aback by the energy swelling in the room. It looked as if the party had been planned over months, not weeks. Del and Phyllis were sitting on red velvet chairs on the stage. Many speakers addressed the energized room of newlyweds, all speaking about equal and civil rights: California State Assemblymember Mark Leno, County Assessor-Recorder Mabel Teng, Reverend Cecil Williams from Glide Memorial Church, to name a few. Molly McKay of Marriage Equality California, wearing her wedding dress and veil, spoke to the crowd. We cheered for the bravery of Gavin Newsom and when Mabel Teng took to the stage to address us, the room roared with gratitude and joy, shaking the walls.

Several times the band played "Chapel of Love" and the crowd of newlyweds sang along with emotion. At one point, a limbo line started and I figured, *Why not?* So, I approached the line, prepared to give the limbo all I had. Well, the ladies lowered the bar and down I went, black velvet dress flying up into the air. What a sight. Yep, I was the only one during the entire limbo to actually fall on her butt. One has to laugh, so I did while people helped me to my feet.

Before the reception ended, I had the honor of meeting Phyllis Lyon. I gave her a rose, a hug, and a copy of my book. I wanted her to know that the work she had been doing truly mattered not only on a civil rights level, but on an emotional level. She was helping save countless young gays and lesbians the fear we had all experienced. I was in awe of her.

As the party began to wind down, I circled the lobby, soaking in the atmosphere and chatting with other newlyweds. I found a wedding guest book sitting atop a linen-covered table in the lobby. I signed it, thanking both Del and Phyllis for their courage and stamina, and congratulating them on their long-awaited marriage. Guests were invited to bring home balloons and flowers, so I helped myself to a decorated balloon weight that now sits upon my altar, four red roses for Renee and I to share, along with one purple and one white balloon for inclusion in my scrapbook. I didn't want the celebration ever to end. Luckily for me, Renee had a treat in store—a romantic dinner at The Equinox on the top floor of the Hyatt. As the restaurant circled, we pointed out buildings and points of interest to each other, and we watched the sun set over the city. Again, I felt blessed.

Since the wedding and reception our lives have continued to become more political. We have been interviewed several times and participated in the upcoming documentary *I Will, I Do, We Did,* by Roland Torres. Our family life has become rather public, and I have allowed that to happen because I do want the world to see just how similar we are to other families. We have many more similarities than differences. In our home, Renee is the provider. She goes to work everyday and provides for our family. I am an artist. I keep the house, maintain the yards, and do our laundry. Renee and I balance each other. We have found that honesty, mutual respect, and communication are key elements in keeping our relationship healthy and fun-loving. It is my hope that when America sees how typical our life is, perhaps they will not be so fearful or judgmental.

As a family we are standing firm for what we believe in: equality for all. Standing up for ourselves and our right to marriage is also teaching our child, at a very impressionable age, to stand up for her beliefs. And she is. Recently Serena wrote an essay that was published in *Collage,* a magazine for children of GLBT parents.

Her friends, from the beginning, were told that Serena had two mommies, and the children have simply accepted it. It is rare to find our house without at least two children running around playing or creating art.

I don't believe there have ever been any two people more meant to be together than myself and Renee. She is my muse, my lover, friend, and confidant. She gives me strength when I feel weak, and together we are raising Serena in a house full of love, creativity, and healthy boundaries. I am one of the luckiest people in the world. I have a smart, loving, beautiful daughter and a beautiful, kind, and generous woman as my wife. What could possibly be better than that? I would hope for the world to accept our love and view our family just like any other family, one that is based on love.

Hitched

DAVID BARRETT

▼

*W*hen *my boyfriend* and I first heard the City of San Francisco was marrying gay couples, we couldn't believe it. We live in both L.A. and San Francisco and had come up north to put hardwood floors into our Potrero Hill condo. But it wasn't long before friends started asking us if we'd gotten married.

"Well, I would," I'd knowingly say in front of Mark, "but no one's proposed to me yet."

Mayor Gavin Newsom, two weeks into his first term, had opened the door for gay marriages on the previous Thursday, but it wasn't until that Sunday night that Mark, my boyfriend of eight years, brought it up over dinner.

"You keep joking that no one's proposed to you," he said, "But what if someone did?"

I stammered for an answer. I hadn't really considered it. Then, the more we discussed it, the more I realized someone was proposing. *He* was proposing.

After eight years, we were still madly in love, and were as legally joined as any gay couple could be: We owned property together. We'd registered as domestic partners with the City of West Hollywood back in 1996. That granted us visitation rights in jails and hospitals. It was nice. But since West Hollywood has neither jails nor hospitals, it was less useful than our membership at Costco.

We'd attended our share of gay commitment ceremonies and had told ourselves, probably rationalizing, that we were never going to have a fake wedding. We'd only wanted the real deal.

And here it was, marching down the aisle, right at us!

We sat in that café in the Castro, considering that for the first time in history, gay couples were getting legally married in America. So we made two lists, all the reasons we shouldn't (there weren't any); and all the reasons we should (there were so many). It was an act of civil disobedience, a political statement, but more than anything else, it was an act of love. In that moment, it dawned on us both that we wanted it. We wanted to be married and we wanted to be part of this historic week.

I said, "Yes."

And luckily, so did he.

The next day was the President's Day holiday, but the City was marrying people all weekend long. We'd heard that the demand was so great that they were turning couples away, so we agreed to show up early and give it a try. Everyone's wedding day should come with such low expectations.

We were at City Hall the next day by 5:00 a.m. The line already circled the entire city block. There we stood, in the dark, cold, wind, and rain, under our umbrellas, and not encouraged to learn that *every* couple on either side of us had been turned away the day before.

A lone man stood in line in front of us. His name was Jude. He was a cab driver in his fifties. The rugged lines of a hard life creased his face. He stood in the rain, not opening his umbrella.

"They're not going to let you do this alone," I said to him with a smile. He told us his lover, Aubrey, had waited in line all day yesterday. They were taking turns.

Behind us was a young, Asian, straight couple, in their pajamas, getting drenched. They must really love each other, we thought, if they're willing to put up with all this. Later, we learned they were saving the place in line for the girl's sister, who was driving down from Sacramento with her partner of ten years. Their mother, in the car with the couple, told them they were not committing to each other, they were committing a sin.

And so we waited.

And waited.

After what seemed like several days, it finally was 8:00 a.m. City Hall opened and the line started moving. From that moment on, it seemed, everything that day was moving. From seeing the city employees working through their holiday weekend, without pay, so we could all get married, to the dozens of others, straight and gay, offering everyone in line bagels, coffee, soup, and even roses to hold while taking our vows.

Jude, the cab driver in line before us, had taken a break and Aubrey, his lover, was now keeping their place. Aubrey was a jolly, good-hearted African-American man in his fifties, with gentle eyes and grey flecks in his goatee. He told us how much he loved Jude, how they couldn't stop making each other laugh, and how Jude only had six months to live. They'd both lost lovers to AIDS and neither had thought they'd ever find love again. But they had, and were determined to marry. Aubrey looked at us with a twinkle in his eye. He said, "You two are so young. You should take naked pictures of yourselves . . . while you still can."

We had decided the night before that we were just going to *try* to get married, so as we started inching closer and closer City Hall's front doors, it dawned on me that we were really about to do it. We were going to get married! My heart sank. I was suddenly nervous. I was excited. I was terrified. I was a bridegroom.

By the time we entered the building it was 1:00 p.m. We went through their post-9/11 security ordeal and got in another line where we filled out an application for the license. This line also took forever. It was like being at a gay DMV. When we finally got into the Clerk's Office, we presented our completed application and check for $82.00, swore an oath that we were telling the truth, and signed our marriage license. Hours earlier, everyone around us in line had gotten to know everyone else, so the receipt of each license was met with cheers, applause, and photo ops.

The San Francisco City Hall rotunda, the fourth-largest domed building in the world, damaged in the 1989 earthquake, was repaired and magnificent. If a couple wants to book it for a wedding, there's a five-month wait. We, however, had to wait only ten hours. Everywhere we looked—up on the balconies, down on the main floor, and all over the grand marble staircase—gay and lesbian couples were getting married. It was a sight I'll never forget.

The entire day, even waiting in line, had been an adrenaline-pumping, mad rush. So when we met Ned Matthews, the minister who was to marry us, we appreciated his calmness. The rush was over. What was about to happen was conducted with reverence and respect. Another volunteer, a newlywed lesbian named Christmas, was our witness.

We had the ceremony on one of the upstairs open balconies overlooking the Rotunda. Christmas took pictures as Mark and I held each other's hands, took a deep breath, and were married. It was a generic justice-of-the-peace ceremony, but it couldn't have been more beautiful. We pledged our eternal love and commitment to one another and were pronounced "spouses for life."

After it was over, we wiped our tears, the minister congratulated us and ushered us into yet another line to have the marriage recorded. Again, we were with the same people we'd spent all day with. Only now, we were married couples and everyone congratulated each other. By the time we were finished and received our "Certification of Vital Record, City and County of San Francisco, License and Certification of Marriage" it was 4:30 p.m. The rain had stopped.

We came out of City Hall's front doors, married, and exhilarated, waving our marriage license. We were greeted by news crews and a sea of well wishers, throwing rice, applauding, and cheering. We were handed two slices of wedding cake, which we fed to each other, and then we kissed. There were more cheers.

We went home and called our families. My two brothers were thrilled, of course. My parents, who had heard about the marriages, were surprisingly blasé. They congratulated us and my dad said, "You two better have sex right away so they can't annul it." Mark's mother, an elderly Texan Republican, even wished us well. His sister in Manhattan still hasn't stopped squealing in delight.

We never got around to the hardwood floors, but that was okay. We had participated in nothing short of a seismic shift. Gay marriage still has a long, rough road ahead of it. But this was its first step. As of this moment, it's no longer just an idea. It has now existed in America. And Gavin Newsom, the hunky and courageous San Francisco mayor, has officially replaced Judy Garland as our community's greatest hero.

The rain started up again. We held each other, a legally married couple, glowing in pride, love, and disbelief over the day's miraculous accomplishment.

Then came the wedding night . . .

I Was Just Tired of Yelling at the Radio

ED SWAYA

▼

I could not believe the mean, dismissive and ignorant things people were saying about the issue of gay people demanding equality in marriage. And the meanness was not about the merits of marriage equality, but about my family and me personally. Hearing them say that my daughter was not better off with married parents or that my marriage to Gregory would somehow undermine all of heterosexual marriage was insulting. And worse still, these people were not muttering these things under their breath, in their churches, or at their dinner tables, they were saying these things, without shame, on national radio and television! I was angry and hurt beyond words. I was tired of yelling at the radio. I wanted and needed to do something.

When my fairly conservative friend Patrick called to tell me he and his partner of seventeen years just got married, I was elated. When he spoke of it changing him in ways he had not expected, I was reminded of my experience at the National March on Washington for Gay and Lesbian Civil Rights. That weekend in D.C. forever changed me because for the first time, I was in the majority in a major city. The march was about making a trek to be seen and to be counted, contradicting the oppression linked to our invisibility. Being surrounded by queers in all parts of the city allowed me to relax in a profoundly new way and made me painfully aware of how much fear and hiding I unconsciously lived with in my day to day "out" life.

After talking to Patrick, I knew I had to go to San Francisco. I had to go there and be seen, counted, and stand up in some loving way to all of the hateful things I was hearing about us. It was my personal political act. My act of defiance. I was excited.

GREGORY AND I had met ten years earlier when a mutual acquaintance of ours decided that we should meet. He was my first date after a couple of painful relationships and I was looking just to date—nothing serious. I wanted a fuck buddy. We played together, traveled together, and laughed a lot. After almost six months, for reasons that were not clear to us, we realized that we were becoming more than just fuck buddies. The following day I was run over by a tram at our house. I broke my pelvis and almost died. Over my three weeks in the hospital and eight weeks in a hospital bed in my living room, Gregory and I got to know one another. I learned that he had a great sense of humor, knew how to stack firewood, could charm my parents, liked fresh-cut tulips, could use a weed whacker, and could have sex in a hospital bed when a nurse did not show up on time. We decided to give our relationship a go. Five years later we got married at a ceremony witnessed by 120 members of our families and community.

BY THE TIME we decided to go to San Francisco, marriage licenses had been issued to same-sex couples on Thursday and Friday, and there were challenges imploring the court to stop the marriages. We all guessed there was only one more day left— the following Monday—to get there before the court would order the marriages to stop. We could not figure out a way to get to San Francisco by that Monday. I was sad. However, by Tuesday the court had not found reason to stop the marriage licenses from being issued. It looked like we had the rest of that week to get there before the court would stop issuing the licenses. We had time to go.

Gregory's sister offered us airline tickets as a pre-wedding gift. We packed up our two-year-old daughter, some snacks, and a diaper bag, and flew from Seattle to Oakland on Thursday, February 19, eight days after our ten-year anniversary.

A COUPLE OF years earlier, my cousin Laura's house was our home base when we began our adoption process. We worked with a Bay Area agency and spent a few weekends at the house while we did paperwork and attended workshops preparing to adopt our daughter. Since we had been the *padrinos*—the godfathers—at Laura and her husband Teo's wedding a year earlier, they were thrilled to be a part of our getting married. So, here we were again, hanging out with Laura and Teo as we were about to be one of the first same-sex couples in the country to be legally married.

My cousin greeted us at the airport. Our flight was almost four hours late and we landed after 10:00 p.m. Laura and Teo picked us up, fed us, plied us with some wine, laughed with us, and tucked us into bed around 12:30 a.m.

I expected the next day to be fun, interesting and empowering. I wanted one of the first wedding licenses offered to a same-sex couple. I wanted to be seen and counted and acknowledged by some governmental agency.

I was not expecting the day to be emotional.

THE NEXT MORNING, I woke up at 4:30 a.m. and groggily dashed to the BART station, exiting at Civic Center. I meandered to Starbucks, got my latte, then found my way to City Hall. I was surprised to see a long line. I was number 116 in line that day. They had married 193 couples the previous day, so I relaxed and sipped my coffee. Gregory and Vivian joined me at 7:30 a. m. and we laughed and played.

Being in line was a gift. The atmosphere was so embracing. There were people driving by and honking their horns in support, there were bags of bagels and cream cheese magically appearing and moving up the line. People walked by with doughnuts and coffee while the couples in line were all telling their stories.

The mean-spirited Christians were there too. There were a couple of the expected caricatures there—the ones with bad posture, bad clothes, and bad hair ranting the same old rants about God hating homosexuals and how hell was the only reward for our "lifestyle choices." But they were a mere annoyance. The really scary mean-spirited Christians were the young, good-looking ones. These kids in their early twenties looked like people I would like to be friends with. They were outwardly comfortable, approachable, and, well, good-looking. They were still delivering the same hateful messages as the bad-toothed ones, but they didn't look crazy. They looked like people I like. That scared me. The people that would deny my access to the rights and responsibilities of marriage (and parenthood and employment and health care and . . .) are people who do not look different from me and my community. Very scary.

There was buzz along the line about whether we would get in that day or whether we would be turned away because of the volumes of people. The licensing office was short-staffed and the office had orders to close at exactly 4:00 p.m. The line moved very slowly, if at all. At 11:00 a.m. I was hopeful; at noon I was depressed; at 1:30 I was giddy and hungry; by 2:00 I was feeling despondent; at 3:00 I was numb; and by 3:40 I was convinced we would not make the cut. All day we kept in touch with family and friends in Seattle to let them know what was going on. We had rounded the bend in the line and could see the County Clerk's Office door, but we were by no means going to get our licenses that day. They issued "tickets" to couples to guarantee them a moment before the county clerk to get their licenses. By 3:50, couples fifteen spaces in front of us (all day I regretted taking the time for my early visit to Starbucks) got their tickets. It looked like they were done giving tickets for the day, and I was convinced we would be turned away. My stomach ached from disappointment. We would have had to fly home that night unmarried.

Then they gave out five more tickets, and then five more, and we still were not sure we would make it. Finally we got our tickets and we both burst into tears. The tears of relief, excitement, anger, and hope were overwhelming to both of us. We called all of our family and friends who were rooting for us. All tears. At least four hundred couples behind us did not get tickets to marry that day.

We literally did not stop crying until we left City Hall (through the mean-spirited Christians). Getting our license, having our ceremony, and filing it with the county were cup-runneth-over experiences for us. We restated our vows, reexchanged our rings; we ate wedding cake brought by our dear friend Jennifer.

THESE EXPERIENCES WERE full of joy and hope and validation of us as a couple and us as a family. Before City Hall I had no idea how much a legal wedding mattered to me. It was one of those things I assumed I would never have. But, we were married, while our daughter napped in her stroller, and in that little part of the world, we experienced what it's like to be recognized by the state for who we were and what our relationship was all about. And it felt great. It mattered.

Months later, I still yell at the radio all of the time. But, my yelling does not feel quite as hopeless or disempowered. I have a bit of a cocky, defiant tone to my rants now. Marriage equality is something I will likely see in my lifetime. Even if these licenses are invalidated, we were a part of history and we as a couple will not go back. As my Republican dad said about marriage equality, "The train has left the station!"

Since we considered ourselves a married couple prior to our arrival at City Hall, it was hard to imagine that our license and small ceremony on the steps would feel so big. But it was bigger than my words can convey. Being legally married was much more than the "stand up and be counted" act of civil disobedience I expected. It was about commitment, hope, connection, family, community, and—well—love.

A Married Community

CHERYL

▼

A song of joy. That is what we experienced all day Sunday, all of Sunday night, and Monday morning. That is how long we waited. In the sunshine and through pouring rain as we camped out all night, couple number 3 in line to be married Monday. The pictures, the news articles, the video—none of them carry the true emotions we experienced and witnessed. We were exhausted, we were cold to the bone, we were wet to the core. But all of us who braved the storm Sunday night were filled with a warmth that we will never lose—the warmth of knowing we were part of history, the warmth of knowing we were to be married, even if only for a day. That warmth carried us through the night and will continue to carry my wife and me through the rest of our lives. We have our marriage license. At this moment, it is legal. *We are legally married.* No one can take away this time or experience. I am a lesbian. *I have a wife.*

MY WIFE AND I met online. The *old* online when we paid $3.95 an hour for AOL. We consider ourselves the "old guard" of the online, lesbian community. We met in person for the first time in February 1995 and we had a handfasting ceremony in July of that year. We had what we considered a "wedding." We had our friends and family around us to celebrate our union, and we did many of the traditional marriage things, treasuring each and every one of them. In our minds nothing could top our wedding day.

In some ways that is still true. But it has been almost a week since my wife and I left our home to make the four-hour drive to San Francisco for our second wedding, and both of us have come back from San Francisco changed in some way. I don't think either one of us ever really felt discriminated against before now; I mean really felt it to the core. Being a butch woman, I have always felt different in some respects. I have walked through this world knowing that many people did not know quite what to do with me, but I never felt truly discriminated against. Now that we have experienced being married, actually married like "they" are, and after bonding with people who were total strangers thirty-six hours before our marriage, we feel eerily different. If and when our marriage is disallowed, we will feel a sense of profound loss, a bone-aching loss that neither of us is quite sure what to do with. We may feel the need to try to lessen that loss through a lawsuit. We have never sued anyone in our lives, but we may join other couples and sue the State of California. We shall see.

TODAY WE RECEIVED a card from two women we met in San Francisco. I pulled the envelope out of the mailbox, checked the return address, and immediately knew who it was from. We had met the couple inside City Hall on Monday. We spoke with them as we waited, while the media swarmed, filming us because we were the group who had spent thirty-six hours in the rain, the group who was called stubborn and unreasonable because we had refused to leave.

I am a public school teacher, and one of these women was an elementary teacher in a private school. Both of us were a little nervous about our pictures appearing in the media. Both of us went to San Francisco knowing we were taking a risk. Her risk was much greater than mine since she taught at a private, religious school.

After avoiding the media for hours, both of us finally said, "The hell with it." The experience of finally being legitimized, of being publicly recognized, of being officially married, even if only for that one day, was more important to us than any job. She said, "I'm not turning away from another camera. I knew when we came here, there was a risk. I now know there was more of an emotional risk in *not* coming, in *not* being part of this historic day, in *not* feeling ever in my lifetime what I am feeling now." I whole-heartedly agreed. We both turned toward the camera and smiled. At the time of this writing, I think we both still have our jobs.

A few minutes later, we were escorted to another room in City Hall, and the wedding license process began. We did not see this couple again, but when I opened our mailbox today, and I saw their names on the return address line, I cried. The front of the elaborate, white card read, "Partners for Life." That is what all of us are, partners for life. We newlyweds share something as cou-ples and as a community. We are married partners, but we are also a married community.

We Are Going to Win

NINA WOUK

▼

essie and I met in the mid-1970s, at a Women Against Violence
Against Women gathering at the Common Woman Bookstore
in Austin, Texas, which was a usual way to meet. We spent three
years as friends, exploring central Texas, a deteriorating American
left, *The Rocky Horror Picture Show,* my first stumbling attempts at
Passover Seders, and getting arrested, among other experiences.
During that time, we each went through a number of lovers, fuck
buddies, and chicks on the side. Eventually we started to explore
sex with each other, after which we fell in love and pretty much
simultaneously realized that we wanted to grow old together.

So far we have succeeded at that. Since we started out with
nothing, we found it easy to merge resources and have never
thought of doing otherwise. Everything we own is in both of our
names. We continue to explore new experiences together, and
also separately, excluding outside sexual adventures, which aren't
worth the emotional cost. My birth family considers us married,
and Jessie's birth family considers me a member, although the
exact reason for that remains unstated.

Over the years, Jessie and I have discussed having some sort of
public ceremony to celebrate our relationship, however Jessie
always said that anything short of a legal wedding would dis-
honor all the time we had been together. And besides, we are

both rather shy. However, when we heard about the weddings taking place at San Francisco City Hall, the opportunity to be part of history turned out to be quite persuasive.

The first same-sex weddings were performed on Thursday, February 12, with no advance publicity. City Hall officials kept the first weddings secret to stop the usual reactionaries from filing a lawsuit based on California's "Defense of Marriage Act" (which is undoubtedly unconstitutional but hasn't yet been deemed such by the California State Supreme Court). The usual reactionaries did file suit Friday, but the judge said he wouldn't hear arguments until Tuesday afternoon. On Friday, so many couples showed up at City Hall that staff members volunteered to come back on Saturday, staying from 10:00 to 4:00 to process those who didn't get their chance marry on Friday. By 4:00 p.m. Saturday, 320 couples were still in line, so those couples received numbers and were told to come back Sunday. Then word was put out that marriages would be performed 10:00 to 4:00 on both Sunday and Monday of the three-day weekend.

Since Jews don't get married on Shabbat, we figured we would get to City Hall early Sunday, which was a clear, beautiful day. We joined the line, which stretched all the way around City Hall, around 8:45 a.m., well before the 10:00 opening. However, due to the overflow from Saturday, they could take only eighty new couples. We were about the one hundredth couple. So we went home, planning to return even earlier on Monday.

Our plan meant getting up at 5:00 a.m., and driving to San Francisco in time to get in line at 6:10 a.m., where we waited in the dark and the rain, in almost exactly the same place we had been standing when we were told to go home the day before. We brought lawn chairs, ponchos, trash bags, and umbrellas, and at first managed to stay reasonably dry. Before sunrise, winds gusted enough to turn some people's umbrellas inside out, but the wind died down after dawn, and the rain slacked off, though it never entirely stopped.

While it was still dark out, a young woman stopped by the line to talk to us, telling us, "This is so historic I just had to be here." Then she asked, "Can I get you some coffee or anything?"

I said, "I wish we had chocolate-covered coffee beans—I don't want to drink liquids and have to get married with my legs crossed."

Later she actually came back with the coffee beans and a foil-covered chocolate rose on a long stem. This was the first of many unexpected acts of generosity we witnessed. People showed up with coffee, donuts, bagels, muffins, biscotti, candy, orange juice, fresh garbage bags, gloves, dry socks, and all kinds of stuff that they wanted to honor us with. A guy passing out coffee, bagels, and moist towelettes drew a lot of appreciative laughter because that was such a gay thing to do. One woman handing out home-made blueberry and sunflower seed muffins with little frosting hearts on top told us, "I was at the fall of the Berlin Wall and this has the same feel about it."

In this joyful atmosphere, those of us who were waiting in line intermittently burst into song, mostly "Chapel of Love." Meanwhile, reporters circled the block looking to interview people who had flown in from places like New York or people who spoke Spanish. An encampment of news trucks filled the parking spots across from City Hall.

From drivers on the street we received much supportive honking and waving, including from tour busses. One guy with a Bible circled the block a couple of times on foot. He said, "G-d loves you!"

"G-d loves you, too!" I replied.

On his second round, he said, "This is the day that G-d made, let us be happy and rejoice in it."

I sang back the original words in Hebrew. I think he was well-meaning in his soul-saving way, but I was glad when he gave up and left.

Soon after we had arrived at City Hall, a guy had walked up to the people behind us and told them they were the 263rd couple in line, and should have no trouble getting in, even if only 400 couples could be married. This was of course an unofficial count and did nothing to stop Jessie from worrying that we would get cut off again. Throughout the morning we heard many rumors, which changed regularly. Later, word was passed down the line that Mabel Teng, the county assessor-recorder, would get the doors to City Hall open early so we wouldn't be out in the rain longer than necessary, and that she intended to get five hundred couples married that day. This rumor turned out to be true. Way around the corner, where we couldn't see, when the doors first opened at 7:30 a.m., the line moved one big jump, and then in little jumps after. People kept arriving to join the line after us— some in taxis, others on foot, all looking hopeful and deter- mined, and just as cold and wet as we were. I hoped they would get to get married too.

As the line fitted and started around the block, rain fell on our little lawn chairs, soaking my seat so that when I sat down my pants got wet. After that I gave my chair to a guy with a proper rain suit and took to standing. We could tell that the line was going to start moving again when we saw the umbrellas up ahead, bright and colorful once the sun came up behind the clouds, moving around the corner. Then we would pack up the chairs and get ready for another ten-foot jump. Each jump came when a group of married couples left City Hall and a bunch of yet-to-be married couples were admitted. Therefore each jump was accompanied by loud cheering from people who were waiting on the steps, handing out wedding cake to the newly married. We were very excited when cars started driving by with people inside holding their marriage certificates up to the window for us to see.

Around 10:00 a.m., members of our little camp started head- ing to the public toilets in the square. Two were regular porta cans, and then there were what Jessie calls the "scary self-clean- ing pay toilets." Next to the pay toilet, a guy in an official van handed out free tokens, which he tried not to give to homeless people, but the marriage line folks shared them anyway. After fif- teen minutes I was second in line for the pay toilets, but back in front of City Hall I could see the umbrellas moving so fast and hear the cheers rising so often that I was afraid of losing my place in the getting-married line. I ditched the toilet line and went back to City Hall, where I heard that we were about an hour from being admitted. So I headed back to the toilet line, since I was by now in pain. People with cell phones called back and forth between the two lines, keeping each other updated.

Twenty minutes later, still waiting for a toilet, I was seriously considering whether I could slip between two parked cars. But I wasn't back in Texas, so there was nothing to do but wait for a toi- let and hope to G-d I would make it back in time. We were all mov- ing as fast as we could, unzipping rain suits and unbuttoning coats during the toilet cleaning cycle. I didn't even fasten my pants until

I was finished and back outside. Then I ran back to City Hall where Jessie was waiting on the stairs, quite on pins and needles with fear that she would reach the head of the line and have to give up our place because I wasn't with her (although that would likely have set us back only a few minutes). Our group was already nearing the building's entrance, so we ran and just made it in with them. It was 11:00 a.m.

Once inside, we cleared security—lawn-chairs, soggy coats, luggage, and all. The halls were full of volunteers, many recently married themselves, who helped us not get too lost. They gave us a form to fill in. I kept scribbling on it, using the floor for a writing surface every time the line stood still. Then along came another volunteer telling us not to fill in the form yet. Then came another asking to check what we had filled in. He told us that we had gotten enough things wrong that we needed a second form, which he gave us. This time I unfolded a lawn chair, sat down, and filled the form in very carefully, while moving the chair each time the line wound another step through the corridor. Another volunteer came by to check the second form and showed us where the first guy had given us inaccurate instructions. But the second form was fixable, so then all we had to do was follow the line up the stairs and over the river and through the woods to the Clerk's Office, where we could show our form and driver's licenses to a clerk who would take our check, give us our marriage license, and send us to wait in another line.

By now we were starting to see a few people we knew from Congregation Sha'ar Zahav, including the rabbi, who was empowered to perform civil ceremonies, and said she would marry us when we got that far. Jessie says she was like a familiar lifeline thrown out into a sea of friendly but unknown faces.

Every time a couple left the Clerk's Office holding their marriage license, the people waiting in line cheered for them. I got to yell a lot of *Yee-haws!*—a mitzvah to gladden the hearts of those who are getting married.

When we finally arrived in the Clerk's Office, it was jam-packed. Usually they issue maybe thirty licenses on a busy day. So far today they had issued about three hundred, and it wasn't over yet. Several couples had babies, toddlers, small children, and preteens with them, making substantial family groups. Some of them had camped out all night, one partner holding a place in line while the other stayed home with the kids. While we were waiting in the office, one woman told the kids they would have to mind her now, because after the marriage she would be their mom.

To control the crowding in the office, outside in the hallway, volunteers watched people's luggage, chairs, sleeping bags, and other belongings. After we got our license, one of the volunteers carried our chairs for us from the license office to the getting-married line, as I high-femmed along, waving at the people who were waiting, and Jessie followed with her usual reserve.

In the rotunda, still more volunteers pointed us in the general direction of the marble staircase where several weddings were going on at once—on the stairs, on the landing, and among the pillars of the second-floor mezzanine—while pictures were taken and volunteer musicians played romantic songs. As soon as we stashed our lawn chairs and luggage, my foot cramped up—probably from jumping up and down while cheering for everybody else—and I had to sit down in the middle of the line, which fortunately was moving slowly. As soon as Rabbi Angel found us, I got another cramp and had to sit down on the steps while she rounded up Jewish witnesses. Even though our civil wedding would have been legal with any witnesses, having witnesses from our own congregation made us feel part of, and important to, our community.

Then, after hours of waiting, our ceremony happened in a flash. When Rabbi Angel pronounced us spouses for life, we hugged and cried and did the various things that people do at times of great emotion. Next, we were shuffled by weepily congratulatory volunteers to the County Assessor-Recorder's Office to get our official copy of the marriage certificate. We arrived in the office just as Mabel Teng was giving one of her many press conferences of the day, talking about how she and her people really believe in equality and love, how great it was that we gave them the chance to make this happen, and how, whatever happens in court tomorrow, we are making history today. She was really sincere, not just another politician. If she ever runs for any office that I can vote for, she has my vote for sure. She also said they had issued marriage license to 1,639 same-sex couples so far, and they aimed to marry 650 couples that day.

Before leaving the Assessor-Recorder's Office, we paid our $13 at one of many counters, and waited next to a big folding table where volunteers were stamping official seals onto piles of licenses, in the midst of the excited crowd. Volunteers with impressively loud voices called combinations of first names that rang throughout the enormous room, where couples were still having their pictures taken, one with the groom-girl in a tux and the bride-girl in platform heels and red chiffon.

Our marriage certificate looks just like a death certificate only with different words. That shocked me at first but then I looked at the content. There we are: really married. It doesn't feel like a change in legal status, but it does feel like an accomplishment. We are the silver platter on which liberation will be served.

By 2:45 p.m. we were out of there. Couples were still lined up outside, but only for half a block. Instead of parading down the front steps, we took our slices of wedding cake down the wheel-chair ramp to the car so we could get home and collapse.

Upon hearing about our wedding, people at work kept asking what we were going to do for our honeymoon, and I keep telling them we had that twenty-five years ago. The couples we had met in line at City Hall had been together upwards of three years, most upwards of ten years, and were undertaking a serious commit-ment, not just making a political statement (although making a political statement shouldn't be underrated). People around us had driven in from Los Angeles and San Diego, as well as from various suburbs like our own. We will all be parties to any legal proceedings arising out of those twenty-nine days of weddings in San Francisco. We all have legal standing and committed rela-tionships to back up our moral position, and we are going to win.

Two Weddings and a Funeral

JUDITH L. DANCER

▼

It's the end of July, and we just got back from Eileen's niece's wedding in New Jersey, a trip I took with some trepidation. The niece is twenty-six, Jewish, and married a Catholic boy. I haven't been to too many weddings in my lifetime, and I felt very nervous to be there. What were the expectations? How would the night go? Would there be any gays or lesbians there besides us?

Eileen's mom had died of cancer in March, which added another layer of emotion to the trip. Flying back to the East Coast from San Francisco brought all those feelings of loss and grief back. Although she was not my mother, I felt very close to her, talking to her on the phone weekly and hearing about the progression of the disease after Eileen's daily calls to her mom.

Add to those emotional pressures the fact that going to the East Coast feels to me like traveling to a foreign land: the brick buildings, the malls, the accents. And this was going to be a brief trip—leaving on Friday, coming home Sunday night. The time crunch enhanced the feeling of strangeness. I didn't think I had time even to get jet lag. Would my body have time to catch up to what was happening and where we were? I carried all these concerns on the plane with me.

■   ■   ■

FIRST THING OFF the plane, I noticed the humidity. I had been ready for the hot weather but hadn't anticipated the moisture in the air. Not being from the East Coast, I haven't experienced all the seasons there. We usually just dropped in for a week, often in winter, for a craft show in Baltimore where Eileen sells her beautiful, lyric ceramic work. After the show we would head up to New York to visit her mom in Brooklyn, in the house where Eileen was raised. Both her brothers live nearby in Connecticut and New Jersey.

As we got the rental car and drove out of the Newark Airport, everything looked so green. I am used to California's brown hills in summer and was surprised by this vibrant, lush color. The greenery refreshed me, and my spirit soared. I am a tree lover from way back. Trees connect the earth with the sky, grounding me into the rich hummus and extending out into the cosmos. As we flew at 60 mph across the New Jersey Turnpike, the trees danced in the wind, heightening my sense of spirit and connectedness.

After checking into the hotel, a box of metal, glass, and floral carpeting, we decided to go out to dinner at the food court in a nearby mall. We wanted to see what malls were like in New Jersey. Eileen told me they originated in this state. I'm not totally sure if that's true or not, but they do have it down there—the mall was huge, so huge that we were unsure where to enter it. We drove around the circumference, wondering how we would penetrate this monstrosity. After getting directions, we slid through a giant glass door and entered the food court area. It was a gastronomical practice in grease, grease, and more grease. We found some vegetables in a Chinese section and faired pretty well. Then, walking around, we marveled that the target age of displays and stores seemed to be about fifteen. The place was packed and hopping. That's what teenagers do on a Friday night there.

Saturday we spent anticipating the evening wedding. I was anxious about fitting in. I am a femme, but I often feel like a butch around straight girls, especially New Jersey straight girls, who seem like a different breed. While I was debating between high heels and sensible black sandals, my really butch gal had decided on wearing a tux. She was angry that when we got married we didn't get all the hoopla that her niece was getting for her marriage. She carried that anger around like an aggressive weight. I felt her rebellious side slide into her body, making her stance more taut and bracing. As the day wore on, all the trans-gressions of her brothers and their difficulty in accepting her as a lesbian came to the surface. I wanted to run away. I wanted to make nice and be pleasant. I was finding it hard to sit in the car with her as we navigated around back roads, taking a "nice drive."

CHOOSING TO MARRY Eileen in February was a no-brainer. On the morning of Friday, February 13, we read in the *San Francisco Chronicle* that Phyllis Lyon and Del Martin, two icons of lesbian culture in San Francisco, had gotten married on Thursday, along with many other couples. I was in the tub, taking a bath, when Eileen called out, "Do you want to go?" I said, "Yes!" immediately. I jumped out of the bath, dripping wet, and got dressed. While Eileen took the dog to the park for her daily constitution, I got ready for work, called a coworker to let him know I would be late (his response was an excited "Take your time!" for which I am eternally grateful), and hightailed it out of there. When she fin-ished up with the dog, Eileen would follow on her scooter. We agreed to meet at the Van Ness side of City Hall.

Eileen and I actually had married each other years before, on the Big Island of Hawaii. Throughout our two-week visit to the island, we said vows to each other at different spots that felt mag-ical to us. We built a rock cairn on the volcano, symbolizing our love and commitment to each other. We exchanged rings. That was enough for us, until this opportunity to get married "for real" presented itself.

When I got to City Hall, I saw several couples hanging out at the door, all men. I looked around and said, "Where are the les-bians? I thought they'd be into this." They all laughed, bonding in our desire to partake in this ritual called marriage. We were let in and went straight to the licensing room. Although I was early in the line, Eileen wasn't there yet, and both parties had to be present even to take a number. She squeaked in a few minutes later, and we became couple number twenty-two, married on Friday the thir-teenth, which we laugh about to this day.

For the next hour or so, the excitement in my body was at an all-time peak. Rarely had I felt this combination of awe, disbelief, and joy all at once. I was glad City Hall's ceilings were so high, so my energy could fly up into that space to meet with other people's energies of ecstasy and wonder. After we were married, we came out of the building, dazed and disoriented. I walked Eileen to her scooter, and I went back to the car. I drove to work and arrived by 9:30 a.m.

People acknowledged our wedding with cards, well wishes, and, to our surprise, gifts. While we were at the funeral and sitting shivah for Eileen's mom, several cousins came and congratulated us. Acknowledgment was slower coming from Eileen's immediate family. She had to tell them several times what it meant to her to be able to get married, and they still don't really understand.

ON THE DAY of her niece's wedding, the layering of experiences—attending a very traditional straight wedding, Eileen's mom passing only four months earlier, and her family's reaction to our marriage in February—made for a compilation of much angst and rebellion. I finally talked to Eileen about the whole thing and we cried together, releasing some of the disappointment, sadness, and loss. We decided that we were up for this and would do our best. We would have several ally cousins that we could talk to if we needed to, who would understand all the layers of emotions and experience.

During our conversation, Eileen asked me if I had been one of those girls who fantasized during childhood about how my wedding would be. Frankly, I don't remember ever being too interested in creating that ceremony as a child. I was more interested in playing house, when I was eight or nine years old, with my girlfriend Lorraine, taking turns being the man and the woman. We would actually make out by pressing our lips to each other's, a dry kiss with feigned passion. It was a repetitive game we played regularly at her house, with the door to her room closed.

IN THE END, Eileen's cousin's wedding was a beautiful melding of Catholic and Jewish tradition. I cried when I saw Eileen's brother cry, when I saw how proud he was of his daughter. I felt my deep support and caring for this family, knowing they were in the middle of a meaningful ritual. I took in the fact that the last time we were together, we were deeply grieving for a woman whose life had gone out of her. I had grown closer to Eileen's family, going through that ordeal with them. I actually talk on the phone to her brothers when they call now. I feel their respect for me as Eileen's spouse, and I respect them.

A few things from the evening stand out. I fit right in with my cute, girly dress and painted nails. I was glad I went for the sensible black sandals instead of ridiculous high heels, because women were dropping around me with cramps in their toes. I especially remember the sheer joy and happiness on so many people's faces, especially the niece and her father. I loved witnessing this, especially when they partook in the father-daughter dance. I cried. Eileen and her brothers looked so cute together in their tuxes. I took several pictures. They were in their comic element, posing and joking around. And we danced. We danced most of the night to a live band. Though I am a dancer, it's not Eileen's element, but she was a trooper getting out there on the dance floor over and over again. Everybody was out there: the niece and all her friends, the brothers and their wives, and all the cousins.

I was happy to see the niece dancing with her girlfriends in playful sensuality: bumping each other, dancing close, laughing, and touching. It gave me hope for the straight world. At one point she introduced me as Eileen's wife, which I appreciated so much. She gets it, and she participates in her acceptance of us by using the term wife.

OUR WEDDING WAS so different from Eileen's niece's. It was a milestone for us, after eleven years of being together and after marrying on the Big Island in 1995. Our reception, which we had at our house with a few dozen friends, happened after Eileen got back from visiting and taking care of her sick mom. The joy was palpable, and people honored our commitment to and caring for each other. It was not the big wedding and reception we had just come from, and that is okay with me. Our wedding was an act of revolution, as much of my life feels like, just being out as a lesbian in my daily life. Our wedding was also an act of sheer joy. The fact that so many of us were being married that day, that week, and within the next month was mind-boggling to me. Our wedding was about intimacy between Eileen and me, pure and simple, and it was about participating in something bigger than us. In my heart, we are married, no matter what the courts say. Society will catch up and see this someday. I hope it happens soon.

My Husband, My Hero

▼

My husband, Robert, and I were married in San Francisco on February 16, 2004, after waiting outside during the cold and rainy night. We didn't get married for a political statement and aren't activists. We just love each other and decided to take the possibly once-in-a-lifetime opportunity provided to us by the City of San Francisco to get married and celebrate our love of ten years.

After the wedding, we returned to Los Angeles and settled back into our normal day-to-day routine. The weather in L.A. was unseasonably warm for winter, almost summerlike at eighty-six degrees. So one night, before bed, I opened our window to let in some cool air—an unusual thing for me to do during the winter. Around 2:30 a.m., Robert smelled smoke coming through the window, and then noticed the popping and crackling sounds of fire. He got up to look out the window and saw flames licking at the back of the condo next door to us. Without waking me, immediately Robert threw on some clothes and ran down our three flights of stairs to go outside and wake the family living there, to get them out of harm's way. He saw no lights on in the condo, so he knew the family inside was sleeping, unaware of the danger they were in. When Robert arrived at their condo, he realized that in his haste he had forgotten his cell phone, so he ran all the way back upstairs and grabbed it, calling 911 as he ran back down the stairs, two at a time, and outside.

By the time Robert returned to the front of our neighbor's place, flames were lapping at their second-story balcony, but still he saw no signs of the sleeping couple and their little girl. He pounded and pounded on their door, yelling, "Fire! Wake up!" over and over for what seemed like five minutes. This is what woke me up. Finally, the couple heard Robert too, and as the fire trucks, police car, helicopter, and ambulance approached, the family evacuated their home through the thick smoke, the young man guiding his seven-and-a-half-months pregnant wife who was holding their little girl.

Later they told us that the smoke downstairs was so thick that they couldn't see their way out. They were so grateful to my husband for rousing them, saving them from very possibly losing their lives. The young man later told Robert that he had third degree burns on his feet. He kept telling my hero that they couldn't thank him enough.

As I watched all this unfold last night, an incredible feeling of pride in my new husband welled up inside of me. I just couldn't believe that this kind of hero is my spouse. In the middle of all the chaos, a neighbor lady said, "With a partner like Robert, you don't have anything to worry about." We all marveled at his clear thinking, alertness to signs of danger, and brave actions. And yet something was troubling my heart—the way Robert's parents treated him when he told them we had gotten married. You'd be correct to surmise that they didn't take it well. Robert's parents have a tremendous son to be proud of, and yet they were treating him like dirt.

I come from a conservative Mormon background. And yet all of my extended family and our friends have reacted favorably to our civil marriage. They know that we weren't married in the Mormon Temple and that we aren't asking for their church's religious seal of approval. Even though our relationship doesn't conform to the way Mormons are taught things should be, they can separate their own strong religious views from the politics of it all and continue expressing their love and support to us. They can still be happy for us, congratulate us on our marriage, and celebrate our ten years of happiness together. For example, my staunch

Republican and strict Mormon brother told me, "I would officially welcome Robert to the family, but welcoming him now feels kind of odd because he's been part of the family right from the very beginning." My mother told me that my father, now deceased, would be immensely proud and happy for us. She did admit that this had not been an easy issue for them to cope with as parents, but she couldn't imagine not loving us or not being together as a family as a result.

Robert's parents' reaction was the polar opposite. His brothers have all been fine. But Robert's parents are apparently unable to reconcile this with their fundamentalist religious beliefs or separate themselves from the hatred, ignorance, and prejudice they've latched onto. His parents are not even big enough to congratulate us or wish us happiness in the smallest way. They couldn't even say, "We're happy if you're happy." In hindsight, this reaction is not entirely surprising, since Robert's dad didn't speak to his son for years after Robert came out. For several years after Robert and I started living together, they wouldn't permit me in their house. They didn't relent until they realized that Robert would never attend any family events, such as Christmas dinner, unless they welcomed me. After that, for years we were a part of the family, attending get-togethers, and except for a little coolness toward me on the part of Robert's father, everything was fine. Now they are shunning us again, and we are back to square one.

With this as a backdrop, Robert's brother, who has lived with a woman for six years and fathered children out of wedlock, was busy with his fiancée, planning their wedding. Though Robert and I were were having our own wedding reception dinner, his brother's wedding was all his parents could talk about. They informed us that they wouldn't be coming to our reception, and asked us not to send them an invitation either. Further, they have a tradition of giving extravagant wedding gifts. We didn't receive even a token gift, because to them we are second-class citizens and deserve treatment as such. Instead of gifts, we asked people to make a donation to either of two cancer funds, and we are very happy to say we raised quite a bit of money. His parents, with another son dying of cancer, would not even make a donation in his name, since that is what we asked for our wedding. The contradiction of his parents turning their backs on our marriage and then talking nonstop about his other brother's upcoming wedding makes me very sad.

My therapist (this *is* L.A., after all) has told me that Robert's parents are living with a powerful poison, and if I lower myself to their level and go off on them, I will risk taking on the poison myself. I am going to try to take the high road, but it's hard for me to accept their second-class treatment, especially of Robert. It's not fun sitting at the back of the bus. His heroism underscores how misguided his parents' actions are. They've done nothing to deserve a son like Robert.

Since becoming married, we've been discussing adopting. I find myself thinking that, however hard it is for me to put up with this kind of treatment from my in-laws, if we did adopt and I found them treating my child as a second-class citizen, I would be fighting mad. I wouldn't tolerate it one bit. Considering my feelings as a hypothetical parent, I wonder how Robert's parents can treat him no better than a mongrel dog. Where is the love?

In clips for the movie *The Passion of the Christ,* when I saw Judas kiss Christ—his betrayal—I thought, *That would be Robert's mom.* When they were nailing Christ to the cross, I thought, "*That would be his father.*" To us their unkind words and lack of support for our marriage seem to be the ultimate betrayal. The perversion or abomination here is not our marriage, but the way Robert's parents, and others, are twisting Christ's teachings, using a literal interpretation of a few select lines from the Bible to the justify banning our love for each other. "Forgive them, for they know not what they do" is an appropriate prayer in light of their actions. I believe that the greatest teaching Christ gave us was to love and that he would be very unhappy with this current state of affairs.

I am so happy and blessed that my family chose to react to our marriage with love and support. I only hope that in time Robert's parents will see things differently and soften their hardened stance. If my conservative Mormon family can deal with this issue in such a positive way, there is hope that Robert's family will come to an acceptance of us as well. It is my prayer that other couples whose families have divided over their same-sex marriages will find reconciliation with their families, or will at least be able to move on with their lives.

It Will Make Us All Equal

ANN SEIFERT

▼

There is nothing extraordinary about my life that would separate me from anyone else walking this earth. We all struggle. Some people's struggles are more visible than others, but we all ride the waves of ups and downs that make up the human condition.

Ours was a Christian family, and we lived in the southern part of the country known as the Bible Belt. I was raised to be good, which meant that I would remain chaste until married, not succumb to vices, respect my elders, attend church every Sunday, exhibit proper manners at all times, be honest and truthful, complete chores and schoolwork without complaint, attend college, and then marry. But as I have matured I have learned that being a good person isn't always enough. You see, until your simple little life begins to bother a large segment of the population, until you become a target in your country, you really don't understand how difficult life can be when you are culled from the pack.

Throughout childhood, I was living a "normal" life in almost every way. I was the fourth child of five, and relatively well behaved at home. I attended church on Sundays with minimal groaning, had a lot of friends in high school, and was very active in after-school activities. I was a member of the tennis, volleyball, and basketball team, a member of the homecoming court in my freshman year, and was voted most friendly my senior year. I had small brushes with trouble, but nothing major. Mine was an average, middle-class, white, American childhood. Things were going along pretty well until I started dating boys.

When my older brother was preparing to marry, I asked his future bride if there was ever a time when she thought that she wouldn't marry. With a laugh she said, "Never!" She went on talking about this and that, not seeming to give my silly question a second thought. But boy, I was suddenly very scared. I was beginning to realize that some parts of "me" were not fitting in as well as they used to. I was getting off track from what everybody else was doing. I was getting close to what was supposed to be my next step, and for the first time I couldn't see that step. I didn't think I would ever marry a man. I hadn't experienced any of the feelings that all of my friends were already having toward boys. Nothing. I began imagining the disappointment this would bring to my parents' eyes when they looked at me. It seemed that up to now my focus had been to live up to their expectations, and it frightened me to notice that my course was veering away from what they expected. I was heading into uncharted territory. I decided to stick with the "normal" course, and hope my feelings would somehow change. I sent my confused feelings underground and just stayed in the pack, doing whatever my friends were doing, waiting to feel the change come over me. Hoping for it.

IN THE EIGHTH grade I began dating a wonderful boy. We were quite an established item by the time we reached our senior year. Our dates were fun and interesting, and I enjoyed being social with other couples our age, but there was always the moment in the date when the problem would surface. I loved him and wanted very much to be able to marry him. But we had a huge block in our ability to be intimate: me. I knew physical intimacy was expected of me, and I still wasn't interested. I tried, but could not make myself available for anything beyond heavy petting and deep kisses. Worries about my feelings began to deepen, and I couldn't figure out what was wrong with me. How could I love him so deeply, but be so repulsed by sexual intimacy with him? Why wasn't my focus in life all about having and enjoying sex like it was for all of my friends during these years? The pressure by then was enormous, but there was nobody in my life that I felt I could talk to about this growing problem. I was scared. It was too bizarre and frightening. You see, I now had a small inkling of what was going on with me, but I wasn't ready to accept it.

OFF TO COLLEGE and still a virgin. I became more involved socially and began doing what other normal female college students did in the late seventies: I studied for classes, attended a lot of parties, and further explored my sexuality. During my first two years at college, although I had casual dates with several boys, I dated only one seriously, a nice young man. With him I first experienced sexual intercourse. I was still trying to find a way to enjoy sexual intimacy. I had imagined that the act of performing sex would feel like a deeply shared, intimate experience. I went through the motions, trying to arouse sexual feelings in myself, but it always just felt stressful and embarrassing. Afterward I felt as if he had taken something important away from me. I knew this was not the normal reaction to a consensual sexual encounter. I was so worried. I was beginning to realize that I would not be able to force myself into acceptable behavior. How would I ever find happiness? I mean, isn't *sex* everything? I kept trying to fit in, kept trying to make it work. In 1977 I met a man with whom I thought I could build a romantic relationship. We had been together for about two years when he proposed marriage. Because I was still struggling so with our sexual encounters, I knew marrying him was the wrong thing to do and totally unfair to him, so I broke off the relationship. The pressure just kept building and building. I was constantly fearful and worried about how I was going to live my life. How am I going to do this? I thought a little distance from home might help.

IN 1980, ALMOST immediately after graduating from Georgia State University in Atlanta, I boarded a plane bound for Los Angeles and began a new life. After several months I had set up my new home, found a good job, and made love fully and passionately with a person of the same gender for the first time. Oh, sweet mystery of life, I found you! Now I understood what all of the hoopla surrounding sex was about. Yes sir. Thank you very much. It is lovely indeed. And that feeling I had with my male sexual partners before, the one that left me feeling as if someone had taken something from me, well, it didn't exist in this new world I had discovered. I felt so free and fulfilled and loved and loving and gentle and happy and glowing and peaceful. It should have been something to sing from the rooftops to my friends and family. I had been so worried for so long, so scared, and now I had finally found the answers, become illuminated, found the opportunity for true happiness and bliss that I had seen friends and family enjoy with their mates. But these wonderful feelings lasted all too short a time. It is sad to me now to think about how quickly the euphoric feelings were replaced by feelings of dread. My falling in love with a woman and sharing sexual intimacy with her was *way* against the rules, against the rules in the *biggest* way possible. I wouldn't be able to share it with my family and friends after all. Well, at least it was an improvement. At least I had found my ability to experience sexual love deeply, intimately, and with passion. Being a stranger to the rest of the world and my family? Well, by this time I was becoming accustomed to that. My life was now broken into two separate realities: one was my true life, offering personal and spiritual fulfillment; in the other I was an actor on the stage, moving always on cue. My true life, without the love and support of my family, was incomplete and disappointing. Living my life as an actor was becoming more and more unacceptable.

I HAD THREE relationships with females while in Southern California, but at work I remained deep inside the closet. I had a middle-management position with a Fortune 500 company in Los Angeles. Although the income was wonderful, the high pressure of a sales position involved a lifestyle that was wearing me down. There was a lot of drinking during sales lunches and conferences, and I constantly had to fend off aggressive sexual advances from my boss and other men on the sales staff. A woman who is not in a relationship with a man and who denies advances from men around the office is highly suspect. I was so tired of all of the games and pressure. So life moved on and so did I.

I LEFT LOS ANGELES in 1986 and moved north to the small community of Big Sur, California. This small town is made up of rugged terrain nestled between the Santa Lucia mountain range and the Pacific Ocean. A person has to love the outdoors and hard work to live here, and to me it was heaven. Six years later I met Jennifer Mahoney, my life partner.

Jennifer had moved with her family to Big Sur when she was twelve years old and had deep roots in the community. Although Jennifer's first marriage failed, she and her ex-husband were blessed with two sons. When Jennifer and I met, her boys, Toby and Kenny, were three and five years old. They lived together in a rustic home next door to Jennifer's mother. Jennifer managed life as a single mother, juggling so many responsibilities.

I was the director of a preschool at the time and taught there as well. I was always busy with the children, parents, and other teachers at the school. I had a wonderful teacher/student relationship with Jennifer's sons, but was so busy during pickup time at the end of each day that, although I saw Jennifer and had pleasant, light interactions with her, I really didn't have a chance to get to know her. She had invited me for visits outside of work several times, but I was always too busy. I finally accepted an invitation to join Jennifer, Toby, and Kenny at a New Year's Eve party. We celebrated the entrance of 1992 together and were having so much fun that I stayed for the next three days. We quickly became good friends and got together often during the next few months. Our relationship was deepening. One evening when the boys were staying with Jennifer's mother for the night, we made love for the first time. Jennifer and I fell deeply and passionately in love with each other. After several months of driving back and forth to be together, I gave up my apartment and moved in with Jennifer and her boys. We knew we wanted to stride through life together.

WE LIVED AND worked in our community like other couples, sharing the parental duties required by two young boys. During those early years it seemed we were always pulling together money for soccer, football, camps, school clothes, medical and dental visits, and all of the other costs involved in raising two boys. We felt it was important to take family trips to relax and enjoy different activities together, like weekend camping at the lake and our once-a-year ski trips in the Sierras. We became a family and had to work through the difficulties that I guess all divorced couples and their children face. We made every effort to create a household that was safe, consistent, and centered around raising the children. It was (and still is) hard, loving work.

As time passed, the members of the Big Sur community accepted our relationship, and they were able to see the two of us as we were, without the label "homosexual" foremost in their minds. Jennifer was (and still is) a loved and respected member of the community. Although shocked, her friends and neighbors never turned against her when they discovered she was having intimate relations with another female. I was still such a newcomer when our relationship began, and I have since felt happily accepted as a part of this wonderful community.

My family has lovingly accepted Jennifer as my partner and her children as my stepchildren. Some members of my family also pray for our souls because, according to their religious beliefs, our choice to be together sexually will keep us from the kingdom of heaven. Jennifer and I embrace and support each one of them and are glad they remain part of our family.

When we first met, Jennifer worked at the Big Sur Health Center. She also had been taking classes as she could afford to, both in time and money, to work toward earning a degree in nursing. I took on more of the load, financially and in caring for the children, in order to afford her the opportunity to take her nursing classes on a full-time basis. We felt it was the best thing for our family's future, so we both worked hard to reach this goal.

The drive from home to Jennifer's school was an hour long on twisting mountain roads, so our days began early and ended late. Jennifer and I were up at 5:00 a.m. each day to get her ready to head out for school. Once I got her out of the house, I would wake Toby and Kenny to start the showers, breakfasts, and last minute homework checks before I would get myself ready. Then out the door we would fly. Off to work I would go until it was time to pick up the boys after school, start dinner, and get on the homework. Jennifer would arrive home in time to read a bit to the boys and then I would warm up her dinner. Finally to bed. Weekends were filled with soccer and football games, cheering for the boys. Our lives remained pretty much the same for the next two years. The boys and I were so proud of Jennifer on graduation day, and she was so grateful for all of the hard work we had done to support her. Today she is a respected registered nurse working on the cardiac floor of our local hospital, and she helps as a hospice nurse for members of our community whenever the need arises.

During this time I was working full-time, managing the business of a world-renowned animal sculptor who was also availing himself to teach me the art of sculpting. I managed to find time to study for and create my first works. I have since created a line of animal and figurative works and set up my business, which supplements our income. Toby once asked me why I worked 24/7. I didn't understand his question at first, but then I realized that he saw me as a person who works all the time. I just told him that I felt there was so much to do and not ever enough time.

WHEN THE HONORABLE Mayor of San Francisco, California, Gavin Newsom, ordered the issuance of marriage licenses to same-sex couples, Jennifer and I had already lived, worked, and loved together in our home, with her two children, for twelve years. The first same-sex weddings took place while I was away on a trip to Atlanta. Upon my return, I was late leaving for work on Thursday, February 19. As I dashed out the door, Jennifer called to me, asking, "Want to go up to the city tomorrow and get married?"

I replied, "Okay."

It was just like that for us.

JENNIFER AND I had never attended a gay protest or rally or parade or anything. We had heterosexual and homosexual friends and acquaintances. We have never chosen our friends based on their sexual preference and practices. (How surprising!) It isn't something we focus on very much. We live our lives and become friends with other people who have common interests, ideas, and life goals. My point is that we had never been involved as gay activists. But when they started issuing marriage licenses in San Francisco, we wanted to dance through the small window of opportunity that had opened and get ourselves married.

In a broader view, we also felt this was very important to the country. We viewed this as a civil rights issue first and foremost. The civil rights of our citizens have been tested often throughout our country's history. This time it was testing the rights of homosexuals to be wed in a civil ceremony and receive the same rights offered to heterosexual couples who make the same commitment to each other. Well, we were gay, in a committed relationship, and unmarried. That meant it fell on us to participate and stand up for these rights.

WHEN HE HEARD of our plans to get married, Jennifer's younger son Toby, now sixteen years old, loaned us his video camera so we could film bits and pieces of the day's events. It took him four years of saving allowance and the money he earned by selling the most raffle tickets at school to buy that camera. We were so touched by his offering it to us for our wedding.

That Thursday night, we had a family dinner with the boys and Jennifer's mom, and they gave us hugs and kisses, wishing us well on our wedding adventure. What a shame we had no time to plan to have our family with us on such an earth shatteringly important day in our lives. Well, we had no choice—we had to move and take advantage of the opportunity.

WE ROSE EARLY Friday morning, February 20, 2004, and began our drive up the coast to reach San Francisco City Hall before dawn, to line up behind 109 other couples who had arrived before us. Our wait began at 5:40 a.m.

From the beginning, we felt anxious about the fact that no one knew if we would actually be married that day. A case had been filed by a group of people who wanted to stop the same-sex weddings, and the judge was scheduled to rule on the issue sometime that afternoon. During our eleven-hour wait, people from the City Hall staff would come around periodically and give us updates concerning our prospects for obtaining our marriage licenses. I cannot say enough about the high level of performance shown by the staff and volunteers with whom we came in contact throughout the day. They had worked for eight days straight, through Saturday, Sunday, and Monday of the holiday weekend, since Mayor Newsom had ordered the issuance of same-sex marriage licenses. The maximum number of licenses issued on any normal day was thirty. But in the past week they had been processing hundreds a day. They were visibly tired. These people behaved in a manner I would expect from any of our governmental employees in this country. It is their job to follow and

uphold the law. They may not like or agree with any number of
the duties they are called upon to perform, but their personal
views had no place. They love our country, respect the freedoms
awarded to our citizens, and carry out the work. From the officers
controlling the crowds to the clerks issuing the licenses, they were
professional, efficient, kind, and courteous. I applaud each and
every one of them.

THE LIGHT OF day began to gently push away the darkness of
night, and our line began to move at the pace of snails. Off and
on the rain came down in a light drizzle and the air was cool and
damp. Feelings of excitement and anticipation pulsed through
all of us waiting in that line. It was palpable. Inch by inch, hour
by hour we moved together. The experience bonded us from the
first moments as we made introductions, always asking each
other, "How many years have you been together?" Most responses
were between ten and twenty years. It was evident in watching
these couples throughout the day that they had weathered a lot
of life together.

WE WERE VERY excited when, after about two hours, we had finally
made it around the first street corner and were now on the same
side of the building as the front doors we were expecting to enter
sometime that day. Our joy began to fade into mild apprehension
as we realized our new position had brought us face-to-face with the
protesters representing themselves as Christians. They were the
most hateful looking people I have ever encountered in my life.
They said they were there to save us. One look at their angry,
unhappy faces told me that I did not want what they were selling.
These did not seem like happy, healthy people to me.
    As any normal, thoughtful person would do in such a situation
as this, several members of our line attempted to dialogue with
the Christians. How astonishing to find that these protesters
were incapable of dialogue. It was like trying to have a discussion
with a child who has memorized a set of rules, say like at summer
camp: no running by the pool; you must make your bed each
morning; stay in groups of three; lights out at 9:00 p.m.—no
exceptions. Their response to any thoughtful question was to
shout out a "rule" of God. One can only have a discussion with a

person who is willing and capable of exchanging thoughts and ideas. It is quite impossible to dialogue with people who respond only by shouting rules. Did they have a right to be there? Of course. It is a fundamental right granted to all citizens of this country. Still, this was the first time I had put myself in a position to receive the full-blown "love messages" from *this type* of Christian trying to save me. To me these religious zealots seem to be sort of brainwashed—everything washed out except a set of rules: black and white, good and evil—very frightening.

If you have ever spent hours arguing with your child about whether or not he should do his homework—working with arguments like "You can't make me!"—you will understand the sense of relief I felt when we left the protesters behind. After about three hours we made it into the building, and I must say it was a relief.

AH, INSIDE! WHERE were we going? Down a set of stairs, past hundreds of people in line, around a corner, and down the hall. The nice thing was moving at a slow walk all the way to the end of the line before we had to stop and start waiting again. It felt good to put away my umbrella, remove my coat, move my legs, and escape from the protesters. I guess they weren't allowed inside. So, we made it into the building in about three hours, and it was another eight hours before we first saw the City Clerk's Office window at the end of a long corridor.

Despite the long wait, everyone remained pleasant and full of hope. As the hours dragged on and we continued to move slowly (I mean, city hall isn't *that* big), we fretted over whether or not we would be married that day. Just the day before, both the couple ahead of us and the family two places behind us had spent ten hours waiting, without success. The day was grueling emotionally and physically. I cannot imagine how they were able to hold up.

At 4:15 in the afternoon, we were half the way down the corridor to the City Clerk's Office when the announcement was made that if we did not receive a number by 4:30 p.m. we would not be served that day. They had been handing out numbers ten at a time all day. Our little group comprised the next ten couples. There were hundreds of people in line behind us. We felt we still had a chance. At 4:28 p.m. a staff worker rushed out and began passing out numbers. We got one! Volunteers brought a set of posts and ropes out to separate us from those behind us who had not received a number. The distance between us began to grow. The couple ahead of us quickly decided to give their number to the family behind us who just missed the cutoff again, after waiting there for two days with their children. It was a loving and kind thing to do.

Before the generous couple made it out of the building, one of the city workers stopped them. The staff member had heard about what the couple had done and told the couple that the city would marry them, too. This is what I mean about those employees and volunteers at City Hall. They are real human beings and treated us all in such a personal manner. They were so much a part of the goodness of the experience.

WE LEFT THE City Clerk's Office at about 4:50 p.m., having been told in no uncertain terms that we would be legally married. We walked out to the rotunda and met a man named Bill Jones who had volunteered to perform our wedding ceremony. He was lovely. He spoke to us about the historical impact of our actions and counseled us to put our marriage certificate in a safe place. Then he took us through our vows, which had more impact on me than I ever would have believed.

A married couple, we exited City Hall at about 5:30 p.m., twelve hours after our arrival that morning. The Christian protesters were packing up their signs and leaving. At the bottom of the stairs, a young man and woman were dancing the jitterbug without any music, just the sounds of the city. It was perfect. We love San Francisco and are so pleased to have been married in that fair city full of such diversity and beauty. Jennifer and I were so happy. We had a chance to spend the day with some wonderful, loving people, and I was able to see clearly that we are a good group of people full of positive strengths and gifts that we contribute to our various communities. I recognize that whether a person is homosexual or heterosexual is immaterial—there are good and bad in each group.

JENNIFER AND I are building a life together and raising a family. Shouldn't Jennifer receive my Social Security payments if I should die first? Shouldn't she receive full ownership of all that has been shared in our combined estate without devastating taxation? Regardless of which one of us dies first, shouldn't her sons inherit all that we built for their futures? Our answer is yes, absolutely. Same-sex couples should be allowed to formally legalize their commitment to a life partnership via a civil contract. The legal aspects of the contract should afford them exactly the same protections and provisions now awarded, at all levels of government, to different-sex couples choosing to commit their lives to each other. In order for this to become a reality, in order for us to sleep more peacefully each night, we need a legal contract recognized at both state and federal levels, one that is equal to the one given to different-sex couples who marry.

We should not be thinking of amending our constitution to block this goal, we should be upholding our constitution in order to reach this goal. Legalizing same-sex marriage will rub some people the wrong way, *but it will make us all equal.* Isn't that what the United States is all about? Leave the other issues in the churches where they belong. It is our beloved constitution that sets us apart as a nation. We should preserve it.

Yes, Be With Her

HEIDI LaMOREAUX AND PANTHER TOMARROCK

▼

Panther says that her first thought when she saw me with my husband in the foyer of a Mormon church in Georgia was *What is that gay guy doing married to that lesbian?* I looked over at Panther and thought, *Combat boots with a cranberry crushed velvet skirt—different, but I like it.* We struck up a conversation. I found that Panther was my daughter's Sunday school teacher. Panther loved my daughter, Lauriann, before she knew me.

We were both married to men at the time and believed the Mormon church's line that being gay is one of the worst sins imaginable—something you can get excommunicated for, and something that certainly neither of us thought we were, despite the fact that we had both felt attracted to women in the past. I was born and raised a Mormon—with polygamist great-great-grandparents—straight from Utah. Panther had converted seven years earlier when she married her Mormon husband.

As we got to know each other, we couldn't stand each other at first. I thought Panther was "hard," she thought I was a "spoiled princess." Both of us were right. We took some tae kwon do classes together and a friendship formed somewhere between the sidekicks and sparring. Friendship turned into long talks, then innocent sleepovers when Panther's husband, a trucker, was away—just holding each other through the night and sharing details of our days, of our pasts, becoming closest friends. Then came kisses on my stomach to help me learn to love my body. Then a life-altering kiss in a dimly lit mental health center parking lot as I said, "I can't, can I?" and Panther showed me that I definitely could. There was no turning back.

The next few months were full of stolen moments. We'd tuck the husbands and kids in for the night and go out together to "talk," or to "get a bite to eat." We were extremely careful not to be affectionate in public. We'd spend from early evening to early morning at the local 50's-style, twenty-four-hour café talking, then move to deserted parking lots, or to my windowless science lab with the doors bolted. We would disappear for weekends so Panther could help me with my dissertation fieldwork. Those times were filled with hardworking days in the peat bogs, followed by private nights in motel rooms. Our lives were becoming beautifully intertwined. It was hard not to be open about our feelings for each other. At the Atlanta Lilith Fair, we had to pretend that we weren't a couple, surrounded by people who openly were.

Then I finished most of my schoolwork and got an interview for my dream job in California. I wouldn't have had the confidence to get the job without Panther's help. As I nervously prepared to get on the plane, Panther handed me three days' worth of encouragement cards, each with explicit instructions about which day to open them. Nightly phone calls from Panther helped keep me focused and enthused. When the job offer came a few weeks later, feelings were mixed, because I would be moving to California, but Panther was planning to stay in Georgia, especially because her daughter, Natalia, was about to begin her senior year of high school. Besides, we weren't officially "together." No one knew about "us" yet, though Panther's mother thought something was up because of how protective I was of her daughter when Panther had surgery.

My husband and daughter left for California in early August so that I could write my research without distractions, and so that they could get settled in the new area. Panther and I spent almost 24/7 together during that time, with me writing all of the days and into the nights, and Panther supporting me. During this time Panther realized that she wanted to be with me—no husband, no Mormonism, just living in genuine love. I was too scared to admit that I was beginning to feel the same way. I was too afraid of being excommunicated and leaving the only way of life—the only way of being—that I had ever known. While I would sleep between writing sessions, Panther spent time online seeking advice about the situation and comfort from strangers in gay chat rooms. She was sharing her feelings with people, telling them that this woman she loved was about to leave, possibly for good. Panther knew she couldn't share her feelings with me. I wasn't ready yet.

I left Georgia with the intention of staying married to my husband, spending stolen moments with Panther only during vacations. I wanted Panther to be my mistress. It was safer that way. No major life change. No excommunication. Panther, on the other hand, was in too much emotional pain to get out of bed. She couldn't wait to talk to me online. She was falling apart, while I was minimizing her pain. Panther felt like she was going to die. She would rather die than share me with anyone. She had stopped sleeping with her husband. She was leaving him and the Mormon church, with or without me. She knew she wanted to be with a woman—even if she couldn't be with me—never again to be with a man. That lie was done. She also knew that she wasn't willing to be my "mistress" anymore.

Panther finally told me to make a choice. I kept telling her, "It isn't God's will that we should be together." To which she replied, "You've always been so concerned about God's will that you don't know what *your* will is. What do *you* want?" I had never entertained the thought that my will counted for anything. I knew I wanted to be with Panther, but like most people brainwashed by a religion, I felt she had to ask the proper authority for permission—in this case, God.

The weekend after I moved to California, my husband and I went to the Oakland Mormon Temple together for the last time. I had an important question to ask in the temple, a place I trusted. I sat down on one of the velvet couches and prayed. I told God that I wanted to be with Panther. I waited for an answer. In my head I heard the words, "Yes, be with her." I couldn't believe it. I was expecting the "your-desire-is-sinful-you-need-to-be-a-good-self-sacrificing-unhappy-wife-for-the-rest-of-your-life" answer, not the "go ahead." I had been told my whole life that homosexuality was a sin, and that sinning was wrong, that I would feel bad if

I broke any commandments or did anything against church policy. Sitting on that couch, I realized that my experiences with Panther, though not "Mormon approved," had never felt wrong. Never. In fact, nothing had ever felt more right.

I called my husband over to sit on the couch next to me, took his hands and told him about my love for Panther, and that I wanted to be with her, not with him. He seemed to take it pretty well. I think that on some level he already suspected, though it took a couple of days for it to really sink in.

When I returned home from the temple that day, I called Panther and told her that I had chosen her over my husband. Panther was not expecting this answer. She didn't think I had the guts to make such a drastic life change. Shocked by the response, Panther decided to "test this one out." She went to the Atlanta temple, and much to her surprise, she got the same answer. However, she didn't care what she heard. Her trip to the temple was more for me than for her. She already knew what she wanted to do. Panther wasn't as married to the Mormon Church as I was. Being a seven-year convert to the church, Panther knew there was life before Mormonism and that there would be life after.

Panther didn't care if she lost everyone in the world in choosing me. She didn't care about her family. She didn't care about her friends. There was only one person who could have kept her from making this life decision—her daughter, Natalia. With trepidation, Panther approached the conversation with her daughter, explaining how our friendship had turned to deeper love, noticing while looking at her daughter's face, there was a smile on it the entire time. As tears began to flow from Natalia's eyes, Panther asked, "Why are you crying?" Natalia replied, "I'm so happy for you guys. I love Heidi. And I *know* she loves you." Panther felt like someone shot her out of a cannon. She couldn't wait to get the fuck out of the Mormon Church. She became a fully out butch lesbian almost overnight. She had her daughter, and she had me, and nothing else mattered. She even faced a group of Mormon Church leaders and told them she was intending to be with me no matter what they said. When they realized there was no changing her mind, they finally left her alone. Within two weeks, Panther had shed the Mormon Church, found an apartment for her and her daughter, and was living life as a fully out, happy lesbian. Panther decided to stay in Georgia until the end of the school year so Natalia could finish high school with her friends.

My coming out was more like touching my toes into cold water. I told my parents, which did *not* go well—they didn't agree, but chose to keep me in their lives. There was a "hearing" about my excommunication from the Mormon Church, which I chose not to attend. My mind was made up.

For Panther and me the year of separation was brutal, full of long, nightly phone calls and flights to California or Georgia every few months. I flew to Georgia in October to spend time with Panther and to defend my dissertation. We both got tattoos to mark the occasion. My tattoo is a gopher tortoise from the peat bogs, with the eastern hemisphere of the earth in the center of the shell. Panther's tattoo is a bear paw enclosing a flower, based on the Lilith Fair poster, with South America—the place of origin of panthers—in the center of the flower, and a hawk feather hanging at the bottom of the paw.

Panther flew to California for a visit at Christmas. I flew to Georgia again in January, rainbow-colored plates and decorations in hand, for our first commitment ceremony, held in a small, white, southern church. Our ceremony was simple—we had a Native American "Blessing Way." We recited our own vows while holding a Native American ceremonial stick. A female shaman friend officiated. Then our guests wrote their blessings and thoughts onto pieces of paper, which we attached to the stick with bright ribbons. Every few years we untie the ribbons and read the messages. That day was one of the most beautiful days of our lives, surrounded by friends expressing their love. Panther felt it was both exhilarating and freeing at the same time, because she felt that we had been hiding our love for so long, and now we were able to stand in front of our community, speaking our love for each other for everyone to hear. It was beautiful.

Panther flew to California again in April. And finally, in June, I dropped Lauriann off with my parents in Utah and flew to Georgia for the obligatory cross-country U-Haul trip to California, our yellow lab, Ela, in tow. Before heading for California by way of Utah to pick up Lauriann, then six years old, we shared our first Pride in Atlanta. I was nearly overcome by the Atlanta humidity, but it was empowering for us to be fully out, as a couple, surrounded by the friends Panther had made in the lesbian community over the past year. Panther took a lot of pictures of the crowd—the cute guy with rainbow water guns, couples in matching sequined outfits, and all of our lesbian friends who attended with us.

As we hooked up the U-Haul to leave Georgia, I was ecstatic, but Panther cried. Leaving her daughter, Natalia, behind in Georgia was one of the most difficult things she had ever had to do. But Natalia, being old enough to make her own decisions about where she wanted to live, decided not to move with us to California.

We arrived in Utah a few days later. Time to meet the Mormon side of the family, pick up Lauriann, and head for our new home. My parents were horrified by my decision to leave the church, and kept the news secret from everyone in the extended family. Thankfully, I had been excommunicated, which made the separation more official and less open to prodding and debate.

I am close to my grandmother and wanted to introduce Panther to her. When we came into town, Grandma was at a birthday party at McDonald's for one of her great-grandchildren. We decided we could meet the family all in one shot. No one knew about our relationship yet. They knew I was divorcing my husband, my parents had shared that part of the story, but they thought that Panther was going to be my new "roommate" in California because it is so expensive to live there. Panther's shaved head, abundant piercings, and visible tattoos raised some eyebrows in the Utah restaurant. I introduced Panther around. Aunt Elaine, the family grapevine, upon meeting Panther, figuring no woman would "choose" to shave her head, sympathetically decided that Panther must be going through chemotherapy. Humorously, we allowed Aunt Elaine her assumptions. Only one of my older cousins figured out what was really going on between Panther and me. She saw the way I looked at Panther and recognized the look as love. Luckily, by the time my cousin told her mother, Aunt Elaine, and the news spread through the family, we were already safely on our way to California.

To their credit, my parents were polite during our stay. They went out of their way to fix vegetarian food for Panther. They accepted us into their home. They tried to be kind, but the underlying current of nonacceptance remained unspoken and present in everything. Finally three long days later, we loaded Lauriann into the car next to the dog, and thankfully headed for California, anxious to start our new life together.

The next few months were filled with settling into our new family, and integrating joint custody arrangements with my soon-to-be-ex-husband into the mix. Panther and Natalia's separation was more painful than either had anticipated. So when Natalia came to visit for our first Christmas together, she decided to stay in California. Now both our daughters were living with us.

We became legal domestic partners as soon as my divorce was final, and Panther and Natalia were added to my insurance. It was a good thing. Natalia was now a student in college, and during this time Panther was diagnosed with rheumatoid arthritis, and it hit her hard. Within a few months she was completely disabled, and a few months after that was in a wheelchair. Not that she took the disease "sitting down." Every day, Panther would wheel to the edge of the ten-foot stairs in the back of our Victorian house, determined to conquer the obstacle. She finally tied her studded belt to her wheelchair, and sitting on the stairs, she lowered the chair and followed on her butt, one step at a time. At this point, there was no stopping her. I came home from work one day to find that Panther had mowed the lawn—quite a task, considering she didn't have an electric wheelchair and we didn't have a self-propelled push lawn mower. She would push the lawn mower, then push her wheelchair to catch up, and then repeat until the entire lawn was cut. Even in the worst times, when Panther was hospitalized for adverse reactions to her medications, her indomitable spirit shone through. She is one of those people who do everything they can, and then some, despite physical limitations. The illness redefined the roles in our relationship a bit, but it has drawn all of our family closer together.

About four years after we moved in together, I arrived at work on Friday, February 13, 2004, to be told by one of my colleagues, who lives in the Castro, "Same-sex couples are getting married at City Hall." All day long, I could think of nothing but the possibility of getting legally married. I called Panther and told her the news. Neither of us could leave that day, and we didn't want to deal with the crowds on Valentine's Day because we needed some time to plan how to do this with Panther's health issues. Waiting in the cold and rain would cause Panther a lot of pain for a couple of days. I asked Panther if she was sure she could physically do this. She replied "I could never forgive myself if I didn't try. A few days of pain to be part of this movement? Are you kidding?" So we decided to try for Sunday, February 15. We took a good friend Amy along as a witness, and with Panther's inseparable companion, her four-pound Chihuahua, Tinkerbell, on her lap, we arrived to be near the front of the line, only to be told that we had to wait for those three hundred plus people given vouchers the day before to get married first. We were told we had a 1 percent chance of getting married that day. Due to the possibility of a court action, we were unsure of the marriages continuing past Monday, and because of the strain of this whole thing on Panther, we knew we couldn't come back. So, we decided that 1 percent was more of a chance than we had a week ago, and chose to stick it out. Approximately eight hours later we were told that we would be among those getting married that day. And by 5:00 p.m. we were!

Natalia and Lauriann are both thrilled that their moms are officially married. Lauriann, now ten, broke into unexpected tears when someone at the Pride Parade asked how she felt about her moms' marriage. She said that she is glad that her moms can have this bond and that people see it as real. She was proud to march with her moms in the parade. Natalia joyfully spread the news to all her friends, and mentions frequently how glad she is that we are together. While the bond between Lauriann and Panther has always been strong, my relationship with Natalia has deepened since her moms' marriage. Natalia has expressed how the legal marriage makes her feel like I am more officially her mom than before. Something indescribable has also shifted in me; a deeper compassion for Natalia has surfaced, which has made our relationship even more loving than it was before. Our family is blessed to be in a place where same-sex marriage is deemed acceptable rather than deviant, as it was in Georgia and Utah. We have a wonderful relationship with my ex, who, though still spiritually opposed to our union, is an excellent father to Lauriann and tolerant of our right to choose. We have our marriage certificate framed in our living room. It reminds us of what we have come through to forge our family into the loving union it is today.

So Many Blessings

ROBERT G. DENOS

FRIDAY, FEBRUARY 13TH, 2004

It was a normal day. Wil and I drove to the office, and as we passed by the newsstand I took a glance at the headlines: "Defiant Gays Marry." This was my first glimpse of what was taking place in San Francisco. For the next few hours all I could think about was *What is so defiant about marriage?* For so long people have tagged us as "ungodly sexual beings that sleep with everyone and everything," shouldn't they be happy that a commitment was on the table here? The day got busy, and as time flew by, my thoughts turned to other daily routines.

SATURDAY, FEBRUARY 14TH, 2004

Valentine's Day! My plans were to get up and cook a nice break-fast and later cook a wonderful Valentine's Day dinner. But first things first—Wil had to read the paper, and I had to check my e-mail. As we both sat on the couch doing our own thing, Wil folded the newspaper, stood up, and with the most serious look on his face, he said, "I have something I want to talk to you about." I was clueless as to what was about to come out of Wil's lips. The next thing I knew, Wil got down on one knee, took me by the hand, and said those magical words: "Will you marry me?"

Anyone who knows Wil and me would *never* guess that he would be the one to pop the question first. This was not how I planned it. I was shocked. First, I never thought the day would even come that we would actually be able to marry. Second, I envisioned that it would be me asking him, at a romantic restaurant, with flowers and a ring. So, of course, I looked Wil in the eyes and asked, "Where are my flowers and my ring?"

He replied, "I was hoping we would go get them now."

After a brief discussion about the limited window of opportunity we had to get married, I responded with a smile and a kiss, "Of course I'll marry you!"

So we skipped my planned breakfast and were off to downtown Los Angeles to buy rings and suits. Our plan was to drive to San Francisco on Sunday and get in line. We had read that City Hall officials were giving out numbers to those who had stood in line but were unable to get married, so they would have a guaranteed place in line the next day. We thought we would get in line on Sunday, get our number, and get married on Monday, which just happened to be Wil's birthday, too. Now he had no excuse for forgetting our anniversary. Our entire day was full of joy.

SUNDAY, FEBRUARY 15, 2004

It was a busy morning. We asked the neighbor to watch our cat, and we had to take the parrot to the sitter's. The pet store didn't open until 10:00 a.m., so we would be getting a late start. Wil was glued to the Internet via his cell phone and came to the conclusion that we should fly to San Francisco instead of driving. So I booked a hotel room and our flight on the Internet prior to taking Einstein, our parrot, to the sitter's. We finished earlier than expected, so we packed our bags and headed to the airport to see if we could go standby on an earlier flight. Along the way we were reading that the line in San Francisco was getting long and that not everyone was going to be able to get in, so we were desperate to get in line as soon as possible. When we arrived at the airport, we checked in and got on the next flight out—our first blessing in this journey.

We arrived in Oakland and took BART to our hotel, which happened to be two blocks away from City Hall. It was about 1:30 p.m. and the hotel was not ready for us to check in, so we left our bags and walked over to City Hall. Remember, we are from Southern California, and we had just left 78 degree weather, so our clothing was not quite up to the standards for northern California. It was cold! And to top it off, it was beginning to sprinkle.

As we approached the City Hall building, we heard a lot of screaming and feared the worst. *Those protesters are at it again,* was all I could think. I was in no mood to read the all too familiar signs: God hates Fags, Homos are going to Hell, Homosexuality is a Sin, and the many others that we so often see. What makes those people believe that anyone could see a loving God behind those signs is beyond me. Much to our surprise, when we arrived at City Hall we found people cheering as each couple walked out of the building with a Marriage Certificate in their hands. An entire family—father, mother, and two young children were standing across the street, yelling and cheering "congratulations" and "best wishes." We were *shocked.* Here all the yelling we had heard was coming from people supporting us! We looked around for those protesters and saw not a single one.

We quickly crossed the street and took our place in line. At around 2:00 p.m., there must have been over one hundred couples in line in front of us. Wil in shorts and I in very thin pants were now standing in line hoping to get our number soon because it was *cold* and we were not prepared for this weather. No sooner did we get in line than a lady approached us and handed us an umbrella, saying "Looks like you guys are going to need this."

Then it started—the beginning of the most wonderful outpouring of love Wil and I have ever received. People were coming down the line with candy Kisses, wishing us the best of happiness; two lovely ladies approached everyone in line with handmade bouquets, since they knew we didn't have time to prepare for any flower arrangements; another couple walked up with homemade cupcakes designed like little wedding cakes. We were floored, to say the least.

As time went on, we learned that we were not going to get in to City Hall on Sunday, but that at 5:00 officials would announce the procedures for Monday. So I ran back to the hotel to check into our room and then returned to the line so Wil could run back to the room and put on some long pants. Five o'clock finally came, and we were told that they were not going to hand out numbers for Monday, and that they were "advising" us to leave and come back in the morning. City Hall would open again at 10:00 a.m. I quickly took notice of the word "advising" and that the words "leave now" were not uttered. This meant that we were in for an all-nighter! So we quickly started making friends in line. We all knew we were in for the long haul. Wil and I called a friend who lived in the area to come visit us and if possible to be our witness on Monday (she did both). People in line were sharing their stories with each other, and we began taking turns leaving the line to buy provisions— chairs, soda, water, and such. But what started happening next shocked us all. People from the community showed up with pizza, homemade sandwiches, drinks, coffee, candy, and, yes, even Porta Potties. Midnight came around and, though it was still very cold, we were lucky that only a few sprinkles had fallen here and there.

MONDAY, FEBRUARY 16, 2004

Wil and I decided that we should take turns getting some sleep. We devised a plan—I would go back to the hotel, sleep until 3:00 a.m., then return to line so Wil could get some sleep. So I went to bed and set the alarm clock, the hotel wake-up service, and my cell phone to make sure I would wake up. Three o'clock came along and all three alarms went off at the same time—enough to make me jump out of my skin. I rushed to get dressed, but before I left the room I looked out the window. What I saw made my heart stop and brought tears to my eyes. It was pouring rain, and the wind was blowing like I have never seen. While I was warm and sleeping in bed, the man who had asked me to marry him was out standing in the rain and wind for *me,* and armed with only an umbrella. I quickly turned the hotel room heater on *high* and ran back to City Hall, weeping for two blocks.

When I got there, again I was not prepared for what I saw. Everyone in line was huddled under blue or green tarps, hidden inside sleeping bags, wrapped in trash bags, or covered one way or another. Apparently, while I was gone, more Good Samaritans had arrived, giving out tarps, sleeping bags, trash bags, and anything people could use for shelter. I ran to where I thought Wil should be and stood there staring at a woman sitting under a large umbrella. As I was trying to control my tears—as if anyone could tell because of the downpour of rain—she softly asked me if she could help me.

"I'm looking for my partner, Wil," I said.

"Oh, I believe he is under that blue tarp over there" she replied, pointing six feet away.

I took five steps to my left and yelled out for Wil.

"Under here" he replied.

"Are you okay?"

I got a soft reply of, "Yes, but a little cold."

When I found Wil, he was sitting in a chair, under a blue tarp, holding an umbrella in one hand to block the wind, and holding the tarp with another. He explained my duties for that position, as one of six people taking refuge under this tarp, then left to get warm and dry. Now it was my turn to brave the elements. Each of the six people under the tarp had a portion of the material to hold down, and everyone had been there all night except for me. It was freezing, and every once in a while the wind would cause one of us to release the tarp which, for me, meant I had water running down my back. Within five minutes of my arrival, I was sitting in a puddle of very cold water. Every time one of us let go of the tarp, all of us would get wet. It was so cold, and the wind was strong, but no one got upset with anyone for releasing the tarp— not once.

Eric, who was sitting next to me, was not looking good. He explained to me that he had to remove his socks because they were soaked. Coming from Alabama, he too was unprepared for this weather. He was shivering, and I could hear his teeth chattering. I started to pray that God would at least stop the wind so that Eric wouldn't get sick, but God had other plans. No sooner did I utter that prayer than I heard a loud call: "Dry socks! Does anyone need dry socks?" The power of prayer. We didn't even see a face, but a hand reached under our tarp and handed Eric a pair of dry socks. I sat there trying to hide my tears.

As I looked up at this blue tarp, with the streetlight shinning through and the rain pouring down, I thought I would try to bring a little humor to the group. So I started a poem: "It was a clear blue night and the moon was shining ever so brightly with tears of joy all around . . ." We all chuckled and began talking, wondering if any straight couple would endure this in order to get married, or if they take marriage for granted.

Around 4:30 a.m. someone came around with duct tape to help fasten down the tarps so that we didn't have to hold them with our freezing hands. Next thing I knew, people showed up with coffee, donuts, and Danish, and as time went by they kept coming, strangers to all of us: "Who wants orange juice?" "Anyone need coffee?" I was amazed by the outpouring of love and support from an entire city of people who knew nothing about me. For me, time flew by.

At around 6:30 a.m., I called Wil to wake him up so that he could take a shower and get dressed. When he arrived in line, I would switch with him, take my shower, and get dressed before they opened the doors at 10:00 a.m. At around 7:00 a.m., an announcement came that City Hall would open early so that they could get as many couples married as possible. Volunteers were showing up in droves, and city and county workers, including members of the sheriff's department, were coming in to work on their own time. Again, I was *floored*—overwhelmed that these people were making such an effort, even though all of us in line believed that the court would put a stop to these weddings the following day. Soon Wil showed up, and I ran back to the hotel to take a quick, *hot* shower and get dressed.

By the time I met Wil back in line, the rain had stopped, the wind had settled down, and I saw my first and only protestor. I wouldn't even call him a protester because all he did was walk up and down the line holding a *very* large Bible, screaming how much God loves us. At first I was angry. Not because he was preaching, but because I wondered, *Where was he at 4:00 in the morning or at 2:00? Heck, for that matter, 6:00? He was nothing but a fair-weather Christian.* Then I stopped and looked back at the last sixteen-plus hours and realized that this man was correct. God did love me and everyone else in that line, so much so that He sent us an umbrella when we first got there. Later, a peanut butter and jelly sandwich, and later still a blue tarp, and then dry socks, duct tape and coffee, flowers, candy, and the list goes on. Yes, God cared enough to shelter us and feed us all throughout the night. It was a "stop and smell the roses" moment, so many blessings in such a short time.

Wil and I made it through the City Hall doors and became couple number sixty-five to get married that day. Upon exiting those front doors, we were cheered on by a large crowd of supporters who stood all around us. Cheers, rice, rose petals, and even bubbles graced us as we walked down the front stairs. An older, obviously straight man greeted me at the bottom of the stairs, touching me on the arm and saying, "You two are the happiest couple I have ever seen come out those doors. Best wishes for a long life together."

How some could characterize those days in San Francisco as "chaos" and "mayhem" I'll never know. I only wish the media would have reported on all the love Wil and I received during the nearly twenty-four hours we spent waiting in line and getting married. It was the first time I could actually say, "I left my heart in San Francisco."

Thank you Mayor Gavin Newsom for your brave stance and for your love toward those you didn't even know. Bless you, city and county workers for your time, support, and hard work to make this day the happiest in my life. Peace to you, City of San Francisco, for demonstrating community at its finest. Words can never express the joy and happiness we now have as husband and husband, spouses for life.

"You Are My Beloved Ones, On Whom My Favor Rests!"

LUKE 4:1–3, THE TEMPTATION OF CHRIST

FROM A SERMON DELIVERED BY REV. RUTH M. FROST
AT ST. FRANCIS LUTHERAN CHURCH,
SAN FRANCISCO, FEBRUARY 29, 2004

Friends and Honored Guests:

In the words of Billy Crystal, "You look marvelous, dahlings!" In fact, you look *married*! I suspect many of you have had that married look for a long time now but our fair city has finally recognized the look and, like God, at the beginning of creation, has pronounced it "good!" And that pronouncement has given *all* marriages an extra special glow.

I can't tell you how honored we are to host you in our midst and celebrate your married love. It has been truly moving to witness the outpouring of love and good will and sheer justice-making at City Hall. And, to use religious language, it has taken a whole cloud of witnesses and a legion of volunteers to bring these gifts into the fullness of time. As one who has both walked down the proverbial aisle and as one who has joined couples in matrimony, I have been privileged to be on both sides of the giving and receiving. And I will never forget it. For those of you gathered here today who have not been down to City Hall to see for yourselves the joy being birthed there every day, please allow me to take a few minutes to give you my own account of it before I address the very serious challenges presented to us in the Gospel for today.

My partner, Phyllis Zillhart, is both my spouse and my colleague in ministry at this church. We first became aware of what our mayor, Gavin Newsom (and other justice-minded officials) had initiated when we opened our newspaper on Friday the thirteenth to see a front page story covering the marriage of Phyllis Martin and Del Lyon, longtime lesbian activists, partners in life, and now revered elders in our community. Phyllis and Del were wed at City Hall after fifty-one years of shared life together. Needless to say, we all know that getting married at City Hall isn't the start of their union. But on February 12, the city recognized their union, celebrated it, and legalized it. Phyllis and Del are a powerful symbol of the love that "dares to claim its name" with pride. And Mayor Gavin Newsom stands tall as a symbol of our many allies engaged in the struggle for equal rights on behalf of all LGBT people.

My partner and I debated ever so briefly whether or not to join the droves of astonished couples flocking to City Hall in response to this new opportunity to have their love recognized. We picked up our ten-year-old daughter, Noelle, from school and beat a hot path to City Hall. We joined a long line of eager applicants, which snaked two stories around the rotunda all the way to the basement level. There were an incredible number of couples like us with children—many with babies in strollers and toddlers in arms, and a few with babies in utero. Cell phones were being passed around to those who needed to make alternate arrangements for children stranded at schools in the mad dash to make it to City Hall in time to get married.

The atmosphere was electric with anticipation, appreciation, and general ebullience. There were many lusty rounds of "Chapel of Love" sung to the reporters covering the event. There were a handful of bemused straight couples who found themselves in a sea of friendly lesbian, gay, bisexual, and transgendered couples. After hours of waiting, it looked like the Biblical story of the feeding of the five thousand as folks began sharing whatever they had brought—Power Bars, water bottles, peanuts, and even champagne. Someone said to our daughter, "You're very patient. You must be getting a little annoyed with the wait." Noelle replied, "All I am is excited for my moms."

We soon discovered that we were beginning a long pilgrimage

involving waiting in three different lines: one for licensing, one for the ceremonies, and another for recording marriages with the registrar. At the top gallery of the rotunda, which was becoming known as the wedding balcony, there were several stations for the ceremonies. One city commissioner, who had come to City Hall for another purpose, took one look at the crowds and exclaimed, "This is marriage triage! Scrub me up, give me a gown, and I'm good for the day!" That was the spirit throughout the day.

When we finally reached the head of the ceremonies line, Supervisor Bevan Dufty greeted us warmly and asked, "Would you like me to do your wedding in the Board of Supervisors's chambers?" Delighted, we said "yes," knowing that the elegant chambers was saturated with the history of Harvey Milk and Mayor Moscone. A gay male couple whom Phyllis had already married accompanied us as our witnesses, together with a lesbian couple who were their witnesses. The six of us, together with our daughter, shared this experience.

While waiting in line, Noelle had salvaged a floral bouquet discarded in a garbage bin but still in perfectly good shape. She quickly became the official flower girl for all three of us couples. For our marriage rite, she stood in the middle with our arms around her as Phyllis and I clasped hands. It was a sweet opportunity to exchange vows with her in our embrace. Afterwards, she pelted all of us with flower petals from her bouquet. Hugs were exchanged all around, together with telephone numbers as we all realized we were no longer strangers to one another, but had become friends who shared a special anniversary.

By the end of the day our mayor had lost his voice and simply had to listen to the crowds chanting "Thank you, thank you!" at him. A member of the press asked us why we got married after nearly twenty years of being together. We answered that we did it for a number of reasons. First, we did it to stand in solidarity with our city and our mayor in this risk-taking action on our behalf. Second, we did it to solidify a written record of who we are as family to one another for our daughter's sake. Third, we did it to claim the future now in anticipation of that time when basic civil rights for all populations will no longer be a debate, but a free-flowing expression of a society based in justice. Finally, we did it to say "yes!" to love between us and among us. And in so doing, I believe all of us have been participating in a great healing which is taking place in this city. There haven't been so many queer people assembled at City Hall since the assassinations of Supervisor Harvey Milk and Mayor Moscone. Thank God—and Mayor Newsom—the wound from that sad event is now finally being healed! We come together today not to remember and mourn what is past, but to dream of the future and celebrate what is present. It was—and is—a joyous turn of events and one that makes us all proud to be San Franciscans and grateful for bold civic leadership.

THE CITY OF San Francisco has been challenging the State of California to live out the principles of equality outlined in our state's constitution. Soon, because of our president's actions, the people of the United States will be challenged to uphold the principles of equality articulated in our nation's constitution. It is not heterosexual marriage that needs protecting these days, but the constitution itself, that charter of freedom for all citizens of this great country. This should not surprise us. Those of us who are people of faith know that whenever the Spirit moves to create something wonderful which challenges the status quo, there are forces waiting to rush in to disrupt and destroy the Spirit's work. We have trials and temptations ahead of us, as our Gospel text for today reminds us.

The story of the testing of Jesus from the Gospel of Luke happens within the larger context of Jesus' baptism. In baptism, the Spirit anoints Jesus for the healing work God has planned for the world. If this were a movie, the scene you would see directly before this would be Jesus in the River Jordan being baptized by his cousin John. As Jesus is being baptized, the heavens open, the clouds part, a dove descends over his head, and the Divine voice pronounces: "You are my Beloved Son, on whom my favor rests." This is the dramatic beginning of Jesus' public life and ministry. But the Spirit knows Jesus needs strengthening against the forces of evil that will try to destroy his ministry by corrupting his intentions for good. Directly following his baptismal blessing, Jesus is taken out into the wilderness, as many holy ones have been before him, to withstand some testing.

In the wilderness, Jesus encounters an enemy which most of us know popularly as "the devil," but what is best translated from the

Greek as "The Worthless One" or "The Obstructer." In a series of visions, Jesus is presented with three temptations. The first test is an economic temptation. Taking advantage of Jesus' hunger, The Worthless One says to him, "If you really are the Son of God, tell this stone to become a loaf of bread and eat it." This is the test that invites Jesus to use God's favor for economic security, to join the Forbes Four Hundred Club and forget the other 95 percent of the population that struggles for daily bread. "Take your divine inheritance and use it to build wealth, Jesus, or at least freedom from discomfort." But Jesus refuses, saying, "It takes more than bread to keep a Child of God alive."

Then The Worthless One shows Jesus in a flash all the kingdoms of the inhabited world and presents Jesus with his second test. The Worthless One says, "I will give you control over all these, and I will give you glory, for it is mine to give to anyone I wish. If you worship me, all of this will be yours." This was the political test, the "power and control over others" test, with a lot of glory thrown in. The lure is: You get all the heads of government and the White House, too. Of what use is a Kingdom of Love without power? But Jesus answers, "Scripture says, 'You must worship the Lord your God, and you must serve *only* God.' So the political test fails."

But there's one more test, the most important one—the spiritual test. The Worthless One takes Jesus to the highest pinnacle of the temple, a place said to be the habitation of Almighty God here on earth. "If you really are the Son of God, fling yourself down, for God will give the angels orders to guard you through all dangers. They will carry you in their arms to ensure that you never strike your foot against a stone." This was the ultimate test, that of spiritual invulnerability. The Worthless One invites Jesus to be on a spiritual plane above it all, removed from the suffering and cares of the world, protected from all hurt and all danger. He could live a safe, risk-free life. He would never lose home, friends, family, or life. He would never have to fear anything. He would no longer be human, but he would be *safe*. Jesus answers, "It has been said, 'You must not test the Lord your God.'" And having exhausted all these ways of tempting him, The Worthless One leaves him until another opportunity should present itself.

Every ordeal of testing is calculated to remove Jesus from the human family, to sever the bonds of solidarity with the poor,

with the vulnerable, with the dispossessed. And if they had succeeded, Jesus would have been removed from God's reach as well,
for God's plan is to reside wherever there are suffering or forgotten people in the world; wherever there are people joyfully
doing the work of healing in the world; wherever there are people engaged in the work of love, whatever the cost in comfort,
power, or worldly recognition.

THE GOSPEL READING for this day certainly brings out a sober
dimension to our celebration of love and commitment. And yet
how prophetic this text is. For we have already seen the dark
shadow of fear and hate issue forth from this administration's
promise to work for a constitutional amendment barring LGBT
people from the right to marry. We have already heard our governor equate what this city's leadership is doing with fomenting
anarchy and lawlessness. The specter of rioting and death has
been suggested as the natural accompaniment to such lawless
actions as our civil marriages. We know that there are a great
many people who want to shut down the joy we have experienced in this miracle at City Hall. They will be, in the long run,
unsuccessful, for love is a greater power than fear. Perfect love,
Jesus assures us, casts out fear, even the fear we carry within us.

But we must be watchful of our own hearts in this process, lest
we fail the tests that must surely await us. We must not give in to
fear of legal reprisals; we must not grow faint in our efforts to create, support, and nurture sound and loving unions; we must not
forget those of our brothers and sisters who live in places that are
hostile to their loving commitments; we must not choose what's
comfortable or what's political over what's right; we must not forget the sufferings of others in our focus on our own struggles;
most importantly, we must not create further divisions in our common life on this earth by returning hatred for hatred.

A wise visitor to our community recently reminded us that the
best response to those who have grown calcified in their hatred
of our relationships is not more hate, but love. Mary Tolbert, a
recent guest speaker at St. Francis, suggested, "What if we took
our bouquets of flowers from these joyous unions and passed
them out to the protestors outside City Hall saying, 'God loves
you'? Would not that be better than countering anger with more

anger?" She went on to say, "Just as Jesus knew that trouble lay ahead of him, so the first Christians living in the time of the Roman Empire knew that as long as evil powers were in charge of the world, the path of faith would lead them into suffering as well as joy. This is because it is part of the movement of the Spirit to disrupt authoritarian power structures that are bent on maintaining privilege for one segment of the population at the expense of justice for another segment of the population."

We know that the health of a country and its government is evidenced in its ability to care for and learn from the most vulnerable of its population. We Christians are called to be in solidarity with those who benefit least by our systems of power. That is why hospitality to the stranger starts first with foreigners, immigrants, and the poor among us. Those of us who have been married in City Hall over this past week and a half and those of you who have surrounded us with your support have experienced the amazing grace of hospitality where there had been none before.

Today, this congregation extends its hospitality to all who worship here but most particularly to those of you who have found little hospitality in God's house in the past. May you be blessed in your life and in your love. May you be given the grace to convert fear into love and tears into shouts of gladness. Today we will anoint you who have been joined in marriage with a blessing from God. In receiving this blessing, we pray that, in some mysterious way you, too, may experience the heavens opening to your relationship, the wind of the Spirit blowing the breath of God into your love, and the Divine voice saying, "You are my beloved ones, on whom my favor rests."

Blessed Be!

We Are Not Deterred

WHITNEY DOUGLAS-WEDDELL

▼

On Sunday after church, Donna and I enjoyed celebrating the marriages of my sister and her partner, as well as a local Bakersfield couple, Donel and Lea Ann. We had cake and toasted the newlyweds, noting the old Meg Christian tune with lyrics by Holly Near, "Can we be like drops of water, falling on the stone? Splashing, breaking, dispersing in air . . . weaker than the stone by far but be aware that as time goes by the rock will wear away." We talked about how, with every marriage license dispensed in San Francisco or anywhere else, truly the rock of homophobia is wearing away.

With that warmth to carry us through a cold ride north, Donna and I hopped into our car with our friends Katy and Joanne to make the drive from Bakersfield to San Francisco.

Arriving in the city around 2:30 a.m., I bitched a lot about the way streets are laid out downtown. I probably broke fifty traffic laws due to total confusion, but we finally found City Hall. In the darkness, we could see there was no one about, so we set off in search of a warm cup somewhere.

Finding a Denny's in a beautiful old brownstone, we donated to the panhandler who swore we did not have to feed the meter at that hour in the morning, who said he'd keep an eye on the car. We went inside for, strangely enough, ice cream shakes, and relaxed for an hour before heading out for the true purpose of our day. True to his word, the fellow had protected our vehicle admirably, so after putting another drop in his cup, we were off to plant ourselves on the steps of City Hall.

This time when we arrived, we saw four people standing on those steps, talking with deputies. This worried us. We knew that a press release had announced that weddings would be performed only by appointment that day, and we feared we might be refused the right to line up. Intrepid Katy went to see what was up. The deputies simply said it was unlikely we'd get in, but we could stay if we liked. At 4:00 in the morning, we were the third couple in line.

OUR HOMETOWN OF Bakersfield has begun to gain a reputation in LGBT circles statewide. That day was no exception. While waiting for City Hall to open, we decorated the police barrier with signs and a couple of rainbow flags provided to us by LJ of Marriage Equality California. Many TV cameras used that blockade as a backdrop for their newscasts, and when Joanne and I decorated the statue of Abraham Lincoln nearby with a We All Deserve the Freedom to Marry sign and a rainbow flag, cameras and videocams came out in droves.

Meanwhile, the opposition made themselves known. Across the street, four Repent America protesters with about twenty nasty signs began to sing their one and only song, but we could barely hear them. We largely ignored them, and sometimes mocked them, because one sign said, God Hates America, and yet they persisted in singing "God Bless America." The bigots just couldn't seem to get their story straight (pun intended).

While ignoring the protestors, we met the fellow newlywed hopefuls standing in line with us. We struck up a pleasant acquaintance with two men from Georgia and two women from Philadelphia. More folks began to arrive, and by 6:00 a.m. the line stretched down the block. We held each others' places as folks made runs to Starbucks and McDonald's, and strangers became friends in minutes.

FINALLY, AT ABOUT 8:00 a.m., a gentleman from the County Clerk's Office announced that we would definitely have to have appointments to get married, and they were giving out only fifty-two appointments that day. When we learned that we had to call to make an appointment, immediately, hundreds of cell phones went into mass action, trying to call one of only three numbers set up for this purpose. Frustration set in and tempers flared when we consistently got busy signals or disconnect messages from the phone system. The folks from Georgia and Philly began to worry that their early arrival might result in nothing, as both couples had to return home that night. We did what we could to assist them, and when one of our phones got an actual ring, we handed off to them, hoping to ensure their ability to marry before returning home. Every ten minutes or so word would come from somewhere in the line that someone had indeed gotten through, and appointments were being made, first, for Tuesday at 2:00 p.m., then we heard 3:00 p.m., and later for March 8. It was becoming abundantly clear that ours was an exercise in futility.

As some people began to leave the line, we started to have some success getting through to the appointment lines. When we connected with a live person, we all mentioned the hard-luck cases from Georgia and Philly, begging them to find a way for those poor folks to be married today. Initially we got hard hearts from the phone operators, but over time we talked to a lot more people in those offices, who told us to wait for a new policy. We held our collective breath. We had no idea at the time that representatives from Marriage Equality California were negotiating with the County Clerk for a change as well.

Because our phone was dying by 10:00 a.m., I went to the parking garage to recharge the battery. While I was gone, someone from the Clerk's Office came out and invited some folks inside. Those people who had traveled long distances to get to San Francisco were lined up in a hallway, filling out papers explaining their situations. Donna dutifully took her place in this new line, hoping against hope that perhaps we would be one of the lucky ones. While waiting there with Katy and Joanne, Donna was interviewed by a delightful French woman writing for a French magazine called the *New Observer*. The reporter seemed thrilled to see this change occurring in the U.S., and expressed her hope that it would spread to her native France within a few years. They spoke again of rocks wearing away.

When I joined Donna in this new line, we talked to a couple of nice fellows from Baltimore, and a pair of women who run the GLSEN chapter in Berkeley. Once again we were reminded how momentous this occasion is for so many of us, and how people put their lives on hold to take this chance to be married. Standing in that line was almost spiritual.

FINALLY, AFTER WAITING in the hallway for a while, we were escorted into an office, where a nice young man talked with us about our long journey and gave us several options for our next step. He explained that today was booked, booked, booked, and just not possible. We didn't want to believe him, but he showed us a long list of appointments for the day, and we had to rethink our strategy. After some negotiation, we agreed to return on Wednesday at 10:00 a.m., this time guaranteed a moment with a Marriage Commissioner.

We left, a bit disappointed, but energized by the amazing people we had met and the excitement that comes with knowing we are participating in something much, much bigger than ourselves. This must be the way people felt at the March on Washington in 1963, or perhaps even at Stonewall. Regardless of what happens next politically, these actions in San Francisco will be a marker in the gay rights movement that no one can take away.

BACK IN THE car, we barely noticed our ride home—we slept while Joanne and Katy took over driving duties. We were relieved to arrive back home in time to rest up for Tuesday's workday—we needed to work double time so we would be free to travel back to San Francisco on Wednesday.

Throughout that first trip to the city, we were grateful to have Katy and Joanne with us, a built-in support structure. They used hundreds of their own cell minutes making calls for us, and Joanne nearly killed herself running back and forth to the car once we were inside the building. (She and the metal detector guy are on a first name basis.) It made a big difference to feel supported and loved through this whole process, and while we didn't ultimately get to marry, we had a fantastic day in the arms of our friends and community. We were not deterred.

A NEW DAY dawned at 2:00 a.m. on Wednesday. Donna and I packed our fancy duds and picked up Katy and Joanne, who apparently had not gotten enough excitement on our first trip to City Hall. Next we made a brief pit stop at Beverly Manor, where Donna works, to get a bag of various bridal necessities that her coworkers had prepared: "Something old, something new, something borrowed, something blue." We were both touched by the generosity and playful spirit of these non-gay women. Sometimes we are amazed by them.

Driving up Interstate 5, we stopped in Kettleman City to stretch. As we were climbing back into the car, Donna, who had removed her shoes for comfort while driving, smashed and broke her little toe on her left foot. After several choice words and some expertly applied medical tape, she was determined not to let this painful injury change our plans. Onward we went.

As the 5 melted into the 580, suddenly traffic slowed to a crawl. It was already about 8:00 a.m., so we became concerned that we might not make our 10:00 appointment at City Hall. That concern became more of a panic at 9:45, when were still trapped on the Bay Bridge and barely moving. Katy, thinking fast, called the Clerk's Office and explained the situation. We were all relieved when they said, "No problem, just get here as quickly as you can."

We finally arrived at City Hall at 11:00, an hour late, but moving very fast. Joanne parked the car while Donna, Katy, and I ran inside the building. As Donna and I sat in the Clerk's Office, Room 168, reviewing our forms, Joanne appeared, videotaping the whole thing. The clerk was most helpful, and very, very friendly. We expressed our gratitude not only for the service, but for the friendliness of everyone in this process. Her reaction was typical of everyone we have dealt with. She said, "We want your special day to be a great one."

From that office, we sprinted, as much as one can sprint with a broken toe, to a restroom stall, where we changed into our froo froo clothes. Joanne and Katy were chatting with some other couples and volunteers when we emerged, ready to get on with the show. We had to wait only a few minutes when Craig, deputized by the County Clerk, arrived to be our celebrant. We found a lovely spot on the second floor, above the grand staircase—much to Donna's toe's chagrin—and the ceremony began.

Craig began to read his prepared but powerful words, and Donna and I were almost giddy. After all the running up and down freeways, waiting in lines, finding ways to get off work, after all the excitement and fun and frustration, here we were, with Katy and Joanne as our witnesses, preparing to utter the simplest and most important words of our life together, "I do." As we slipped the wedding bands onto each other's fingers, as Craig finished, saying, "I now pronounce you spouses for life," I remember feeling overwhelmed by an incredible thought: *spouses for life!* Who would have ever thunk it, that in this bigoted world, two women from podunk Bakersfield would be truly married in the eyes of the law? It was an emotional few minutes, bringing tears to Katy's eyes, and hugs all around after it ended.

We remained in the rotunda, taking photos and chatting with other couples, and then proceeded to the next step: the official recording of the document. It's not legal until the assessor-recorder says it is. We walked to Room 190 and handed over our paperwork, then we waited. And then, as is typical with us, we ran into a problem. Craig, the wonderful fellow who had married us, had used a blue pen to sign the form. No good, we were told. Go back to the beginning and start over. Donna began cussing under her breath as we made our way—broken toe and all—back to Room 168 and the wonderful clerk who wanted our day to be great.

The clerk was not at all happy with the Assessor-Recorder's Office. She marched with us back to Room 190 and corrected the fellow: the form can be signed in blue, but not amended in blue. A fine distinction to be sure, but what it meant for us was that, with a quick payment of $13, we would be legally married. No matter what the powers that be decide, in this moment, we are indeed, spouses for life.

ON THE WAY home, Joanne chauffeured our rather cramped limousine. As Donna and Katy snoozed, Joanne and I chatted about the immensity of this seemingly trivial event. People get married every day, and yet these weddings, simple and concise, are shaking the very foundations of our government. As we were deciding what to wear to our wedding ceremony, the whole world was deciding how to respond to gay and lesbian couples who now have legal marriage licenses. President Bush has called for a constitutional amendment, truly an earth-shattering idea. States throughout America are wrestling with homophobia and liberty, democracy and freedom and justice for all. Regardless of the short-term legal outcomes, in the long run these discussions will bring the kinds of changes that will one day guarantee all lesbian and gay people equal access to marriage rights. Have no fear. The rock of homophobia will continue to wear away. We are not deterred.

Flowers, Tons of Flowers

JAMES HARRIS AND MICHAEL MOULDS

▼

From the beginning, we both knew that we had something special. We had both recently divested ourselves from abusive relationships. Jim had been with a sot, and Michael had been with a still-closeted, unloyal person. Both of us had decided that life was better alone, rather than with the wrong person. So when we met we both carried high expectations, and we were perfectly willing to go on with our lives alone. But we soon learned that our connection to each other was special. It was not a great emotional love, but one that was deep and always grew.

To celebrate our commitment, nine years ago Michael insisted on a holy union ceremony. Jim was willing, but leery, until he was introduced to the Reverend Gregg Dell. Ever since Reverend Gregg Dell performed our holy union ceremony, we have talked about someday having the opportunity to get married legally. We dreamed it would happen. This past Saturday morning, after following the news from San Francisco, we decided that things looked right for us to fly to the Bay Area to get married. Somewhat assured by the news that two judges had decided to let the weddings continue for the time being, we believed our trek would be successful. So we booked our flight and reserved a room at a small hotel just three blocks from City Hall. Our neighbor Florence agreed to babysit our dog, Molly, while we were away.

We told nobody of our plans. Even Michael's mom, in Tucson, did not get her usual Sunday evening phone call from Michael.

We left very early Sunday morning and arrived shortly after noon on Sunday. As we walked from the BART station to our hotel, we passed by City Hall. No one was there, which we expected. While we stood at the steps of that gilded building, a small SUV pulled up to the curb. The woman inside asked us if this was where the weddings were taking place. We replied that we thought so. She then asked, "Are you guys here to get married?" We answered yes. The woman jumped out of her car and gave us both hugs and kisses and then opened up the back door of her SUV. Inside, it was packed with hundreds of roses. She took out a bouquet and gave it to us. She explained that she and her two friends had bought up all the flowers at home and driven nearly 100 miles to come to town to show their support. Then she drove us the rest of the way to our hotel, leaving us with more hugs and kisses. We thought this was our good luck omen.

Taking advantage of the difference in time zones, the following morning we arrived at City Hall shortly after 6:00 a.m., which was 8:00 a.m. to us. About fifty people waited in line in front of us. We stood next to a couple of guys from Chattanooga in their cold shirtsleeves. Behind us we met a couple of girls with their dogs, who had driven all night from Eugene, Oregon. At 7:45 a man came out from City Hall and handed all of us a printed message: procedures had changed over the weekend, and walk-ins were no longer allowed. Now we had to call in on the telephone and make an appointment. Our dreams dropped. We had no cell phone, and we knew the switchboard at City Hall would not handle all the calls anyway. We knew we never would get through. We later learned that City Hall had received so many telephone calls at 8:00 a.m. that the overload had shut down their phone system for a while. We decided that our attempt at a legal wedding was a nice try, but we'd make this a vacation weekend instead. We abandoned our place in the line and went to breakfast. Later we toured the waterfront piers, visited an aquarium, saw sea lions out in the bay, and rode the old trolley cars.

Shortly after noon we headed back to our motel for rest. As we passed by City Hall, we saw another group on the front steps protesting violence against minorities. We lingered there, wondering if anything had happened that we did not know about. The group of people we had been with that morning had gone by now. When a woman approached us, I asked her if anything had changed. I told her that we were from Illinois and had been in line at 6:00 a.m., but were not aware of the procedural change. The woman grabbed Jim by the arm and practically pushed us into City Hall, urging us, "Now you two just go in there and go down the corridor on the right-hand side, down to the end of the hall, and you tell them just what you told me." She went on, "You've come all this way. Now get going," she ordered.

We ended up outside the Mayor's Office of Community Affairs, in a line with many other couples. A gentleman in a tailored suit came down the line taking names and passing out numbers. He handed us a Post-it with the number forty-five on it. As we stood there waiting, several of the others in line learned that we were from Illinois. Suddenly they began trading us their numbers, which were lower than forty-five. "Here, take ours. We're from here. We can always come back. You guys can't." They forced their lower numbers on us. In a matter of seconds we had advanced to the front of the line! A form had been shoved in our hands to sign. Flowers, tons of flowers adorned us. Champagne flowed. Cookies were passed. Hugs and kisses from every passerby. We could hardly hold back the tears for the love and support shown to us by these perfect strangers.

In a matter of minutes we were called inside and talked to a deputy to the mayor. We only hoped to make an appointment for a wedding on a future date. Mike reminded me that he had a week's vacation coming up in two weeks. We could come back. We did not ask anything from the deputy. We only asked if anything could be done for us. He took over the conversation, "What time do you have to be at the airport for your flight home?" We told him we could wait until noon on Tuesday. He made some notes and did something with his computer. "Okay, you guys sit out there in my waiting room for an hour and I'll see what I can do."

We sat in his lobby with eight other couples. On one side of us sat two men from Georgia; on the other side, two men from San Diego. Across from us waited two women who had driven all night from Seattle. Two men from France came into the room. Soon the deputy came out and called the names of four couples.

Among them were the two guys next to us from Georgia. He announced, "Now you are my Monday group. Come with me." He took them down the hall. Soon he returned and announced to us remaining that the County Clerk was in a meeting and that we should sit tight for an hour longer. He would see what he could do.

The longer we sat, the longer our faces got. Maybe we should have insisted on Monday. We looked up and saw the couple from Georgia standing in the hall, holding a copy of their marriage license for us to see. We were elated, and also sad because it looked like that was not going to happen for us.

Twenty minutes later, the deputy came out and called our names. "Now for you people," he said in a glum tone, "I've got news. You're not going to get married on Tuesday." There was a long pause. Faces sank. Hope was gone. "You are getting married right now. Gather up your stuff and come with me." Many of us openly wept.

We went into the County Clerk's Office, filled out necessary forms, and paid our fees. While we were there we ran into the couple from Chattanooga whom we were standing in line with at 6:00 a.m. They were on their way to be married. They hugged us and encouraged us to stay and let the wonderful people there help us. They assured us that it would happen.

Soon we were ushered into the grand rotunda of City Hall. It is a glorious place adorned with crystal, gold, and a huge marble staircase. Observers, volunteers, and newlyweds were milling around. Flowers and flash cameras lit up the space. Amid the seeming confusion, a beautiful lady in a white silk blouse came up to Jim and told us that she was there to help us. We were offered more flowers for our ceremony, then she introduced us to a beautifully silver-haired gentleman named Bill Jones, the Deputy Marriage Commissioner who would perform our wedding. Bill asked, "Now where do you want your ceremony?"

My mind was swimming. Was this really happening? We said that we'd like our ceremony on that landing, and pointed to a large landing in the marble staircase about halfway up. "Let's go," Bill said, and escorted us to our chosen spot. Volunteer witnesses were summoned, and the couple from San Diego, whom we had met earlier in the office, followed us with their cameras.

For a moment, Bill stood on the landing and explained what was going to happen. Cameras were flashing all over the rotunda as other couples were exchanging their vows. By that point, we held at least four-dozen roses, all given to us by strangers. And then it was happening—the vows were read and our rings exchanged. When it came his turn to answer the big question, "Do you promise to love and comfort each other, honor and keep each other in sickness and in health, for richer and for poorer, for better or for worse, and to be faithful to each other as long as you both shall live?"

Michael cried and said, "With all my heart."

Then Bill finished up the ceremony, "By virtue of the authority vested in me by the State of California, I now pronounce you spouses for life." A tremendous applause erupted; cameras clicked and flashed. We could not hold back the tears as we hugged and kissed. I looked at the clock. It was 3:30 p.m.

Because our camera's batteries failed right at the time of the ceremony, other people used their cameras and then took our names and address so that they could mail the photos to us. Now it was time for us to reciprocate. We changed cameras and stood as witnesses to our newfound friends from San Diego. We watched as they too felt the gravity of what they were doing.

Shortly we were in the County Assessor-Recorder's Office, picking up the certified copy of our marriage certificate. A cell phone was shoved in Michael's hand so he could call his mother in Tucson with the happy news. When she answered the phone, he said, "Hello, my dear," their customary telephone greeting.

"Oh, I missed you. You didn't call me yesterday," she replied.

"Mom," he asked, "How many legal son-in-laws do you have?"

"Why, two," she replied.

"No, you are wrong. Now you have three. Jim and I are standing here in City Hall in San Francisco, and we just got married." More tears flowed.

Then we were off to dinner with our friends. As we stepped out of City Hall, cars were honking, people were waving, and more roses were piled on us. At dinner, we talked about what had just happened. We all drank champagne. Jim said that his exhaustion at noon had just faded away under the emotion of what had happened.

The following morning, we went back to City Hall, with new batteries in our camera for more photos. Bill Jones posed with us. Then we were interviewed by local news reporters and reporters from Dallas who wanted to know how we felt about President Bush's announcement that morning of his support for a constitutional amendment to prohibit gay marriages. Of course we voiced our opposition. You cannot impose morality by man's laws. It has never worked. This is clearly and only a matter of civil rights. They may later try to strip away what we have, but they will never, never do it. We will always have this piece of paper as witness to what happened to us and how we feel about each other.

We left City Hall at about 9:00 a.m. on Tuesday and rode BART out to the airport, hoping to get an earlier flight back home. The weather in San Francisco had been beautiful, and spring flowers were in bloom. On the flight back we could see Lake Tahoe through the clouds and then the Great Salt Lake. We got into Midway Airport about 7:00 p.m. local time, and were home with our dog, Molly, by 7:45, safe, sound, and married.

Once home, we developed our photos and made up a marriage announcement to hand out to friends. The following Sunday when we showed up in our Sunday school class, our classmates wanted to know where we had been the previous week. We handed them our announcement. The outpouring of love has been nothing but humbling. Support has come from so many unexpected and wonderful sources, we could never have imagined.

The celebration of our wedding has continued long past our ceremony. Recently we have been in contact with Bill Jones. We hear that the City of San Francisco is inviting newlyweds back to participate in the 2004 San Francisco Pride Parade. Yes, yes, yes we will be there. We have also found out that our wedding photo appeared in the March 26 issue of *Frontiers* magazine (page 80, striped shirt).

Jim will be sixty-five this year, Mike is six years younger. We both know that there will never be anything that will ever separate us. Not even death. We're making preparations for Mike's retirement soon, and look forward to spending all of the rest of our lives together, loving each other, and showing by example how wonderful being together is.

This Is My Husband, Robert

BALTIMORE GONZALEZ

▼

Robert and I met in May of 2002. My roommate Julie was having dinner at the Elephant Bar in Fresno, with a friend who worked at a car dealership nearby. Julie called to say that her friend Marjon had brought a coworker of hers to dinner, and that I should come to the restaurant to meet him. I declined because I was busy working out. But Julie called me a few more times, and I finally decided to go. When I walked into the restaurant, unbeknownst to me, I met the man I would marry.

Robert and I are both Tauruses, which is funny because our personalities clashed at first. When introduced, we felt no connection. Neither one of us seemed interested in the other's conversations. In fact, we both seemed to go out of our way not to acknowledge the other. We later admitted to one another that we each thought the other was "stuck up."

While leaving the restaurant I turned to Julie and said, "He's out of my league."

She asked, "What do you mean?"

I said, "He's young and gorgeous and looks like an Abercrombie model."

She just replied, "Oh please!"

That same evening, after dinner we all went back to Marjon's to watch a movie, and Robert and I ended up speaking by ourselves while smoking on the patio. We stayed there for two hours. It turned out we had many commonalities. We spoke of school, family, drugs, alcohol, and the "gay scene." As a rule, I never spoke about my personal experiences with anyone when I first met them. I was shocked by my own eagerness to share everything with this man I had just met. Robert had the same rule that he had broken. Despite our eight-year age difference, it seemed as though we had walked the paths of our lives side by side.

At the end of the night, we exchanged phone numbers and each waited for the other to call. I pumped Julie for information daily, while Robert pumped Marjon daily for information as well. Knowing the stubborn traits that we shared, both from our life experiences and as Tauruses, I was worried neither one of us would have the guts to call the other. Finally, I gave in and called Robert after a couple of days. After speaking on the phone, we decided to meet at Starbucks for coffee with Marjon and Julie. I knew that Robert had just moved into an apartment, so I surprised him with a housewarming gift from Starbucks, a clear coffee mug with candy inside. Handing it to him, I said, "I bought you a little something as a housewarming gift." He seemed shocked, yet I could tell that he was flattered.

The next time we met for coffee, we went alone. It was dynamic—the intense nervousness of the first time being alone, the butterflies that dance in your stomach the whole time you're in conversation, wondering if the other person is intrigued, interested, or possibly bored? It was great to be in the company of someone who had so much to talk about that I found relevant to myself. It was great to listen to someone who spoke so openly and honestly about himself. It also felt great to have someone listen with such interested ears and passionate eyes. Sparks were flying. We had so much in common. We loved animals, shopping, eating, conversing, and taking drives to the coast. Our life experiences were very similar; we were both homebodies at heart; we had similar goals in life, such as helping others. We connected in so many ways.

Robert and I continued to date after that and spent many evenings at Starbucks, my house, his apartment, movies, and restaurants. It seemed as though we couldn't spend enough time together. We didn't want to be apart. Either Robert would spend the night at my house or I would spend the night at his apartment. About six months later, we decided that we wanted to live together and began our journey as partners.

A few days before Christmas 2003, I purchased a promise ring with the intention of proposing to Robert on New Year's Eve. But neither Robert nor I can keep secrets from each other. I was so excited and nervous at the same time. I had no idea how Robert would react. Finally, on Christmas, I decided this would be the night.

The house was decorated with Christmas candles, wreaths, and lights. I lit the candles and played soft music. When Robert came home from work, I asked him to have a seat on the couch. I could see in his eyes that he was very nervous, not knowing what I was about to do. I knelt down on one knee, pulled a ring out of my pocket, and said, "Will you marry me?"

Robert quickly embraced me and said, "Yes, I will marry you!"

We had no idea what came next. We researched on the Internet to find out what states, if any, were allowing same-sex marriages. We had decided that we would go to Vermont, which was the only place in the United States that we knew of that offered civil unions, the closest thing to a marriage license. There was a resort in Vermont that offered a $3000 all-inclusive package with travel, food, skiing, and lodging.

Then, in February 2004, we started noticing newspaper articles, television news clips, and e-mails regarding San Francisco City Hall allowing same-sex marriages. We immediately decided to make an appointment. We called City Hall and listened to a recording that directed us to their Web site for appointments. We went online and set our wedding day for April 7, 2004. I was very nervous about the date, worried that the marriages would be ordered to a halt due to all of the media coverage they were receiving. It all seemed too good to be true.

On Tuesday, March 9, still nervous about our wedding date, I decided to go online to see if any appointments had been canceled so that we could get married sooner. I was able to change our appointment to March 11 at 11:30 a.m. When Robert arrived home from work, I told him that I had made the change and apologized for not discussing it with him first. Robert knew that I had a bad feeling about our original date. When I told him about the change, he gave me a kiss and said, "I love you!"

The next day we went to Macy's to pick out special suits for our wedding. We notified Robert's sister Susie, who was going to be our witness, and she was excited for us. We then packed our bags and drove from Fresno to Benecia, not far from San Francisco, to spend the night at Susie's house.

On the following morning, bright and early, we headed to San Francisco City Hall for our wedding. One of our favorite parts of the whole experience was seeing all the other couples there, looking so happy, so validated. We filled out the necessary paperwork, then had a beautiful ceremony in the rotunda, performed by Donald Cook. Looking into each other's eyes and exchanging our vows made us giggle quite a bit. We were so excited to be married! Susie and Donald Cook were equally excited for us. After the ceremony, we had lunch in the Castro and returned to Benecia.

Later that day, Robert and I were preparing to leave Benecia to go home to Fresno. I decided to check my e-mail before leaving, and read a message from Molly McKay, Marriage Equality of California director, urging everyone to be in front of City Hall for a demonstration at 5:30 p.m. because the same-sex marriages had been ordered to an immediate halt at 2:30 p.m.

Just hours after our ceremony, in the exact same spot where we had stood exchanging vows, Gavin Newsom now stood in front of television cameras, holding a press conference, addressing the immediate halt of the weddings. Approximately two hours after our ceremony, some of those other happy couples we had seen at San Francisco City Hall had been turned away. Hearing this news, Robert and I experienced a bittersweet feeling. We were excited that we had been married just before the courts ended the weddings. However, we felt saddened by the fact that so many people would be devastated by the news. I knew that I for one would have been devastated. I thought of my coworker, who had an appointment to be married in April.

Robert and I immediately headed back to San Francisco, with our marriage certificate in hand, to join in the rally outside City Hall. We did not know what to expect. Neither one of us had been to a gay protest or rally, much less one of this magnitude. When we arrived at City Hall, we both had chills from seeing all of the people there. There were police cars, bullhorns, huge signs. We couldn't believe our eyes. All these people were upset about the same thing as us. After the rally, we left feeling that we had to do something for the cause. We immediately contacted Marriage Equality of California and became the chapter heads for Fresno.

Upon our return home, Robert and I vowed to continue our celebration and immediately started planning a wedding reception for April 17 at the Ramada Inn. We had white flowers everywhere, Philharmonic Strings playing the entire time, and forty people whom we love surrounding us. It was very romantic. Despite the California State Supreme Court March 11 ruling to stop the weddings and the August 11 ruling to invalidate our wedding licenses, Robert and I are so happy. No other feeling in the world compares to the feeling of being able to say, "This is my husband, Robert."

For Ourselves and Our Children

Cheryl Dumesnil

▼

The rainbow-flag-with-wedding-ring icon flashed on the upper right corner of our TV screen, behind the news anchor's head, so I pressed the volume-up button on the remote and called Tracie out of the kitchen to watch with me.

"Hey, love, you've got to see this."

"What?"

"They're talking about gay weddings."

"What're they saying?"

Her voice wasn't getting any closer, so I knew she was still standing over the dog's bowl in the kitchen, trying to keep the cat away while the pooch was eating.

"Just come here," I insisted, sitting down on the couch and punching the volume up higher. "Gavin Newsom says he'll issue wedding licenses to same-sex couples."

Tracie left the pets to fend for themselves and sat beside me on the couch. We listened as Newsom explained that he'd asked Mabel Teng, the San Francisco county assessor-recorder, to change the language on the county's wedding license application from "Bride" and "Groom" to "Applicant No. 1 and Applicant No. 2." That simple. Change the words and we can get married.

However interested I was in the story, I can't say that I felt called to action in that moment. The urge to call City Hall to find out how we could get married never hit me that night. I simply watched the news and thought, *Cool.* I figured that a small handful of gay and lesbian couples would step up to get married, and then some government official higher in rank than Newsom would stop them, prompting the couples to file a law suit. Then, backed by the Human Rights Campaign or Lambda Legal Defense or Marriage Equality California or maybe even the ACLU, those couples would travel the arduous road through the California court system, attempting to gain the right to marry. That's what was happening in Massachusetts, right? As I saw it, Tracie and I didn't have the time or resources for that kind of court battle. She's a business owner responsible for the educational programs of over thirty children and for the livelihood of twenty-plus employees. I'm a freelance poet, writing instructor, and editor. In addition to our professional commitments, we were in the process of starting a family. After three miscarriages, once again we were in the fourteen-day "maybe, maybe not" period between insemination and taking a pregnancy test. For all we knew, I could have been pregnant at the moment we were watching that news program. So, given our circumstances, we'd have to find a way to support those newly married couples from the sidelines.

At dinner that night, Tracie and I raised our glasses to toast Gavin Newsom, Mabel Teng, and the pioneering couples who would blaze the trail for us. End of story.

THREE DAYS LATER, as the numbers of married couples reached into the hundreds and the front pages of newspapers filled with photos of newlyweds-to-be camping out on folding chairs, my inner activist started itching. This was not Massachusetts. People like us were walking into San Francisco City Hall as domestic partners and walking out carrying certificates that declared them legal spouses—the same marriage certificate my sister and her husband had, the same one my parents had. I wanted to get married. I wanted that piece of paper emblazoned with the seal of the State of California, bearing our two names.

On Sunday afternoon, February 15, Tracie and I were scheduled to attend an event where Arun Gandhi, Mahatma Gandhi's grandson, would speak on the topic "Love Your Enemy." Grumbling that "If we hadn't already spent fifty bucks on these tickets we could be getting married right now," I drove us up a wet, winding road toward the Rheem Theatre, where we learned that the event had been canceled due to illness. Great, now Arun Gandhi had the flu, we couldn't hear him speak, and it was already 3:30—too late to get married.

"Trace," I told her, driving back down the winding road toward home, squinting through the raindrops on the windshield, "I really want to get married."

"I know," she said, with that cautionary note in her voice, "but I've just got so much work to do. I'm backed up on billing. I can't go down there now. My schedule is packed for two or three weeks."

"But this could be our only opportunity—can't you change your schedule around at all?"

"No. I'm booked solid. I can't change it."

This, I believe, is when I began to pout. I *tried* not to pout, but I'm sure Tracie could tell how I felt—she can read and understand the slightest flutter of my left eyelid, so I'm certain she had no problem deciphering a poorly veiled pout. Still, I didn't *want* to pout. I didn't *mean* to pout, but inside my gut felt like the Push-Me-Pull-You, the two-headed, llama-like animal from Doctor Dolittle. One of the animal's opposing heads said, "I can't believe she won't change her schedule for something this important," and pulled me in the direction of "pissed off at Tracie." The other head said, "Chill out. She'd change her schedule if she could. If it's meant to be, you'll get married when her schedule lightens up," and pushed me in the direction of "compassion for my partner," which is where I strive, but sometimes fail, to live. I'd like to say I settled into compassion and chose to wait patiently for the day when we too could descend upon City Hall, but in reality the two heads debated for days:

HEAD 1: Maybe she's just less of an activist than I am. Maybe this really isn't all that important to her.

HEAD 2: Come on, you two already had your wedding two and a half years ago. Don't discount the beauty of the ceremony you had in your own backyard, surrounded by your family and friends.

HEAD 1: I'm not discounting our real wedding, I just really want for us to be a part of this moment in history. It would make our future children proud to know we had fought to have the sanctity of our relationship honored. I can't believe she won't take one day off.

HEAD 2: It's not that easy for her—she owns her own business; she has a full load of clients.

HEAD 1: Don't tell me there aren't two clients she couldn't shift around to free up one day. She's the boss! She can do whatever she wants!

HEAD 2: Put yourself in her shoes. Don't you have appointments that you wouldn't cancel? I mean, what if she wanted to get married on a Tuesday when your poetry workshop meets? Would you cancel on your students?

HEAD 1: No, you're right. I don't cancel on my students (except that one time at the university when I canceled a class so I could go get a tattoo). And I do have a much more flexible schedule than she has, but . . .

The internal debate continued from Sunday until Thursday. While the two heads told each other stories about what was *really* happening here, I persevered, trying, rather obnoxiously I fear, to convince my wife to bag her responsibilities and run away to San Francisco with me. Since my initial, direct approach didn't work, I got creative. First, I told her that two of our friends had offered to camp out in front of City Hall with me and to pose as Tracie so that we could get our piece of paper. Of course, the friends were joking—they knew I wanted to marry *Tracie,* to share this experience with *her.* I didn't just want the piece of paper. But I told Tracie the joke because I'm Irish, and that's how we try to make our most serious points—with humor. That tactic never works on Tracie. In fact, it annoys her, so I'm not sure why I even tried.

Next I attempted to argue the *Antiques Roadshow* point. Tracie's a big fan of the show, and she's certain that one day we too will go to a garage sale and purchase a $65,000 lampshade for a mere twenty-five cents. I love her for her sense of possibility. And I learned the *Antiques Roadshow* argument from her. She uses it when she wants to buy artwork or knickknacks from secondhand stores: "You never know—this could be worth a lot of money to our great-great-grandkids." So, desperate, I tried it: "Tracie, imagine, our great-great-grandchildren will bring this piece of paper to the show—tastefully framed, of course—and the antique dealer will say, 'Well, Ms. Dumesnil-Vickers, this is an amazing piece of civil rights memorabilia. Did you know that in 2004, lesbian couples were not allowed to marry?' And our great-great-grandchild will say, 'No, really? Why not? That's ridiculous!' Then the antiques dealer—who will happen to be a specialist in San Francisco history and civil rights artifacts—will tell our progeny the story of our union, and tears will fill her eyes as he reveals the value of the document—enough for her to send her firstborn to college." Tracie smiled at me in that "nice try" way, then countered my argument with a diversion tactic: "Sure, if we get married in a few weeks, that could happen."

Finally, a well-meaning friend, Becky, who is also a colleague of Tracie's, tried to intervene. On a Thursday night I met Tracie at her office before going out to dinner in downtown Walnut Creek. Just before we left for the restaurant, Becky said, "I know what we can do. I can switch my schedule for Monday and all three of us can go down to City Hall together."

Tracie sighed, defeated by five days of my hard-core pestering, and said, "Becky, I can't. I start a new case on Monday, I have an Individual Education Program meeting with a school district on Tuesday, I see the new client again on Wednesday, I have another IEP meeting on Thursday, on Friday I see a once-a-month client . . ."

Suddenly I heard something I had not heard before. Though Tracie had told me "I can't" several times, she had never told me the specific reasons why she couldn't take off time from work. Now that I heard about the kinds of appointments she had scheduled for each day, I understood. Tracie owns an agency that provides treatment programs for children with autism. In addition to running the administrative side of the business, she directs the programs of many clients. The appointments she described are the kind you cannot change, and she had two and a half weeks' worth of those appointments on her calendar. At that time in San Francisco, couples were waiting upwards of eight hours to get their licenses at City Hall. There was no way Tracie could find eight consecutive free hours in her day. Over dinner that night, Tracie told me how pressured and stressed she had felt, thanks to my pestering. I realized that when Tracie had said "I can't change my schedule," I had heard "I *won't* change my schedule." Because I was so busy believing that Tracie wasn't doing enough to honor my desire to get married, I couldn't hear her messages about her needs, nor could I see how my pressure was affecting her. Not only did I not hear Tracie correctly when she said, "I can't," I did not believe what she had told me until I saw *proof,* until I knew the specifics of her schedule and *I* decided that yes, indeed, it was too full. It was a lesson in humility and communication. That night I ate a big piece of humble pie for dessert. And when we got home after dinner, Tracie pulled out her calendar and chose March 11 as the day we could get married.

Tracie and I had already publicly declared our commitment to one another, on August 18, 2001, in a backyard wedding attended by sixty of our closest and dearest, with our friend Nicole presiding. We had spent that whole summer landscaping our yard in preparation for the event. Our landscape design included the artful distribution of a VW Bug–size pile of river rocks that the local quarry delivered to our driveway, not to mention the twenty fifty-pound bags of gravel we transported from the trunks of our cars to the farthest corner of the yard. By the time our ceremony day arrived, between the digging, hauling, and planting, we were two muscular and bronzed brides. On our wedding day, our gardening work provided a beautiful backdrop for the linen-draped, circular dining tables, the plentiful bouquets of roses, and the dozens of wooden folding chairs filled with people we love. Tracie and I wore long white dresses, and we walked into the ceremony to the sound of friend and vocalist Yvonne Perea singing "Simply" by Sara Hickman. That day far surpassed what we had imagined for our wedding. Love radiated from everyone in attendance, and we felt lifted, inspired, and awed by our community. Though I have attended and officiated many weddings in my life, I learned something unexpected at our ceremony: in its finest incarnation, a wedding becomes a beacon of hope, a reminder of who we are in our best moments, a reflection of our love for each other, and an inspiration to aspire to that pinnacle of love every single day of our lives.

Despite my thoughts about our first wedding, when I went to San Francisco City Hall on February 24 to make an appointment to marry Tracie on March 11, I did not have high expectations for our second wedding day. First of all, we had already celebrated our real wedding—our spiritual, emotional wedding. Second of all, I suspected that the California courts would stop the marriages before March 11. We had more than two weeks to wait for our appointment, and I feared the ax could fall at any time. When California State Attorney General Bill Lockyear filed a brief with the California State Supreme Court, I knew our days were numbered. The court responded by asking San Francisco to file their brief by Friday, March 5. After the city complied, the court fell silent. Tracie and I watched the news on television every night, and I listened to it on the car radio every day, awaiting word from the court.

In fact, I was so busy wondering if the courts would stop the weddings before Thursday, March 11, that I didn't think about what we would do if we *could* get married. Tracie kicked that planning into action on Monday, when she spent her lunch hour picking out a dress. Calling from her car, still in her post-shopping-excursion glow, she left me a detailed phone message, describing a "champagne colored, satin dress, knee-length, sleeveless, with fabric draped at the neck." Her voice sang with excitement. March 11 was only three days away. Maybe we really were going to get married? I followed Tracie's lead and, in two hours of frenzied shopping, bought a pink dress that complemented hers, had my wedding ring polished, spent too much money on the perfect necklace, invested $3.99 in a curling iron (my first one since my high school days), and hunted down just the right shade of nail polish. By March 10 at 7:00 p.m., the courts had taken no action; our friends Becky, Lisa, and LaDonna all had made arrangements to skip work and attend the wedding; and Kristen Boyd from Carole Migden's office had called to confirm that Carole would meet us at City Hall at 10:45 a.m. to officiate our ceremony. The fact started to sink in: we might actually get married.

By the time we arrived at City Hall, fifteen minutes early for our 10:00 a.m. appointment at the County Clerk's Office, I had already visited the building two times: once to volunteer (back in the long-line, hectic-with-media days of the early weddings) and once to make our wedding appointment. Still, upon entering the building on this morning, the sight of the rotunda awed me. Marble flooring and walls reflected light from high windows. A staircase that puts Scarlett O'Hara's to shame stretched upward from the lobby, raising my gaze up more than four stories to an intricately sculpted white dome that looked, honestly, like a wedding cake. Never in my life have I seen a more elegant setting for a wedding. Tracie, Becky, and I paused in the rotunda to take in the view. Still feeling antsy about the pending court decision, I felt an urge to rush first to the bathroom—yes, I was indeed pregnant, though no one but Tracie knew that at the time—and then to the Clerk's Office to fill out our application pronto. But I reminded myself that neither of my companions had witnessed any of the weddings yet. So we remained in the rotunda a few moments longer to watch a couple who were standing on the stairs, against the gold filigree banister, completing their vows. Along with twenty-some other spectators, we applauded as the couple kissed, then Becky spoke for all of us when she said, "You know, by the time my kids grow up, none of this will be an issue."

Over and over, as I have talked with people about the "gay marriage issue," an old fashioned phrase comes to mind "This will all be an amazing story we will tell." I truly believe those words apply to the struggle for gay marriage. As desperate as I was to get our marriage license as soon as possible, as sure as I was that the California court would stop the marriages at some point, like Becky, I am also sure that someday gay marriage will be no big deal. In fact, at that future time, we'll simply call it "marriage." All this struggle will be "an amazing story we'll tell."

When I couldn't wait any longer, I urged Tracie and Becky to proceed down the long corridor to the County Clerk's Office (after the necessary bathroom pit stop, of course). There we found our friend Lisa, who had missed our first wedding because she was busy working with AIDS patients in Chile. Now she works for the San Francisco AIDS Foundation where her supervisor kindly released her for a couple hours to attend our ceremony.

Sitting in the lobby of the Clerk's Office, Tracie and I filled out our light blue application form, then received a number: 430. While we waited for our turn to get our license, we spoke to a couple of women from Ohio who had flown in to get married. They planned to pick up their license and bring it to the First Unitarian Church in San Francisco, where a minister would marry them later that day and sign the document. Then they would fly back to Ohio for a wedding celebration at their home church, sending their signed license back to the Recorder's Office and waiting to receive their marriage certificate by mail. Before they left, we took a picture with them, and they laughed at the look of our dress-up clothes next to their casual pants and shirts.

We also met a couple of men from New York. They had called ahead for an appointment, but by the time they had gotten through all the busy signals, the soonest they could schedule a wedding was May. Suspecting that the courts would intervene and end the marriages before May, these gentlemen booked a flight to San Francisco, hoping that the Clerk's Office staff members would smile upon them and let them slide through without an appointment, which they did. That couple had been together for twenty-seven years.

As I sat there in the lobby, waiting to hear our number called, sipping some water and discreetly nibbling on a scone to quell the morning sickness, I thought about the day, three weeks earlier, when I had sat in that very same chair as a volunteer, helping newlyweds prepare their paperwork and then walking them from this office, marriage licenses in hand, down a hallway full of cheering couples, out to the rotunda for their ceremonies. Now it was our turn. Now Tracie and I would get to proofread our names on the license form. Now we would get to raise our right hands and testify to the truth of the information typed there. Now we would get to walk down the hallway to the rotunda for our ceremony. My spirit filled with appreciation—for my wife and my friends, for the couples waiting with us, for the hard work of the city and county employees and officials who made it possible, for the volunteers, and for the overwhelming feeling of love and support that pervaded every inch of City Hall during this historical time.

"Number 430? Number 430?" One of the women from Ohio poked her head out of the Clerk's Office door to call us. "They called your number—did you hear them? You can come in now."

We grabbed our IDs, our checkbook, and our blue form, and rushed into the office. While we stood at the counter, Becky ran the video camera and Lisa snapped still photos. I'm sure I sounded like turbo bride—nervous, excited, overwhelmed. I kept saying to Tracie, "I can't believe it's our turn. We get to do this." After a small question about the fees we owed and a brief incident with a typo, we had our license and were ready to go. Kristin Boyd from Carole Migden's office found us in the rotunda and brought us to a spot six steps up the main staircase to wait for Carole. Tracie and I were the picture of bridal jitters, holding hands, smiling nervously, making feeble attempts at small talk. I took deep yoga breaths and wiggled my toes in my sandals to try to stay grounded.

Then Kristin said, "Here comes Carole."

I squinted through the lobby to see the backlit shadow of Carole's form moving through the metal detectors. Behind her I saw a television cameraman. Then another one.

"I told you the media would be here," Tracie mumbled.

"I didn't think so," I whispered back. "These weddings have been going on so long, the TV stations aren't down here every day anymore."

"Yes, but when Carole Migden does your wedding, you get the media along with her."

Apparently, when Carole Midgen does your wedding, you get a lot more, too. Just as Carole walked into the rotunda, a group of second grade students on a field trip passed by the staircase where Tracie and I waited. As Carole bounded toward the stairs to introduce herself to Tracie and me, she turned to the children and said, "Hey, do you kids want to come to a wedding?" While I asked Carole's staff member, John, to be our ring bearer, the field trip group's teacher lined the kids up on the stairs behind us. Before I knew it, Carole began the ceremony with an animated, "We are gathered here in the presence of witnesses for the purpose of uniting in matrimony Tracie Vickers and Cheryl Dumesnil," and suddenly we were surrounded. I don't know where all the people came from, but I know that both Lisa, our photographer, and Becky, our videographer, were edged out by the media professionals and had to jockey for a position where they could record our ceremony for us. Camera lights flooded us. In the last glance I took before focusing on my wife, I saw one familiar face in the crowd—my friend LaDonna had finally arrived. In order to stay present in the moment, I listened intently to Carole, making eye contact as she read the words of the ceremony, then I turned to Tracie and felt an explosion of love as I looked into her eyes. When it came time to exchange rings, I looked around for our ring bearer, John, but found him nowhere. I think it was LaDonna who caught my attention and mouthed the words, "Look behind you." Tracie and I looked over our shoulders to find two beautiful little girls with big brown eyes and wide smiles, each holding up an open ring box. What a brilliant surprise.

We picked the rings out of the boxes, slid them on each other's fingers, and said, with Carole's coaching, "I give you this ring, in token and pledge of my constant faith and abiding love. With this ring, I thee wed." Then Carole threw her arms in the air and announced, "By virtue of the authority vested in me by the State of California and by the City and County of San Francisco, I now pronounce you, Tracie and Cheryl, spouses for life."

The ever-growing circle of witnesses erupted into applause as Tracie and I sealed the vows with a kiss. Phenomenal. I felt like a part of me had blasted off out of my shoes and rocketed up to the dome to turn somersaults and figure eights in the air. The rest of me stayed on the rotunda steps, hugging my wife and our friends, overwhelmed by all our good fortune.

In a post-ceremony whirlwind, Carole introduced us to Mabel Teng, the county assessor-recorder and one of the principal heroes of the San Francisco marriage movement; we took a group picture with the field trip class, their teachers, John, Kristen, Carole, and Mabel; we gave photographers our contact information; and then did a brief interview with Channel 4, during which we were asked, "What is it like to be here?" and I, the writer, found myself struck speechless. At some point Carole signed our license. We borrowed a black pen and clipboard from a volunteer so Lisa and Becky could add their signatures as our witnesses. LaDonna snapped all the necessary pictures and helped schlep our belongings to the Assessor-Recorder's Office, where we would get our favorite souvenir of the day, our official marriage certificate.

In the Assessor-Recorder's Office, we sat in front of a staff member's desk as she reviewed our marriage license. Part of me still feared that a glitch on the form would send us back to square one. As her finger moved from box to box on the form, my stomach turned in anticipation. I felt like I was sixteen years old and watching the woman at the DMV correct my driver's test.

Apparently, we passed, because the staff member looked up at us and said, "Okay! How many copies?"

I replied, "Seven hundred, thirty . . ." then laughed. "No, okay, how about two?"

I could hardly concentrate enough to fill out the check for $26. Tracie watched to make sure I didn't make any mistakes. I handed over our check, and then we had them: two marriage certificates decorated with the seal of the State of California, our home state, the state where both of our families have lived for generations.

By 11:30 A.M., Tracie and I were married, exhilarated, and ravenous. Aside from the mouse nibbles I'd taken from my stomach-settling scone, none of us had eaten for hours. Our entourage stopped for one more picture outside the doors of City Hall, then took a cab to Zuni on Market for a brief celebration lunch with our friends, all three of whom needed to get back to work. During lunch we reviewed the pictures on our digital camera and watched what we could see of the video through the camera's tiny view screen, but nothing seemed to capture the essence of those moments in City Hall. I still couldn't answer that interviewer's question, "What is it like to be here?" in any tangible way. No single word, no metaphor, no anecdote could do the job. Until we left Zuni and started walking down Market Street toward the BART station.

Nothing attracts attention like two people in love. A newly-in-love couple walks down the street radiant with their thoughts of each other, and witnesses can't help but smile. An elderly couple, together for years, holds hands in the grocery store, and that image lights something within. Soon after I met Tracie, I was walking across a parking lot alone, apparently smiling to myself about her, when a man getting out of his car took one look at me, grinned, and said, "You are too happy."

I said, "Not possible."

He said, "Then you must be in love."

Precisely. Love begets love. Love begets happiness. Love inspires compassionate actions. Motivated by the loving couples they saw on television, people across the country sent bouquets to City Hall for use during the wedding ceremonies. Good Samaritans showed up on rainy nights to deliver blankets, hot drinks, and food to couples who waited in line. Cab drivers offered free rides to newlyweds. This chain reaction of love and generosity extends far beyond our vision. In this way, love is a powerful force that makes positive things happen in the world.

So there we were, Tracie, Becky, and I, walking the eight blocks from Zuni to the BART station, emanating all the love of the day. A young man walked up to us and asked, "Did you get married?"

"Yes," we said.

"Congratulations! I'm here from Virginia. This is amazing what's happening here. I was watching it on the news in Richmond, and I thought, it's time to visit San Francisco. It's just wonderful."

A few blocks later, a woman caught up with us and asked, "Did you just get married?"

"Yes," we smiled.

"You know, I have to tell you, I'm in town from L.A. for a business meeting. When I was in L.A. watching all this on the news, I thought, well, I could see how some people could argue against these weddings. But now that I'm here and I see it happening in person, I wonder how anyone could argue against love?"

"Have you been to City Hall?" I asked.

"No, I haven't been down there yet."

"You should go," I pressed her. "You really should. There are weddings happening every few minutes. There's amazing energy in there—everyone celebrating, everyone helping each other out."

"I'll try to get there," she said.

I hope she did.

The responses of those strangers captures the essence of what it was like to be at City Hall. Witnessing not only the love of the newlyweds, but also the caring of City Hall employees and volunteers—it changed people, opened their hearts and minds.

BY 3:30 THAT afternoon, Tracie and I had returned home to Walnut Creek. We had hung our dresses up, put our necklaces and earrings back in their boxes, and changed into our jeans. I had driven to doggie day care to pick up the pooch, and now Tracie was out on the front lawn giving the dog a bath. Just as I laid down on our couch for a long overdue nap, the phone rang. I opened my eyes and debated for a second, then decided to answer it.

"Cheryl, it's Lisa—they've stopped the marriages."

"What?" I immediately thought about Doug and Bill, a couple from Atlanta who have been together for fifty years. They had an appointment to get married on March 17 at 8:00 a.m. My stomach sank.

"At 2:30 today the California State Supreme Court stopped the weddings. There's a rally at Castro and Market at 5:30. I'm e-mailing you the information right now."

"This is unbelievable."

"I know—I wasn't sure if I should call you because I didn't want to burst your bubble, but . . ."

"Oh, no—you didn't burst my bubble. I'm glad you called. I'm mean, I was expecting this to happen. I'm just so surprised by the timing. We got home less than an hour ago." For a moment I considered my marrow-deep exhaustion, the logistics of managing nausea while on the road, the odds of finding bathrooms when I needed them (every fifteen minutes) at the demonstration. Despite the urge to demonstrate, I relented to the pregnancy. "Damn, Lisa, I don't think we can get back in the city in time for the rally. You'll have to yell loud enough for all three of us."

"Okay—I'll call you later and let you know how it went."

I hung up the phone and stared at it in disbelief. We were just there. The weddings had been in full swing. And now they were over, just like that. The joy flowing through City Hall had stopped, dried up with the utterance of a few Supreme Court justice words. As reality sank in, my inner activist started chiding me: "So you're going to lounge around on your couch while you could be standing up to be counted?" Good point. I consulted the baby in my belly, and he agreed: nausea, exhaustion, and overactive bladder be damned, we needed to hit the road.

I called out the window to Tracie, "Love, I think we need to go back to San Francisco."

After a quick conversation to fill Tracie in on the news, we called Lisa: "We're packing up the dog and heading back into the city. I'll call you when we get there."

SOME FORM OF grace must have cleared the freeways for us because, during rush hour, we arrived in San Francisco in forty-five minutes, then found parking in the first place we looked.

Maybe love has *that* kind of power, too. We unloaded the dog and walked up to Castro Street, where we found several hundred people standing with signs, candles, copies of marriage licenses, baby strollers, dogs, bullhorns, and drums, preparing to walk to City Hall. When she heard that Tracie and I had gotten married earlier that day, a Channel 2 reporter started asking me questions. One of them resonates with me still. She asked, "Are you sad?"

"No I'm not sad," I said, "I feel energized. I know that love always prevails over hate. Love will prevail over bigotry and love will prevail over closed-mindedness. It's just a matter of time."

Later that evening, though, as we marched the two miles from Castro Street toward City Hall, in the crowd I saw a woman whom I had met a couple weeks earlier. I tapped her on the shoulder and said, "Hi—we met in line at City Hall when we were making wedding appointments."

"Oh yeah, I remember you." She introduced me to her partner and told me, "We had an appointment for tomorrow."

"Yep," her partner said, "we got a phone call from City Hall today."

Now I felt sad. I felt sad for Doug and Bill. I felt disappointment for this couple who had almost gotten through the gate before it closed. I felt concern for the couple from Ohio who had taken their license to the First Unitarian Church this morning—would they be able to file the signed license with the county assessor-recorder? Would they get their marriage certificate? I felt relief for the couple from New York who had taken the bold step of showing up at City Hall without an appointment. I felt frustration on behalf of all the people who were sent back to square one. I caught myself thinking like a guilty survivor of a train wreck, *Why did we make it? Why didn't they? They've been together for fifty-one years, twenty-two years, thirteen years . . .* And I felt more resolved than ever to help affect the changes we need to make in order to gain marriage rights for all people.

THAT NIGHT, AFTER the demonstration, Tracie and I arrived home in time to watch our wedding ceremony replayed on Channel 4's 9:00 news, to hear Carole Migden joyfully announce, "I now pronounce you, Tracie and Cheryl, spouses for life!" At 10:00 on Channel 2, we watched a differently dressed Cheryl and Tracie marching down Market Street with our dog, demanding the right to marry. When I see those juxtaposed images, I am challenged to remember that we are not moving backward in this struggle, only forward, changing the world for ourselves and our children. More importantly, when I replay those tapes, I am reminded of the significance of our first, private wedding—how the memory of that day has become a touchstone for us, a reminder of who we are as a couple, in our very best incarnations of ourselves. Our second, public wedding has become the same kind of touchstone for us, reminding us of who we as a community are in our very best moments, reminding us that anything is possible when we work together, motivated by justice and love.

After Fourteen Years

SANDY ALLEN AND PAM WRIGHT

▼

*W*e *met in* 1990 at the Michigan Womyn's Music Festival. At the time, Sandy's seven-year relationship with a woman had just ended, and she was singing in the festival pickup chorus, needing its warm and caring community to get through her first festival alone in thirteen years. (Admittedly, she also wanted to meet new women.) Pam was at the festival to sing as a ringer from MUSE, Cincinnati's Women's Chorus, to help everyone learn MUSE's repertoire. As a feminist and politically liberal chorus, MUSE performs music that stirs the fervor and passions of women, lesbians in particular. Within a few hours of rehearsal, these feelings were stirring between us. Pam's fifth festival, but her first time attending with her seven year old daughter, was a respite from her traditional marriage and an homage to her inner lesbian. Of all years to find a "festi fling," only to have to juggle the fling with the "mommy" role! But juggle we did.

After the festival, Sandy went home knowing she was ready for major, and happy, changes in her life, and Pam went home knowing that she'd finally found the right woman to motivate her to risk leaving her best friend and husband of almost fifteen years. We needed a "love so strong" to get us each through the nearly overwhelming obstacles to bring our lives together. Within two weeks, Sandy sold her farm, quit her job, and transferred nursing schools to move to Cincinnati. Pam left her husband and beautiful home in the suburbs, then worked daily, if not hourly, helping her two daughters, ages four and seven, cope with a changing lifestyle. We all managed with only rare traumatic and only slightly more frequent dramatic moments.

During our years together, we've had many wonderful experiences as a family, from being asked, as a lesbian couple, to be room parents; to taking part in a doctoral study about lesbian families in which Pam's ex and the girls actively participated; to Pam and Sandy singing together in MUSE; to now being the proud parents of one college senior and one college-bound freshman, both very successful students and happy, well-adjusted, "alternative" young women.

Yet who are we? On the many forms we have filled out in life, sometimes we have felt required to be honest—Sandy was single, Pam divorced. At other times, we felt inspired to be differently "honest," declaring we had "partners," or more boldly as the years moved on, "lesbian partners," and even at rare times claiming ourselves "married." When asked, "Are you married?" Pam would often respond that she was "As married as I'm allowed to be." This question would fill Sandy with angst, wondering what people really wanted to know—if she was happy, or unavailable, or "settled," or had children. We both felt the proper answer to those "Are you married?" questions was "Yes," but that's not the legal truth, and "married" always implied a husband lurking somewhere. We believed definitions needed changing.

Then news of the legalization of marriage for same-sex couples started trickling in from Hawaii. We started to make plans to go, but the weddings stopped seemingly overnight. Sandy wanted to be "made an honest woman of," so she could say, "Yes, I'm married," and Pam wanted to publicly formalize our relationship. When Canada sanctioned same-sex marriages, Sandy was ready to go, but Pam was holding out for a legal U.S. marriage. Vermont was never an option, as we wanted a marriage, not a "civil union." What would we say? "No, we're not *married*, but we are unioned"? The fact that a few, very vocal segments of our society respond so negatively to the concept of same-sex "marriage" suggests the depth of difference between a "civil union" and a "marriage." Clearly civil unions are not considered equal to marriage. Being married is the whole enchilada and anything else is, well, less.

Though what we have is fundamentally no different than a heterosexual marriage, and in our case is better than most marriages, our relationship is labeled "less than"—less than what society upholds, supports, and celebrates as the model for relationships. Barred from access to marriage, we are also barred from access to the privileges and customs surrounding marriage. Getting married is a right of passage into adulthood for our Western culture. Our families do not take seriously relationships that aren't leading up to marriage. Many families hold different expectations from their adult children, based on their marital status—siblings who are not married are expected to make their family of origin their top priority, whereas married siblings are expected to focus on their own spouses and children. Our culture has a role in supporting married couples—celebrating their formation, offering understanding and guidance in times of trouble, trying to uphold taboos related to infidelity, not to mention the vast array of financial and legal support. We want—and deserve—all that.

When things began happening in San Francisco, we watched very closely, holding our breath, worried of a Hawaiian repeat. On February 20, after hearing that the court case to block further marriages wasn't going to proceed right away, Sandy proposed going to California the next day, Saturday. We went online and discovered that licenses were now being issued by appointment only. So the moment the phone lines opened on Monday, Pam was on it, wearing out the redial button for more than three hours, occasionally getting through, only to hear the same recorded message about how to call for an appointment. The phone activity by hundreds, if not thousands, apparently crashed City Hall's phone system that day. But finally, hours after City Hall's stated closing time, we got through to a live person and set our wedding date for March 11.

Shortly after deciding to go to California, Sandy was at a committee meeting at St. John's Unitarian Universalist Church and told the group about our upcoming wedding. Amid the cheers and joy and congratulations, they asked if we were getting married in a church. Sandy told them that we had decided just to go to City Hall because the cost of a church wedding was over $300. Within five minutes our church friends, realizing how significant this was, wrote checks that covered the cost of the church wedding.

Then the planning really took off. We were put in touch with Milo Hanke, a past member of St. John's who was now living in San Francisco. Milo agreed to be one of our witnesses, to help take pictures, and to set up newspaper coverage. Members of our church were beside themselves wishing they could be there to support, participate, and celebrate with us. At the urging of our minister, and based on vague memories of a Society of Friends tradition, we collected 128 signatures the Sunday before we left, on parchment, that reads:

> "You're taking our love there with you."
> from "Every Long Journey" by Ann Reed.
>
> As friends and family of Pam Wright and Sandy Allen, and as members of St. John's Unitarian Universalist church, we've signed this covenant to be with you, in spirit and in our hearts, on the occasion of your marriage, in the City of San Francisco, on March 11, 2004.

We planned to display the signatures in frames on the altarlike table as part of our ceremony.

On the plane to San Francisco, we finalized the ceremony plans—readings, vows, and such—using material e-mailed to us by the minister of the church there. We ordered flowers through a San Francisco florist to be delivered to the church. And we found our second witness, Becky Johnson, the daughter of a MUSE friend, now studying at a seminary in Oakland. We'd known Becky since she was little, and she proved invaluable during our visit, driving us around San Francisco and even reading a statement from one of Pam's daughters during our ceremony.

On March 11, after an exciting forty-five-minute phone interview with Maggie Downs from the *Cincinnati Enquirer,* our local paper, we headed out to City Hall to get our license. What an amazing experience! Shortly after walking into the building, we watched a wedding between two men taking place on the beautiful, winding stone steps in the rotunda. The licensing office was overflowing with same sex-couples, their friends, their parents, and their children, many dressed in their finest with bouton-nieres, corsages, and bouquets. Everyone was so happy, including the staff that was so welcoming and helpful. It was wonderful to talk with these couples, all of whom had been together for many years. We received our license at 10:30 a.m. Then, following lunch at Fisherman's Wharf, we headed to the First Unitarian Universalist Society of San Francisco to prepare for the wedding.

We chose the chapel over the sanctuary as a more intimate and cozy space for a small group. We were surprised to see that almost a dozen members of the local congregation, none of whom we had ever met, came to support us. We had realized only the day before that we had forgotten to ask our daughters if they wanted to add any words to the ceremony. We called them twice, leaving messages both times, giving them the e-mail address of the minister. Just before the ceremony started, we asked the minister, Rali, if she'd received anything from Hannah and Leah. She said, "I'm holding two e-mails right here, but you'll have to wait until they're read during the ceremony."

And this is what we heard: Our oldest daughter Leah, now twenty-one, wrote, "Though Sandy and I got off to a rough start, I can't imagine my life without her. She has helped raise me from the time I was seven. I know that you two love each other and that I was raised in that love. Now I am glad that others are also recognizing the commitment you two have made to each other. I am glad to now officially have Sandy as a mom." And Hannah, age seventeen, had sent these words: "On this amazing day, I am so sorry that no more than my thoughts can be there with you. To see the two of you be pioneers in a movement such as this makes me proud to have you as my mothers. Every day I see how in love you are; it is only right that you should have this opportunity to get married. Fighting for equality and expressing your love for each other are probably two of the most important things you can possibly do. I wish I could be there to witness this. I hope that my love and good thoughts find their way to your hearts."

Pam had walked down the aisle tearing up and now was out-right crying. I'm not sure how much of the following readings we really heard, but the vows brought us right back to the moment. We'd chosen fairly traditional vows, as Sandy felt strongly that the reverence and tradition of these words made them required elements: "I, Pam, take you Sandy, to be my partner in life; to have and to hold, from this day forward; for better, for worse, for richer, for poorer, in sickness and in health; to love and to cherish, till death do us part. Thereto, with my whole heart, and with my earnest and complete devotion, I give you my love." I think it was at that moment that something shifted. We now, somehow, had a greater commitment to each other, and maybe more significantly, to ourselves to fulfill these vows.

For the moment in the ceremony when, traditionally, a couple would exchange rings, we had written a "Blessing of Jewelry": "When Pam and Sandy began to interweave their lives, they wore matching silver necklaces with pendants of a labyris and a symbol of a tree, reminding them of the Michigan Womyn's Music Festival where their relationship began. Today we renew these necklaces, having since been converted to gold on their fifth anniversary, still representing the steadiness of their love for one another. During their first year together, Pam gave Sandy a personally chosen and designed ruby ring, and Sandy gave Pam her grandmother's amethyst solitaire, representing their engaging intent to commit themselves, one to the other. These stones now reside in new, tenth anniversary rings. Each designed her own ring reflecting their ongoing individuality while still honoring the significance of the original gifts. On Pam and Sandy's first anniversary, in a private ceremony at the Michigan night stage, they exchanged lesbian-made and -designed gold rings representing their lifelong love and commitment to each other. With their trillium-cut blue topaz stones, they are also a tribute to the world gay community to which they belong. We now rededicate these rings by which Pam and Sandy originally wed: 'This ring I gave you, as a token and pledge of my constant faith in our togetherness and my abiding love for you. I now renew my pledge.' And finally, at the moment of their marriage, Pam and Sandy each place, on each other's earlobe, a diamond earring, together forming a pair, as they have been already for nearly fourteen years. As a 'first' for each, the bestowing of diamond jewelry has always represented everlasting love, which Pam and Sandy now declare to each other."

Without our glasses on, we nearly needed help from Rali to put these earrings on each other. The rest of the ceremony was a bit of a blur—well, not the kiss of course—but it was beautiful. Our sisters from MUSE were present in song with a recording of "Wood River," and we'll be forever grateful to the San Francisco Unitarian Universalists who celebrated with us. They took pictures, cheered, cried at all the appropriate moments, and gave us many cards and presents.

Following the ceremony, the minister and our two witnesses signed the license, and we shared a champagne toast with all our new friends and surrogate family. It wasn't until about 6:00 p.m. that we heard that the California Supreme Court had shut down the issuance of licenses to same-sex couples at 2:33 p.m. We felt lucky that we'd made it in time.

On the flight home, we realized that because we got married off-site, our license hadn't been recorded right away. What would that mean? We've decided that we are married whether it's been recorded or not. Our completed license has been mailed and should now be at City Hall. It remains to be seen what they'll do with it. In early April, following the usual procedure, we'll mail a request for a copy and see what happens.

Since we've been back, life has been a media whirlwind. The front page *Enquirer* article was very positive, and we've received many e-mails and phone calls of congratulations. On March 13, we appeared on the Channel 9 news, both at 6:00 p.m. and 11:00 p.m., and were used as the news "teaser" all evening. On March 15, we appeared live on a local TV talk news show on Channel 19. In each of these interviews, we wanted to make certain points: we want the public to know we're just like anyone else, there's no reason to hate us, and we deserve the right to marry in the eyes of the government; and we believe that churches, separate from the government, should make their own decisions about whether or not they marry same-sex couples.

After fourteen years together, we didn't think that marrying would affect our relationship, but it has. We feel legitimized and even more committed in our relationship with each other. The public response has been quite positive—not one nasty comment. Sandy was even given a little party at her job, with presents and cake. Pam's mom and our daughters have been totally supportive and would have been there in San Francisco if it had been possible. We culminated our wedding experience with a reception that was originally planned as Pam's fiftieth birthday party. It was elegantly catered, and Pam finally got the "basket" cake she always wanted—a stunning three tiers of it. A professional DJ had everyone dancing, and about 125 of our friends and family attended, excited to be a part of this historical event. We showed the video of our wedding and then danced, ate, and shared libations for three hours. It was a perfect end to our wedding extravaganza.

Now that we have had our taste of marriage equality, we hope to work in the State of Ohio to overturn the so-called "Defense of Marriage Act" so all who want to marry will be able to.

Now I'm Mad as Hell

BILL JONES

▼

I graduated from the College of the Pacific in 1951 with an embedded sense of morality and justice. My professors were mostly young men back from a war that may have been "just," but their nightmares replayed the blood and destruction they fought through and brought about. They were motivated pacifists and adamant about civil rights. They felt the doom of the A-bomb hanging over our heads and they pleaded with us to go out and make wrongs right, to commit our lives to peace, justice, and equality. I thank my lucky stars that I was privileged to have such a unique and wonderful education, and I have tried to live up to their idealism.

And so I marched in the civil rights movement of the sixties, protested the wars, was arrested for the protests, adopted a crack baby and became a single dad, wrote my letters to Congress, and involved myself in the gay rights struggle. Yes, because I took my professors seriously, I am proudly a lifetime activist. So volunteering to help a brilliant new movement that started at City Hall in San Francisco on February 12 was the natural thing for me to do.

On February 16 I was deputized to be a deputy marriage commissioner for the City and County of San Francisco. For the following three weeks, for nine hours a day, I married couples, both same-sex and opposite-sex. The experience was both euphoric and exhausting, an emotional roller coaster, where I found myself choking up as I gave these committed couples their vows to repeat. I'm seventy-five years old and, because I am gay, I have lived as a second-class citizen of the United States all my life. I've been denied the right to defend my country and denied the right to share the obligations and responsibilities of a family united in marriage. I thought I'd be dead and buried before these rights would be granted to me. So, actively participating in this histori-cal event was a dream come true for me.

For three weeks I was allowed to share the most important moments in the lives of 457 teary-eyed couples, and I thanked each one of them for giving me the privilege of performing their nuptials. I just wish that the protesters out on the sidewalk and those who object to these marriages could have come and stood as witnesses to any one ceremony. To see in the couples' eyes the long-term tenderness, the intensity, and the tears would surely change their minds.

Most of the couples I married had been "partners" for years, decades really. When I asked one lesbian couple what they planned to do to celebrate, one of the women answered, wiping away a tear, "Go home and feed the dog." Many such moments took me by surprise, like the time a three-year-old took off his shirt and pants just as his moms were promising to "love and comfort each other, honor and keep each other in sickness and in health." They just smiled and kept going.

Another couple of men asked that I declare them "husbands" instead of "spouses" for life. It sounded great to me. Only one transgender couple asked me to say, "By virtue of the authority vested in me by the State of California, I now pronounce you hus-band and wife" instead of "spouses for life." "Spouses" seemed a perfectly good word for most people, even for a straight couple I married.

After waiting on the sidewalk for two days in the rain that first weekend, a soaking wet couple bragged to me that they had stood in line longer than Britney Spears had been married! I mar-ried a couple who read love poems in German and couples who had to have their vows translated into sign language. I married four different couples where one was in a wheelchair or on oxygen. I married men with AIDS and women who were pregnant; men who were crippled and women in the last stages of MS; two New York City policemen who had been together eight years and two professors at the University of Hawaii who had been lovers for thirty-seven years; and a couple of farm boys from Nebraska who needed to be reassured over and over that it was okay to touch each other and actually kiss in public after they exchanged rings.

The toughest part of the ceremony for so many was the exchange of rings, "in token and pledge of my constant faith and abiding love, with this ring I thee wed"—difficult only because they had already exchanged rings ten, twenty, thirty years ago and had never before removed them over their aging, swollen knuckles. So to get the rings off and then to put them back on offered the comic relief that we all needed.

Then, what all started as an exhilarating shock on February 12, ended with a mallet's blow on March 11, at 2:33 p.m. I had just started up the marble stairs in the rotunda with my 457th couple, Raul and Robert from West Hollywood (together for fifteen years), when someone grabbed my arm and told me to run with it. The California State Supreme Court had just issued a stay on the same-sex marriages. Raul, Robert, their two witnesses (one lugging a portable lavender tape player), and I literally ran up the stairs to the top where we, panting, performed the wedding ceremony, surrounded by television cameras and reporters. The boom box was playing "We've Only Just Begun" by the Carpenters, and wasn't *that* appropriate?

While I was signing the certificate and license, reporters were asking me how I felt. Well, besides feeling like I was going to burst out in tears any second, I felt like I'd just been kicked in the ass and slapped in the face at the same time. Really, it iced me over. I still can't comprehend the self-righteousness of anyone who would want to snatch this away from the couples who had been together for decades and had already gone through "keeping each other in sickness and in health, for richer and for poorer, for better or for worse." How mean-spirited and spiteful can you get?

These wedding ceremonies were not about sex. They were about love, commitment, and family. So the Christian Right-wingers claim that only their heterosexual members are "entitled" to love, commitment, and family, and their God would never have anything to do with gay families. Give me a break.

With these thoughts running through my head, I went to the County Clerk's Office to check in with Nancy Alfaro to see if there was an official declaration from her office. When she told me that the weddings were officially over, my mood changed. I actually felt relieved and started thinking about all the time I'd have for myself now. My taxes weren't done. The house and garden were in a mess, and my cats needed a bath. I had given my word to stay to the end—for the long haul—and I meant it, but this abrupt ending got me off the hook. I was free to go out and enjoy this great weather, even maybe sit in a chair when I ate a lunch.

So I left Nancy's office feeling better, until I opened the door to the hallway. There stood couples dressed in tuxedos, suits, ties, boutonnieres, Levi's, and wedding dresses, holding bouquets, looking stunned and hurt. Many were wiping away their tears. I saw a mother and father who had just flown in from Dallas, comforting their son and his lover. Just minutes before they had been giddily standing in line to register for a marriage license at the County Clerk's Office. A dream all lovers dream was about to come true for them, then it was snatched away and they were left there, drifting in space. It hit me hardest when I watched a young woman slump to the floor, open her blouse, and start to breast-feed her baby, all the time clutching her wedding bouquet. Her bride-to-be stood by her side staring into space.

Now I'm mad as hell.

"Gentle, Angry People"

MARNIE H. SINGER

▼

*R**eed and I* went to City Hall on Friday, March 12, at 11:00 a.m. for our appointment to get our marriage license, knowing that we would be turned down. We were wearing the same clothes we had worn for our church wedding last June 14—matching royal blue silk vests made by a friend. After the gentle and apologetic man behind the counter turned us down, we remained in and around City Hall all day. We struck up conversations with happy male-female couples going in for their licenses. When we congratulated them on their marriages, without exception they gave us warm, supportive words in response. After they walked out of the Clerk's Office with their licenses in hand, Reed went back in the office and asked again for our license.

Wanting to put a personal face on the marriage equality struggle, we worked the press. We had conversations with reporters from the *San Francisco Chronicle* and Associated Press, and we told people at the various TV vans that we planned to remain at City Hall until they granted us our marriage license, or until they escorted us out. The day is blurring together already in my mind, so I can't remember which TV stations recorded us saying what. I felt fairly articulate when talking to Fox, explaining that we see civil marriage as the fourth aspect of marriage, and no court action or marriage equality opponent could take the other

three away from us—the commitment between us, the commitment we made in front of family and friends, and the religious
marriage.

After taking a break for lunch, we headed to the Mayor's
Office to thank him or his representative for his wonderful support. As we opened the door to his outer office, the first person
who greeted us was a man standing right near the door with an
outstretched hand, saying, "Hi, I'm Gavin." We introduced ourselves and then noticed that the other people in the room were
either holding TV cameras or microphones, or they were part of
the mayor's security detail. We had walked in on an interview!
Since he had been so welcoming, we were put at ease and shared
our words of appreciation. Mayor Newsom apologized for the discrimination we were facing, and he assured us that he was continuing to do all that he could. We explained to him why civil
marriage is important for us, and we acknowledged that we knew
that he and his staff didn't intend to discriminate against us, that
they were just doing their jobs. After we stepped out of the room,
someone with a clipboard followed to get us to sign releases for
MTV News.

Having met Mayor Newsom, we made the rounds of the TV
vans again, telling them that we would still be inside City Hall at
the 8:00 p.m. closing time. After the Clerk's Office closed at 4:00
p.m., we pulled chairs out to the rotunda and settled down with
books. TV cameras and a reporter returned at about 7:30. Reed
read aloud to me from Audre Lorde, and then we started singing.
We sang a couple verses of Holly Near's "Singing for Our Lives,"
then "I Ain't Afraid," and Maura Volante's "A Woman's Voice
Raised Up in the Silence." The rotunda has wonderful
acoustics—it was like singing in a very, very large bathroom, but
it felt daunting. Our resolve made us strong.

Sometime after 8:00 p.m., a uniformed man from the Sheriff's
Office came up to us and told us we needed to leave. His outstretched hand and my handshake assured all of us that we had
peaceful intent. We told him why we were there, and he reiterated
that we needed to leave. Reed asked if she could make a statement, and he agreed. As he stepped back, the cameras stepped
forward. Reed read her statement: "For nearly a month, I have
volunteered here at City Hall. Those of us who have been here

have celebrated the right to marry the people we love. This is not about any church marrying us. It is about claiming our civil right to marry and to enjoy all rights and responsibilities legally married couples enjoy. Historically, we are not the first to fight this battle. Slaves were denied this right. Interracial couples have had to fight for it, also against strong popular opinion. Marnie and I stand here for this right."

When Reed finished, the officer stepped back to my side and walked with us to the door. We picked up our singing, and the cameras followed us out. When we reached the sidewalk, we hugged and kissed, and then continued walking toward BART, singing.

Fifty Years Together, Then Six Days Late

DOUG JOHNSON AND BILL WEAVER

▼

How does it feel to be a gay couple for fifty years? Sometimes it feels as if we met last month, but more often it's as if we have been together forever. Now that we are in our seventies, the view back to 1953 is a long one. What was our gay background before our lives merged? Very briefly, we like to say the initial event was being born with penises, and the enabling event was puberty with unambiguous same-sex erotic fantasies. From then on our stories become more complex.

IT WAS THE END OF WORLD WAR II

Before we met each other, we had both experienced encounters with other men. Bill's family lived in Norfolk, Virginia, and at age fourteen he amateurishly picked up a sailor to explore a few minutes of privacy in an alley. Afterward Bill was sick at heart for a week. But he did it again, and soon accepted his orientation. When Doug was eighteen and an enlisted man in the navy, he was seduced by a navy lieutenant. Their intimacy was agreeable, but Doug was shocked when the lieutenant said, "Someday you will make someone a good wife." Horrified, Doug resolved to remain chaste until he grew up, which he reasoned (naively), would be when he graduated from college.

We met in 1948, a few months before we both enrolled at The University of Florida. Then finding common interests, we became close friends. Although our relationship was platonic, we did many things courting couples do. We ate meals together, attended concerts and movies together, and visited each other's parents. One Christmas we even traveled together to visit New York City.

After earning undergraduate degrees, we went to different graduate schools. Doug remained at Florida, and Bill went to Eastman School of Music in Rochester, New York. After Doug graduated with his PhD in pharmacology, he finally understood that his sexuality would never change. He wrote about this to Bill.

THE 1950S: GAY IN ATLANTA

In 1953 we were both seeking employment and found positions in Atlanta—Bill as organist-choirmaster for an Episcopal church, Doug as faculty member of a local college of pharmacy. With our past friendship and now common orientation, it seemed natural to move in together. We rented a six hundred-square-foot, unfurnished garage apartment, and set up housekeeping.

Doug was eligible for a GI home loan, so a year later we bought a starter house southeast of Atlanta. Our neighbors were other postwar families with similar interests—starting lawns, buying furniture, establishing credit, and such. We fit in easily with no questions asked.

Still, living in a homophobic society during the 1950s was difficult. Tight closeting was obligatory, and this interfered with more than social life. It meant no gay or lesbian could speak honestly with an employer, doctor, pastor, lawyer, coworker, or family member. On the other hand, homosexuality was not a subject of general public awareness. It was rarely mentioned in news media, and few straights were suspicious. Gays who kept "the secret" were routinely assumed to be straight, and in Atlanta this worked even for "nelly" types—after all, in the 1950s, the public persona of a straight man with a thick, old-school southern drawl was not much different.

In Atlanta of the 1950s there were no public places for homosexuals to meet and socialize. There were a few notorious public restrooms to be cruised, but pickups were not friendship material. New friends were met mostly in homes. Gays and lesbians with culinary skills hosted small dinner parties regularly; those not so gifted hosted an annual catered cocktail party.

In these early times in our relationship we formulated rules to maintain public security and private integrity: 1) in public we would never reveal gayness by touch or comment; 2) for personal integrity, we would not engage in pseudo-heterosexual dating; 3) we would establish a known style of accepting social invitations, only when both were included, and at heterosexual gatherings we would circulate as singles.

Though long-term gay commitments and monogamous relationships were unknown in the 1950s, with time, we grew into both. Today we believe that the major cements of long-term relationships are sex and companionship. The relative importance of these varies with time however. Sex is the more compelling for many years, then gradually becomes routine. With time companionship grows to such importance that it takes over as the lasting cement. Both motivations are fulfilling, but in different ways.

THE 1960S: BUILDING OUR HOME

In 1963, Doug joined the faculty of the University of Georgia College of Pharmacy in Athens, sixty-five miles from Atlanta. Rather than commute daily, he rented an apartment there, and drove to work on Mondays and returned on Fridays. Though together only on weekends, we spoke daily by telephone. This situation prevailed for twenty-seven years until Doug retired.

Bill changed employment in 1960, and became organist-choirmaster of St. Anne's Episcopal Church in northwest Atlanta. The parish was young and growing, and Bill arrived in time to influence the selection of a pipe organ—an excellent tracker instrument built by DA Flentrop in Holland. Doug sang in the choir, and St. Anne's was our church home for many years.

Although Atlanta was segregated during the 1950s, we had African-American friends we sometimes invited to dinner. The first time a friend visited, he was stopped by a policeman who wanted to know why he was driving in a white neighborhood. Integration came to Atlanta in the 1960s, and it was under Bill's leadership that the Atlanta Chapter of the American Guild of Organists integrated its membership.

In 1966 we built our permanent home in the suburb of Dunwoody, north of Atlanta. Except for its large music room, the floor plan was "interesting but modest." By 1971 our music room was furnished with a fine stereo system, a Steinway B piano, and a 10-rank Flentrop pipe organ. Life was good, and we continued to entertain as usual.

THE 1970S: CELEBRATING TWENTY-FIVE YEARS

When our twenty-fifth anniversary arrived in 1978, we decided for the first time to celebrate with a party. Still closeted, we invited only gay friends, two dozen or so, into our home. An older couple from Virginia were out-of-town guests. The night's celebration was fun, but disaster hit the next morning when one of the Virginians had a heart attack. We quickly drove him to a hospital where he had his most severe attack of all. During the two weeks before he died, we cared for and supported his partner.

THE 1980S: COMING OUT

In the 1980's, AIDS struck many Atlanta gays. Our special concern was for our friend Rex and his partner John. Rex developed full-blown AIDS at a time when there was no really effective therapy. We helped tend to Rex during his last days, staying overnight when needed. When there was no hope left for Rex and John, they initiated their end plan. John consolidated his various leave times so he could be home for six weeks, and Rex discontinued his medications. It was a sad time for all as the dire disease took its toll.

By the late 1980s, many older gays lived in their closets as much by habit as necessity. Our decision to break the habit came when we transferred church membership to a new parish. At the first conference with our new rector, we asked to be considered one family, making one pledge and receiving one mailing. All reservations about our relationship becoming general information were soon dispelled.

Shortly after we joined the Episcopal Church of the Epiphany, an adult education series on *Family Lifestyles in the Parish* was scheduled. Weekly segments were devoted to nuclear families, blended families, interracial families, gay and lesbian families, and people who live alone. Each unit concluded with interaction between audience members and the panelists representing the "lifestyle-of-the-day." We appeared on the gay and lesbian panel, and it was our first time to speak publicly about our personal lives. We received some naive questions, but no hostile comments, and it was a good experience. The later response was also positive. We had suppressed the emotional onus of closeting so long that, once out, we felt a surprising euphoria. We also felt a serenity being in church that we had not known we had lacked.

Among our straight friends, none were surprised when we came out. All said they had known for years that we were gay. We found that they did vary, however, in their comfort level in talking about gay issues.

THE 1990S: LIFE AFTER RETIREMENT

In 1990, we retired, and applied newly available time to activist causes. We spoke of our life experiences whenever and wherever we were invited—religious and secular groups, Georgia State University, the University of the South in Sewanee, Tennessee, among others. We appeared in educational television tapes prepared by the Episcopal Media Foundation, and our story was recounted in Larry Kent Graham's book on pastoral care of lesbians and gays, *Discovering Images of God.* For many years we delivered Project Open Hand meals to AIDS patients in Atlanta, stopping only when short-term memory lapses made it difficult to keep track of who needed what diet. We also served on Project Open Hand's speakers' bureau.

When our fortieth anniversary came around in 1993, we hosted a second anniversary party at home. This time the guest list was mixed gay and straight. At our forty-fifth anniversary in 1998, our Episcopal church celebrated a Eucharist in thanksgiving for our milestone. There was no same-sex blessing, but emotionally and spiritually we declared our commitment before two hundred of our faith community and friends.

THE NEW MILLENNIUM:
PLANNING OUR FUTURE, CELEBRATING OUR PAST

By 2001, it was time to make terminal housing plans. Atlanta had no gay retirement facilities, so our only option was to approach a straight-oriented facility. There we were told we would be welcome individually, but we could not live together in one apartment because we were not related by blood or marriage. It took several months of lobbying, as well as a bit of legal persuasion, but eventually the admission policy was changed.

When we move in at the end of 2005, we will be the first gay couple in residence. We will have a 1,434-square-foot apartment in a new building now under construction. In the meantime, we remain at home, with support from close friends and a part-time companion-housekeeper from an agency.

Our long-awaited fiftieth anniversary came in 2003. We had two celebrations, one public and one private. In June, we served as honorary grand marshals for the Atlanta Pride Parade. Seated at the rear of a bright orange Volkswagen convertible, we were driven through the cheering crowds lining Peachtree Street. Banners on the car read, "Together in Atlanta Since 1953."

Our private celebration was attended by seventy friends at the Lowe Gallery in November. With gourmet food in generous supply, and fine art on the walls, the party was a great success. Guests who had planned to visit briefly remained for the entire evening. Will Headlee, our friend since 1949, came from Syracuse, New York, to reminisce about old times together for the group.

THE NEXT STEP: MARRIAGE

We began to hear talk of formal recognition of homosexual couples about fifteen years ago. People discussed sacred approaches such as marriage or holy union. Secular approaches included civil marriage and civil unions. The Episcopal Diocese of Atlanta is liberal in providing pastoral care for lesbians and gays, but does not permit rites not approved by the national church. Our Eucharist at our forty-fifth anniversary was sanctioned as a thanksgiving, but not a blessing of commitment or holy union.

Ideally, we still hope for the day when same-sex marriage will be sanctioned by our diocese. We are not interested in secular civil union, but we did retain interest in civil marriage. The Episcopal prayer book includes a rite for blessing heterosexual civil marriage, and someday, we hope, this will be extended to same-sex civil marriage.

On February 12, 2004, San Francisco City Hall began issuing marriage licenses to and marrying homosexual couples. The next day, our San Francisco friends Jon-Ivan Weaver and Diego Sans were married. The Sans-Weavers knew we would be in Los Angeles on March 13 for the ordination of a friend. They suggested we extend our trip to include a wedding in San Francisco. Considering our ages, our interest in secular marriage, and no prospect of such in Georgia, we decided to do just that. When we were unable to reach City Hall by phone, Jon-Ivan visited the license office and obtained the necessary appointment for March 17. What happened next came as a depressing surprise. On March 11, the California Supreme Court halted issuance of marriage licenses to same-sex couples.

Our San Francisco friends had arranged a celebratory champagne brunch at the Garden Room of the Palace Hotel. Despite dampened spirits, we kept the appointment. Our waiter, who had observed similar groups, diplomatically asked if we were marking a special event. When we related our situation, he brought forth a complimentary dessert with banner proclaiming: "Happy Anniversary!"

For most of our time together we did not consider, much less desire, public recognition of our relationship. Closet maintenance left little time for useless speculation. Only when gay unions were instituted in Europe did we begin to rethink our position. Our initial reassessment was hypothetical, but once the movement crossed the Atlantic, it became personal. Civil marriage became a focused desire once we knew we planned to visit San Francisco. When San Francisco same-sex marriage licenses ceased six days before our arrival, we were greatly distressed. It seemed our hope had been foolish. However, we retained hope for realization of our desire at some future time.

The idea of marking an anniversary with civil marriage remained attractive, but how long would we have to wait? Which anniversary?

POSTSCRIPT

In July 2004 we attended the Organ Historical Society convention in Buffalo, New York. Shortly before departing Atlanta, we realized that Ontario is one of the Canadian provinces that sanctions homosexual marriage. Also that Niagara Falls, Ontario, is only a thirty-minute drive from Buffalo. So we asked Will Headlee who lives in Syracuse, New York, to drive to the convention so he could join us as wedding chauffeur, witness, and photographer.

We knew we needed to go to Niagara Falls City Hall to get our license. There we found no line, and were met by a very pleasant young lady. As we filed our application, she inquired, "Did you plan to get married today?" We nodded yes, and she responded that there was no one at City Hall who could officiate, but that there were three people in the city who would do so. "Would you like me to telephone one of them?" We did, and she did.

When we arrived at the address that the clerk at City Hall had given us, we found ourselves at the Two Hearts Wedding Chapel with hanging baskets of lavender petunias in front. We laughed. As we chatted with the lady minister we found her to be friendly and sympathetic to gay marriage. Asked if we preferred a religious or civil ceremony, we chose the latter. During the first portion of the ceremony, facing her, we affirmed our desire to be married. Then, as we faced each other and held hands, she led us through our vows. Midway through, Bill said, "Doug, you're holding too tight and hurting." We laughed for a second time. After the ceremony, we completed the paperwork, and our party of three Americans adjourned to a local bar and grill for a banquet of sandwiches and beer. On our way back to Buffalo, we calculated we had been in Canada no more than three hours. Convention friends celebrated with us that night, and at the final banquet our marriage was announced from the podium.

We had always wondered what impact marriage would have on

us. Our vows of love and support were not new thoughts, but repeating them in full while holding hands and looking into each other's eyes had unexpected emotional impact for both of us. And recognition by a major governmental entity was sincerely a welcome affirmation of us as first-class citizens. Finally, after fifty-one years.

We Couldn't Be More Married

ISOBEL T. WHITE

▼

Exactly six months ago, my partner, Angela, and I stood in line at San Francisco City Hall to exchange vows. We were joyful and excited as we waited for hours, watching the couples around us. There were the two women behind us, one of whom clearly was ill, her scarf masking a bald head. Her partner stood in line while she found comfortable places to sit. There was the couple whose sister, mother, and daughter all joined them in line. There were the two men we had seen around town with their adorable little boys. And us. I was newly pregnant—just five weeks at the time. A shotgun wedding, we joked. One day our child would look at the date on the marriage certificate and say, "Wait a minute . . ."

Today, August 11, 2004, five months after the last same-sex wedding was performed in San Francisco, the California State Supreme Court ruled our marriage license invalid. But the truth is, despite their ruling, my partner and I couldn't *be* more married than we are now. I'm over seven months pregnant, my fingers too swollen to wear my wedding ring, full of hope and anticipating the birth of our daughter. Angela's mother just got out of the hospital after back surgery. She'll be staying with us for a week. We're in the midst of remodeling our home—after all, as our plumber said, "If I had a nickel for every couple who found out they were pregnant and started remodeling. . . ." Angela is struggling to balance the demands of her pregnant wife, her recovering mother, and her torn-up house. How much more married could we be?

So married, in fact, that we won't be protesting the court's decision today. We're too busy right now just trying to keep our family afloat. But we know there will be other opportunities to get married and other opportunities to protest, with our daughter in tow. We know that someday, she'll be stunned by the discriminatory laws we fought against, and proud of us for standing up to be counted.

In the meantime, in lieu of the rights that would be granted to us by a legal marriage, in a few weeks we'll be meeting with a lawyer to secure Angela's rights to care for both me and our child in the hospital. And in the meantime, we'll frame that marriage certificate we received months ago, along with photos and our congratulatory letter from the City of San Francisco. That is, as soon as we can find it in all this remodeling mess.

Afterword

CHERYL DUMESNIL

▼

On the morning of Thursday, August 11, I left home, heading to Seven Hills School to teach my last in a series of summer creative writing classes. I had given myself enough time to swing by Safeway to pick up treats for the kids, who had done an amazing job of focusing on their writing projects, despite the distractions of middle school hormones, beautiful weather, and a swimming pool glimmering just outside the window of the school library where we met.

A few blocks from home, I remembered to turn on the car radio to see if the California State Supreme Court had announced their latest decision yet. I was waiting to find out if the court would rule that Mayor Gavin Newsom had overstepped his authority when he urged the City Clerk to issue marriage licenses to same-sex couples, or if they would validate Mayor Newsom's actions and honor the marriage certificates of the 4,037 couples who married between February 12 and March 11, 2004.

Honestly, I think most of us newlyweds knew what to expect from the court. Mayor Newsom's action was a kind, forward-thinking, just, and bold gesture. But it was also, according to California's (yet-to-be deemed unconstitutional) "Defense of Marriage" law, an illegal action. So I wasn't surprised when, stopped at a traffic light on Geary Road, I heard the court's decision announced on the radio: yes, Mayor Newsom had over-stepped his legal authority; yes, our marriage certificates were rendered invalid. What did surprise me was my emotional reaction to the ruling. Each time I heard the word "invalid"—and I heard it several times as I flipped from news station to news station—I felt a physical tightening in my stomach. One station announced that state officials would be sending the newlyweds letters, notifying us of our status. Four thousand and thirty-seven letters let loose in the U.S. mail, reiterating the bad news. Another jab to the abs.

After years of activism, I certainly wasn't naive about what could—what most probably would—happen that morning. But caught in that gap between my intellectual understanding and the emotional reality of hearing the news, I was stunned. Never had discrimination felt more real to me. In a fog, I pulled into the Safeway parking lot and exited my car. As I stepped through the automatic doors into the grocery store's air conditioned interior, an employee stacking cantaloupes in the produce department looked up at me and said, "Hello, welcome to Safeway." I couldn't even muster a smile. I looked at the wedding band on her ring finger and wanted to ask, "How would you feel if they invalidated your marriage certificate?" I wanted to ask this question of every married person I saw in the store—the man next to me, filling his cart with potato chips as I chose cookies for my students, the checker who asked, "So how are you doing today?" Usually a chatty person, usually ripe for an opportunity to educate people about injustice, instead of telling her the truth, I offered what probably looked like a smirk. I just couldn't get the words out yet. I felt both saddened by the news and shocked by my response to it.

Arriving at the school library a few minutes early, I was greeted by three gregarious middle school girls who bounded up to me, shouting, "We have a performance for you!" They instantly grabbed hands, forming a circle around my body like I was a maypole, then galloped clockwise around me and sang a chanting song I hardly remember—something about frogs? They are adorable girls—so full of energy and creativity that they don't care what others think about their full expression of it. And I love them for that. As much as possible, I tried to let their exuberance penetrate the shell of my disappointment, and I thanked them for their crazy dance. Then my coteacher and friend, Judy, sensing I wasn't all there, told the girls to go run at least one lap around campus before class started.

As they burst out the door, Judy asked me, "Okay, so what's up?" I filled her in on the court ruling and my response to it, then shrugged and said, "This is what it feels like to be part of a civil rights movement."

Immediately she asked, "What can I do?"

And that's just it—that's what I'm used to: a supportive community of friends, and sometimes strangers, who ask, "What can we do?" I live in the San Francisco Bay Area. In my middle-class, suburban neighborhood, my wife and I have found that our straight neighbors celebrate the milestones of our lives—wedding, dog adoption, pregnancy—as they would anyone else's. In this environment, I rarely encounter discrimination. Perhaps that's why I feel stunned when I finally do. Perhaps that supportive community is exactly what gives me the strength and energy to fight discrimination when I see it.

With this thought in mind, as our students gathered in the library, I felt the fog start to lift from my brain. After Judy and I got the kids going on their first creative task of the day, Judy retreated to her office to send protest e-mails to every California state official she could think of, and I did what I always do in times of distress—I picked up my pen and started writing in my journal. Quickly, the act of writing moved me out of my "victim of discrimination" mindset and back into the empowered, informed activist mindset I had enjoyed before I heard the verdict.

Historically, civil rights actions move two steps forward and get pushed one step back. But they *do* move forward. The court's August 11 decision closed one legal avenue to marriage equality, but many other avenues remain open. As I write this, San Francisco newlyweds are engaged in a lawsuit challenging the constitutionality of California's law that restricts marriage to heterosexual couples. California State Assemblymember Mark Leno's Marriage Non-Discrimination Act continues to move forward in Sacramento. On its first go-around, the Federal Marriage Act—the fruit of President Bush's promise to write marriage discrimination into the United States Constitution—died on the vine. Thanks to the City and County of San Francisco's actions in February and March, public opinion about marriage equality has shifted, permanently. And despite the anti-gay marriage laws passing in several states across the country, opinion polls confirm that marriage equality will become a reality as the older generation of voters gives way to the younger—it's only a matter of time. Though the marriage certificates issued to us at San Francisco City Hall guarantee no legal rights, the experiences we had waiting in line, taking our vows, and publicly celebrating our relationships remain valid, essential, and powerful moments in our lives and in the history of this civil rights movement. As we continue to move toward marriage equality, through the frustrating shuffle of two steps forward and the one step back, may we all remember the sense of liberation we felt at San Francisco City Hall. No court action can take that away.